BLACK SCIENCE

IMAGE COMICS, INC.
Robert Kirkman – Chief Operating Officer
Erik Larsen – Chief Financial Officer
Todd McFarlane – President
Marc Silvestri – Chief Executive Officer
Jim Valentino – Vice-President

Eric Stephenson – Publisher
Ron Richards – Director of Business Development
Jennifer de Guzman – Director of Trade Book Sales
Kat Salazar – Director of PR & Marketing
Corey Murphy – Director of Retail Sales
Jeremy Sullivan – Director of Digital Sales
Emilio Bautista – Sales Assistant
Branwyn Bigglestone – Senior Accounts Manager
Emily Miller – Accounts Manager
Jessica Ambriz – Administrative Assistant
Tyler Shainline – Events Coordinator
David Brothers – Content Manager
Jonathan Chan – Production Manager
Drew Gill – Art Director
Meredith Wallace – Print Manager
Monica Garcia – Senior Production Artist
Addison Duke – Production Artist
Vincent Kukua – Production Artist
Tricia Ramos – Production Assistant
IMAGECOMICS.COM

COLLECTION DESIGN: JEFF POWELL

BLACK SCIENCE VOLUME 2: WELCOME, NOWHERE. First Printing. January 2015. Published by Image Comics, Inc. Office of publication: 2001 Center Street, 6th Floor, Berkeley, CA 94704. Copyright © 2015 Rick Remender & Matteo Scalera. All rights reserved. Originally published in single magazine form as BLACK SCIENCE #7-11. BLACK SCIENCE™ (including all prominent characters featured herein), its logo and all character likenesses are trademarks of Rick Remender & Matteo Scalera, unless otherwise noted. Image Comics® and its logos are registered trademarks of Image Comics, Inc. No part of this publication may be reproduced or transmitted, in any form or by any means (except for short excerpts for review purposes) without the express written permission of Image Comics, Inc. All names, characters, events and locales in this publication are entirely fictional. Any resemblance to actual persons (living or dead), events or places, without satiric intent, is coincidental. PRINTED IN THE U.S.A. For information regarding the CPSIA on this printed material call: 203-595-3636 and provide reference #RICH-602096. For international rights inquiries, contact: foreignlicensing@imagecomics.com.

ISBN 978-1-63215-018-9

RICK REMENDER
WRITER

MATTEO SCALERA
ARTIST

DEAN WHITE (#7-10)
MICHAEL SPICER (#11)
PAINTED ART

RUS WOOTON
LETTERING + LOGO DESIGN

SEBASTIAN GIRNER
EDITOR

BLACK SCIENCE CREATED BY
RICK REMENDER & MATTEO SCALERA

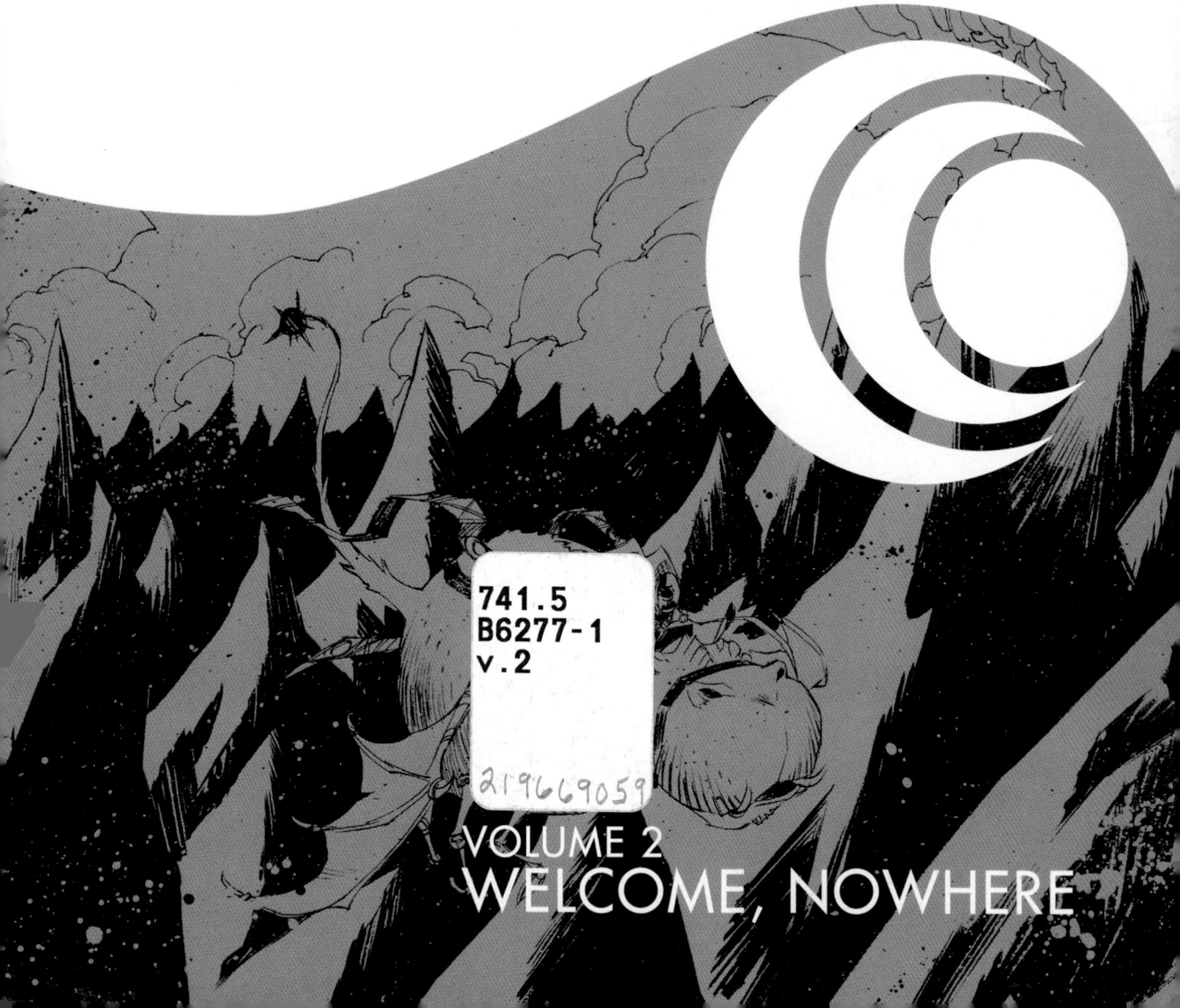

VOLUME 2
WELCOME, NOWHERE

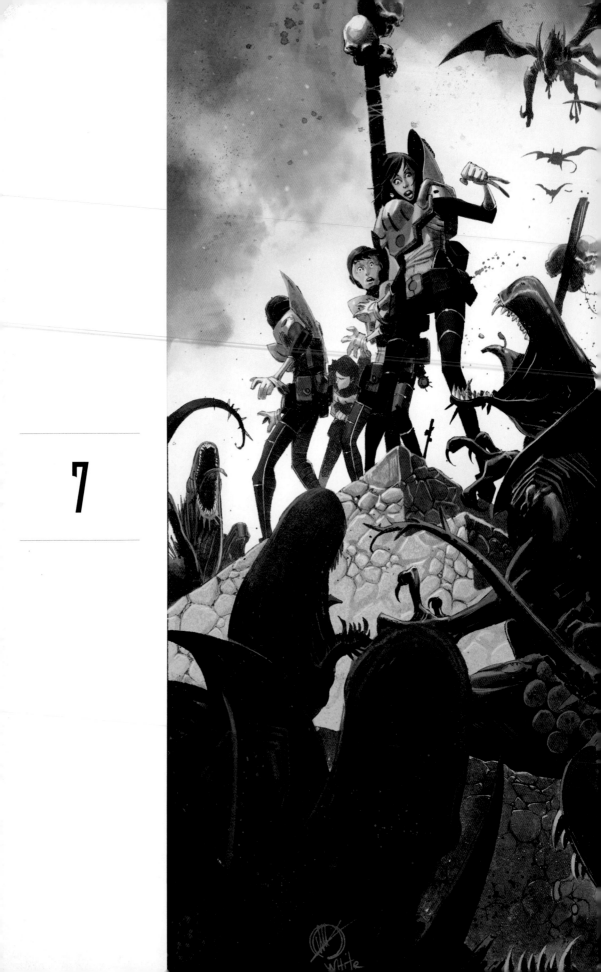

7

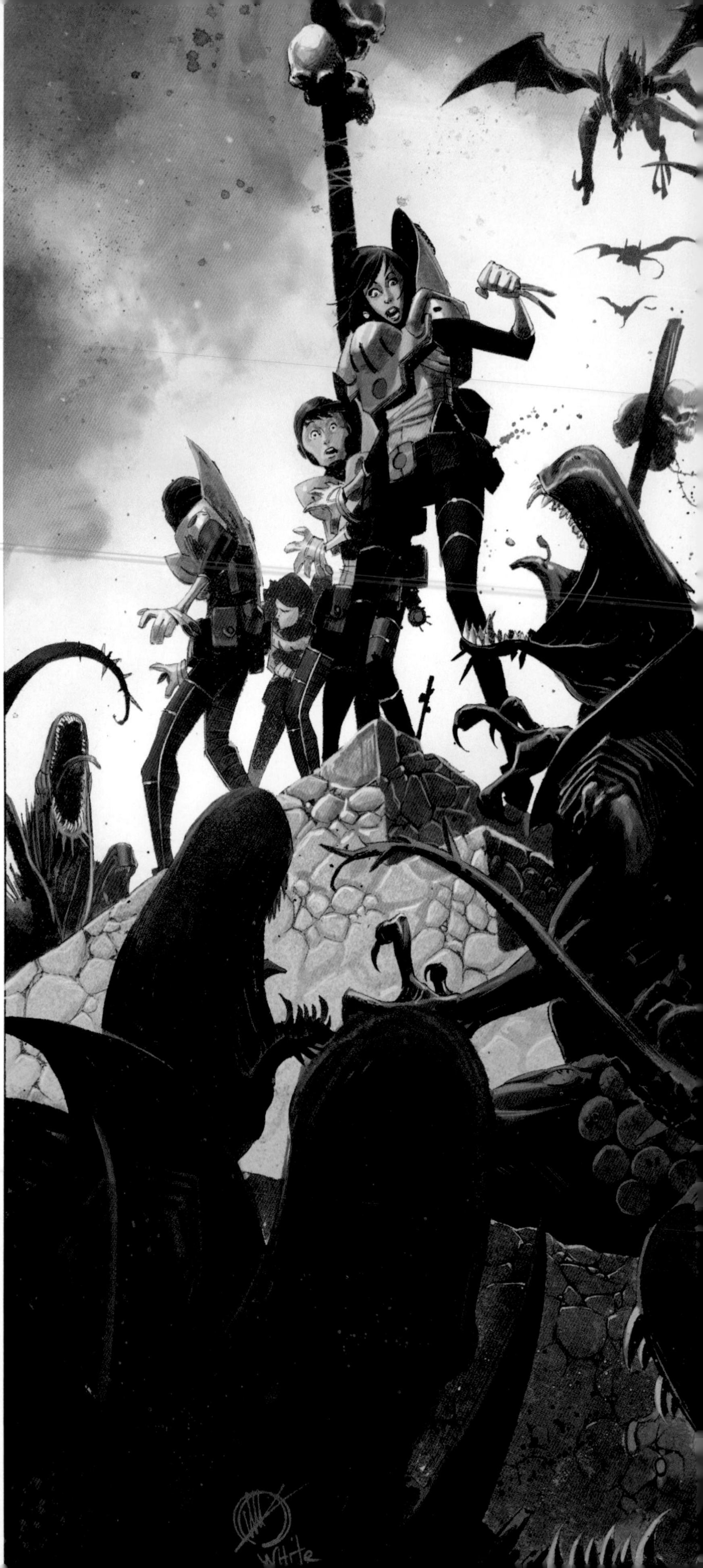

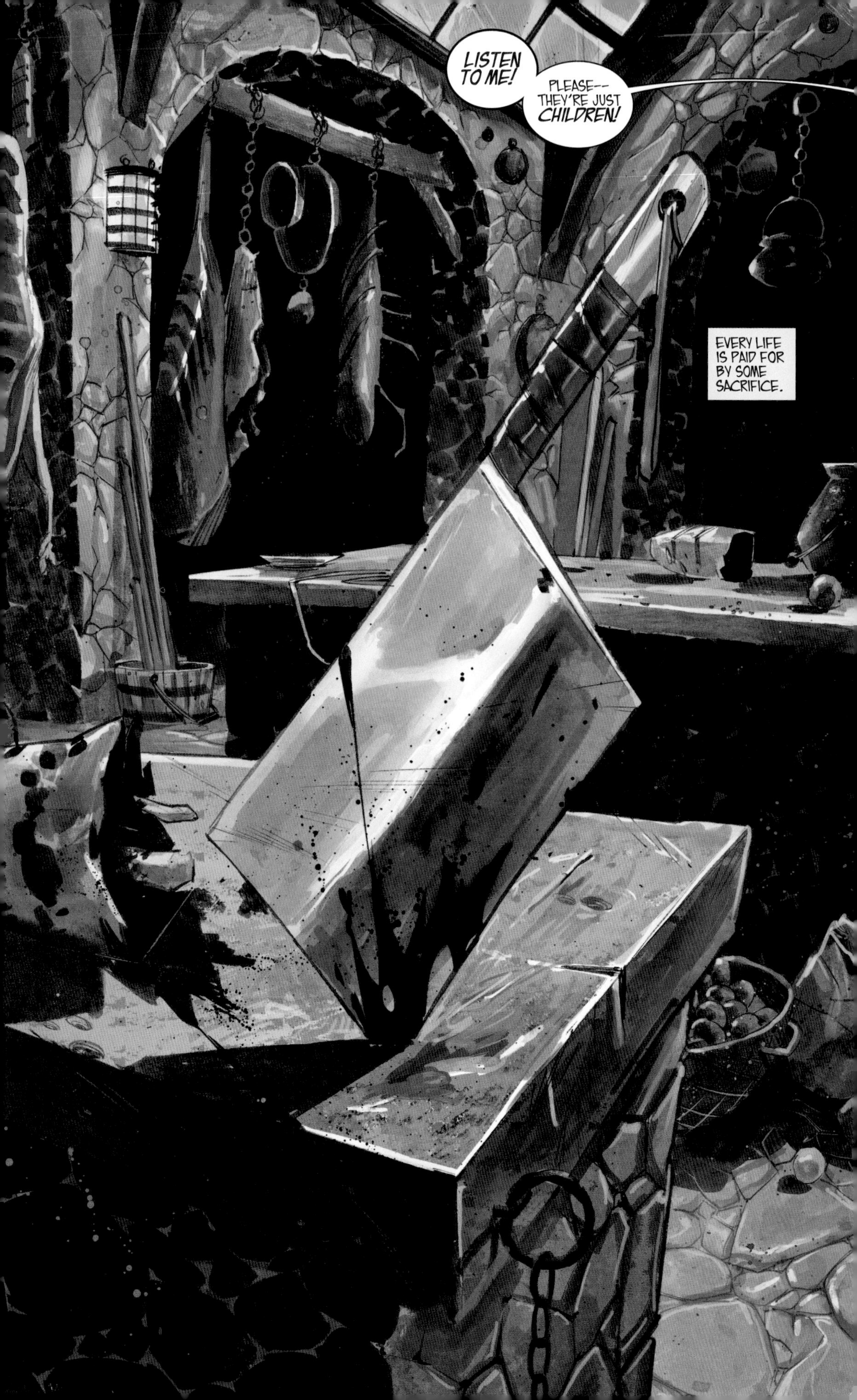

LISTEN TO ME!
PLEASE-- THEY'RE JUST CHILDREN!
EVERY LIFE IS PAID FOR BY SOME SACRIFICE.

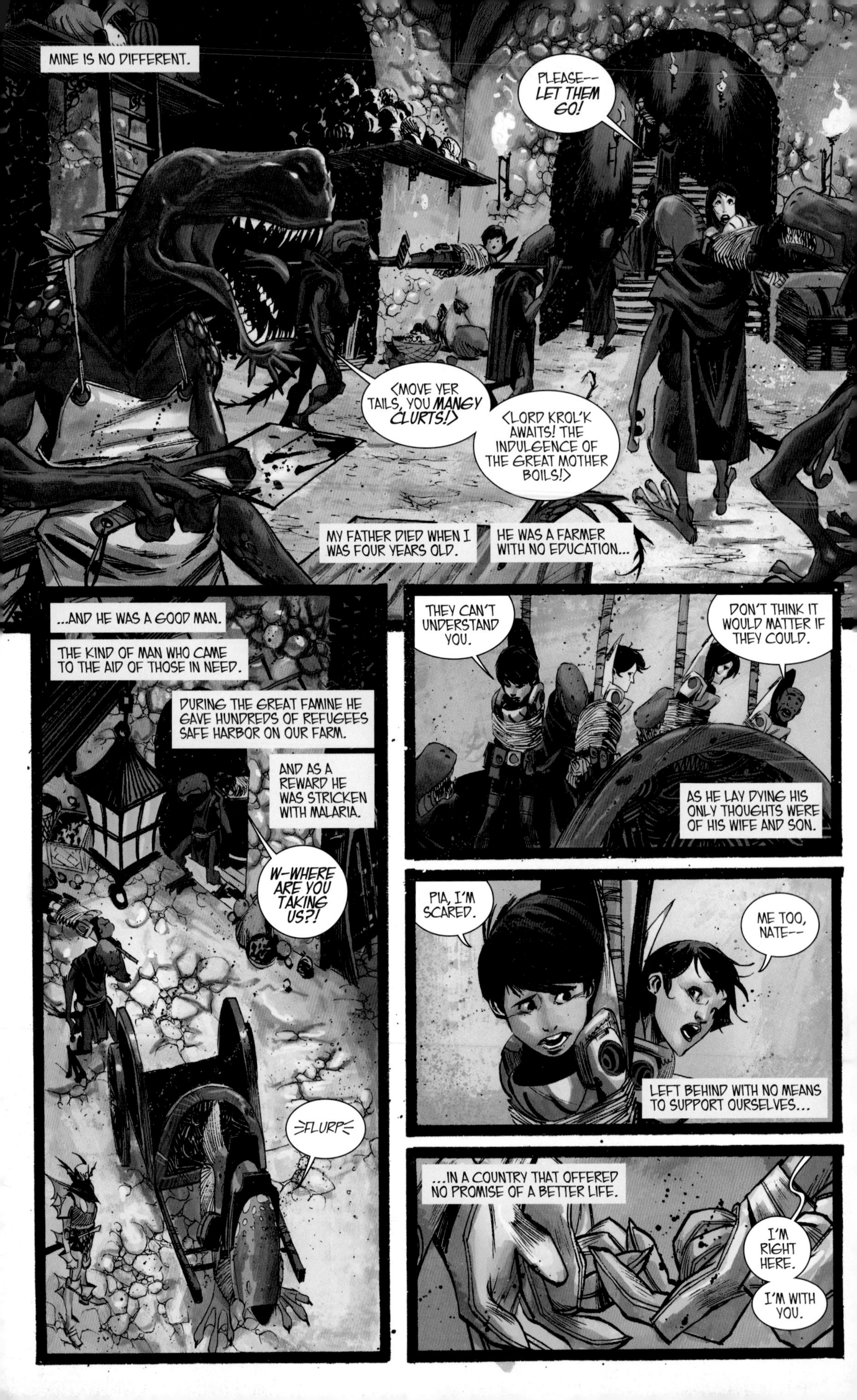

MINE IS NO DIFFERENT.
PLEASE-- LET THEM GO!
<MOVE YER TAILS, YOU MANGY CLURTS!>
<LORD KROL'K AWAITS! THE INDULGENCE OF THE GREAT MOTHER BOILS!>
MY FATHER DIED WHEN I WAS FOUR YEARS OLD.
HE WAS A FARMER WITH NO EDUCATION...
...AND HE WAS A GOOD MAN.
THE KIND OF MAN WHO CAME TO THE AID OF THOSE IN NEED.
DURING THE GREAT FAMINE HE GAVE HUNDREDS OF REFUGEES SAFE HARBOR ON OUR FARM.
AND AS A REWARD HE WAS STRICKEN WITH MALARIA.
W-WHERE ARE YOU TAKING US?!
FLURP
THEY CAN'T UNDERSTAND YOU.
DON'T THINK IT WOULD MATTER IF THEY COULD.
AS HE LAY DYING HIS ONLY THOUGHTS WERE OF HIS WIFE AND SON.
PIA, I'M SCARED.
ME TOO, NATE--
LEFT BEHIND WITH NO MEANS TO SUPPORT OURSELVES...
...IN A COUNTRY THAT OFFERED NO PROMISE OF A BETTER LIFE.
I'M RIGHT HERE.
I'M WITH YOU.

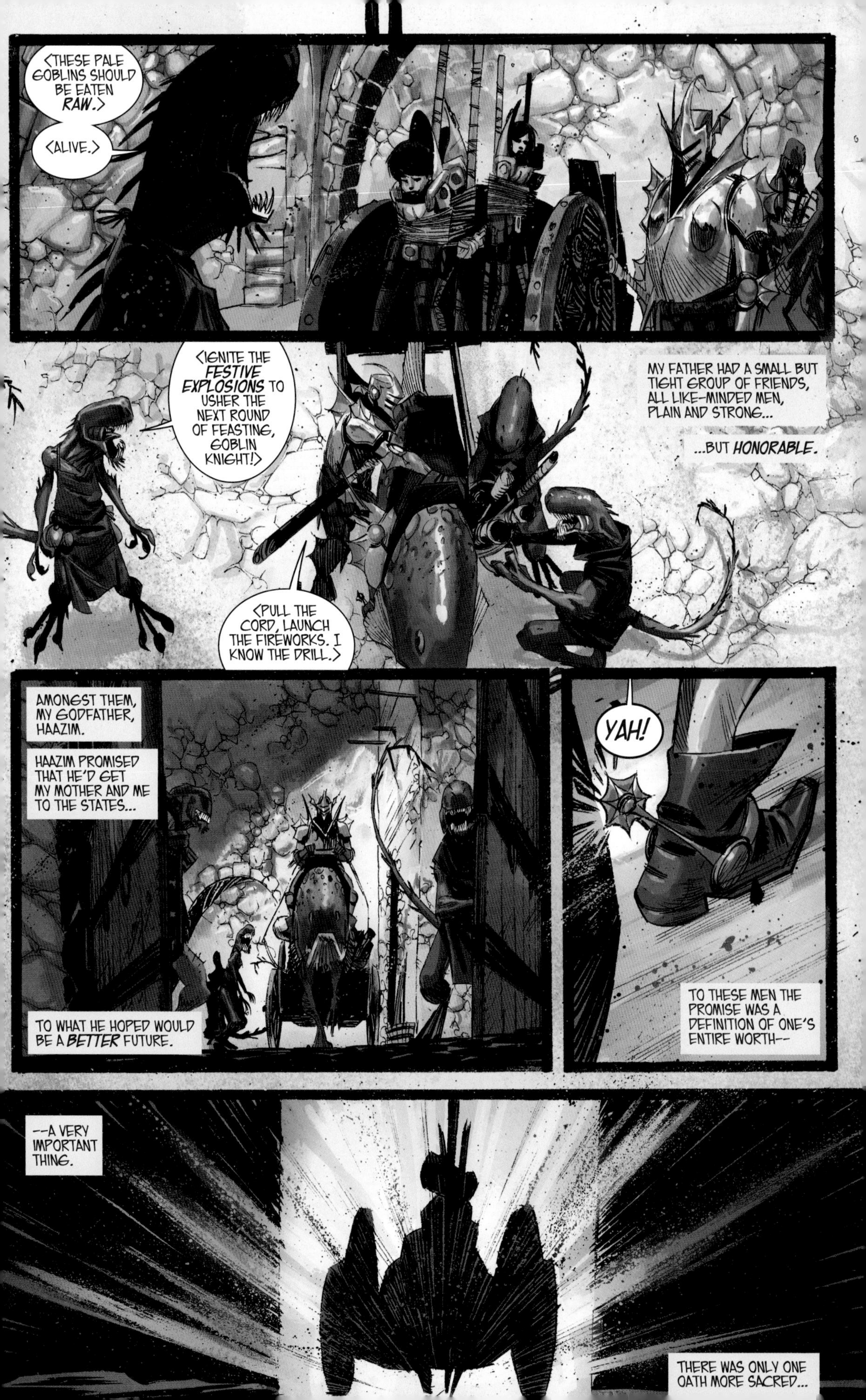

<THESE PALE GOBLINS SHOULD BE EATEN RAW.>
<ALIVE.>
<IGNITE THE FESTIVE EXPLOSIONS TO USHER THE NEXT ROUND OF FEASTING, GOBLIN KNIGHT!>
MY FATHER HAD A SMALL BUT TIGHT GROUP OF FRIENDS, ALL LIKE-MINDED MEN, PLAIN AND STRONG...
...BUT HONORABLE.
<PULL THE CORD, LAUNCH THE FIREWORKS. I KNOW THE DRILL.>
AMONGST THEM, MY GODFATHER, HAAZIM.
HAAZIM PROMISED THAT HE'D GET MY MOTHER AND ME TO THE STATES...
TO WHAT HE HOPED WOULD BE A BETTER FUTURE.
YAH!
TO THESE MEN THE PROMISE WAS A DEFINITION OF ONE'S ENTIRE WORTH--
--A VERY IMPORTANT THING.
THERE WAS ONLY ONE OATH MORE SACRED...

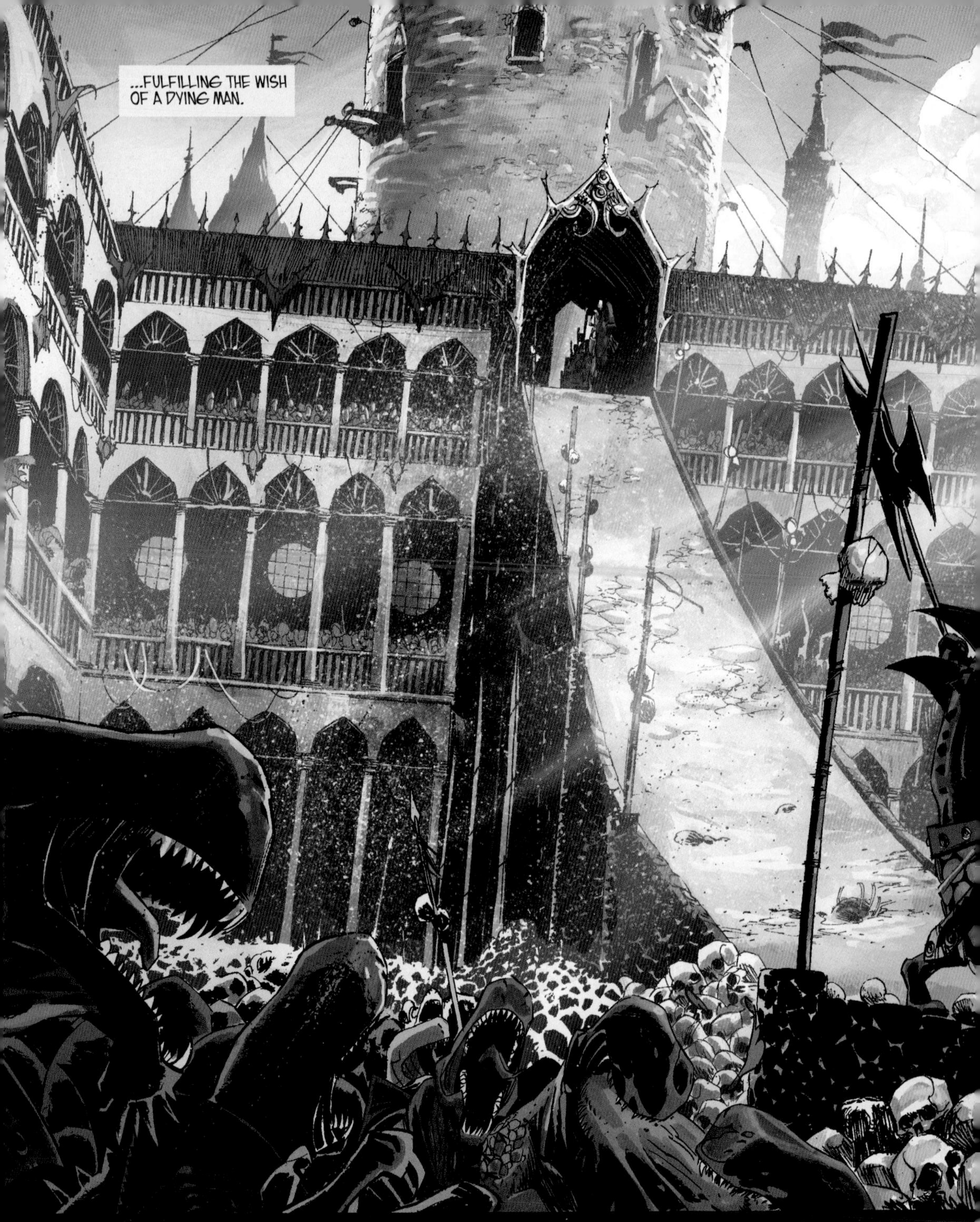
...FULFILLING THE WISH OF A DYING MAN.

BLACK

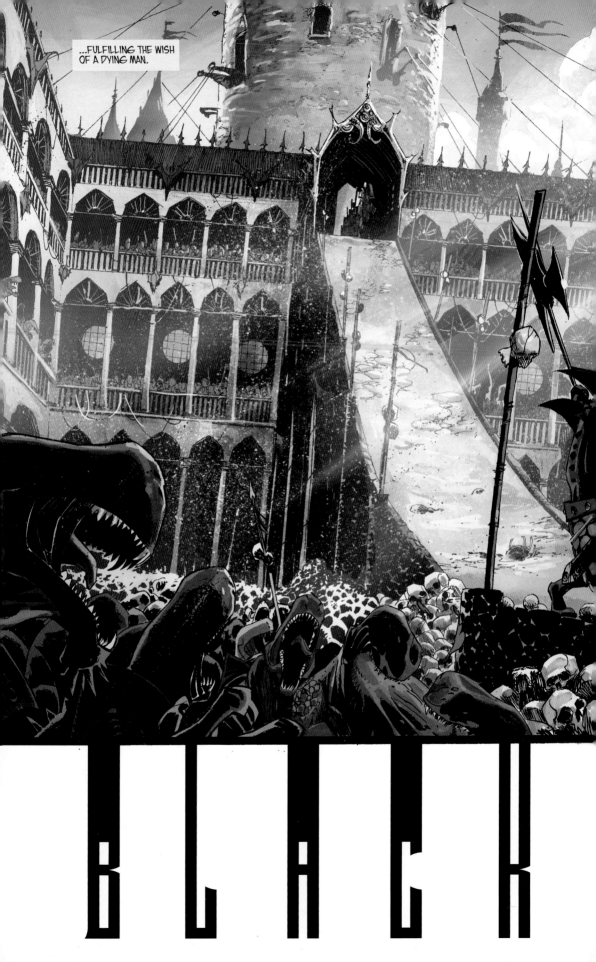

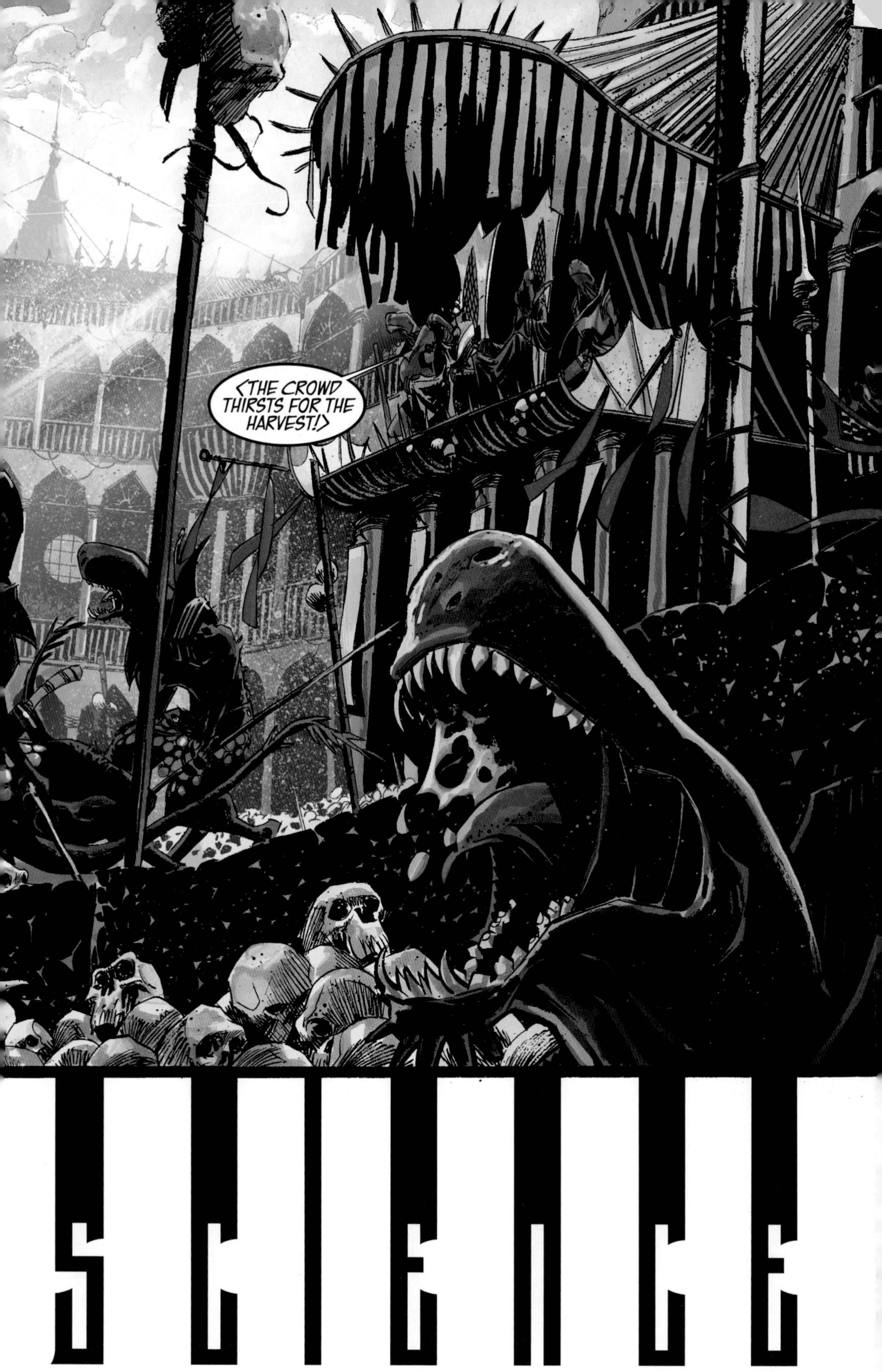
<THE CROWD THIRSTS FOR THE HARVEST!>

SCIENCE

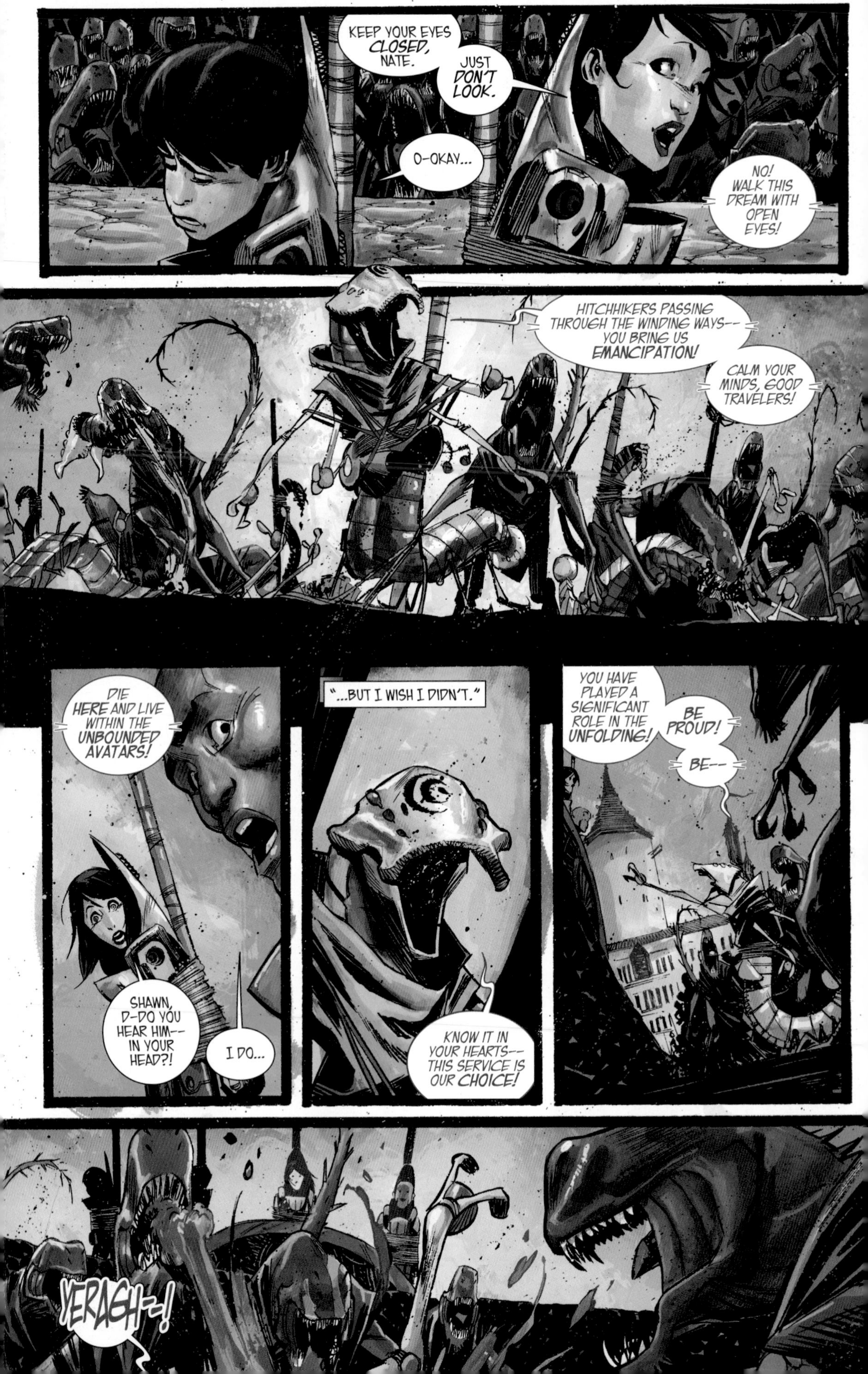
KEEP YOUR EYES CLOSED, NATE.
JUST DON'T LOOK.
O-OKAY...
NO! WALK THIS DREAM WITH OPEN EYES!
HITCHHIKERS PASSING THROUGH THE WINDING WAYS-- YOU BRING US EMANCIPATION!
CALM YOUR MINDS, GOOD TRAVELERS!
DIE HERE AND LIVE WITHIN THE UNBOUNDED AVATARS!
SHAWN, D-DO YOU HEAR HIM-- IN YOUR HEAD?!
I DO...
"...BUT I WISH I DIDN'T."
KNOW IT IN YOUR HEARTS-- THIS SERVICE IS OUR CHOICE!
YOU HAVE PLAYED A SIGNIFICANT ROLE IN THE UNFOLDING!
BE PROUD!
BE--
YERAGH--!

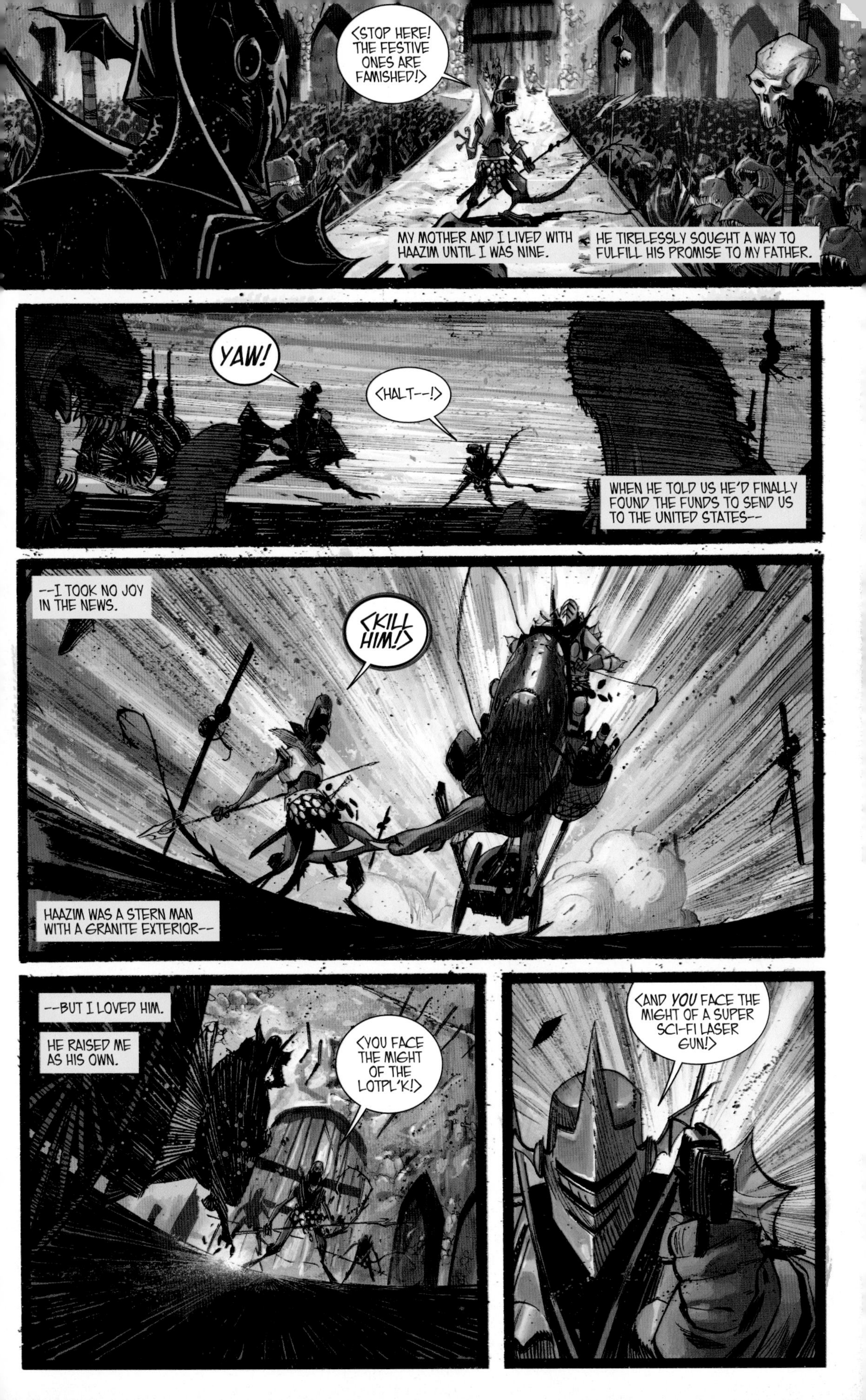
<STOP HERE! THE FESTIVE ONES ARE FAMISHED!>
MY MOTHER AND I LIVED WITH HAAZIM UNTIL I WAS NINE.
HE TIRELESSLY SOUGHT A WAY TO FULFILL HIS PROMISE TO MY FATHER.
YAW!
<HALT--!>
WHEN HE TOLD US HE'D FINALLY FOUND THE FUNDS TO SEND US TO THE UNITED STATES--
--I TOOK NO JOY IN THE NEWS.
<KILL HIM!>
HAAZIM WAS A STERN MAN WITH A GRANITE EXTERIOR--
--BUT I LOVED HIM.
HE RAISED ME AS HIS OWN.
<YOU FACE THE MIGHT OF THE LOTPL'K!>
<AND YOU FACE THE MIGHT OF A SUPER SCI-FI LASER GUN!>

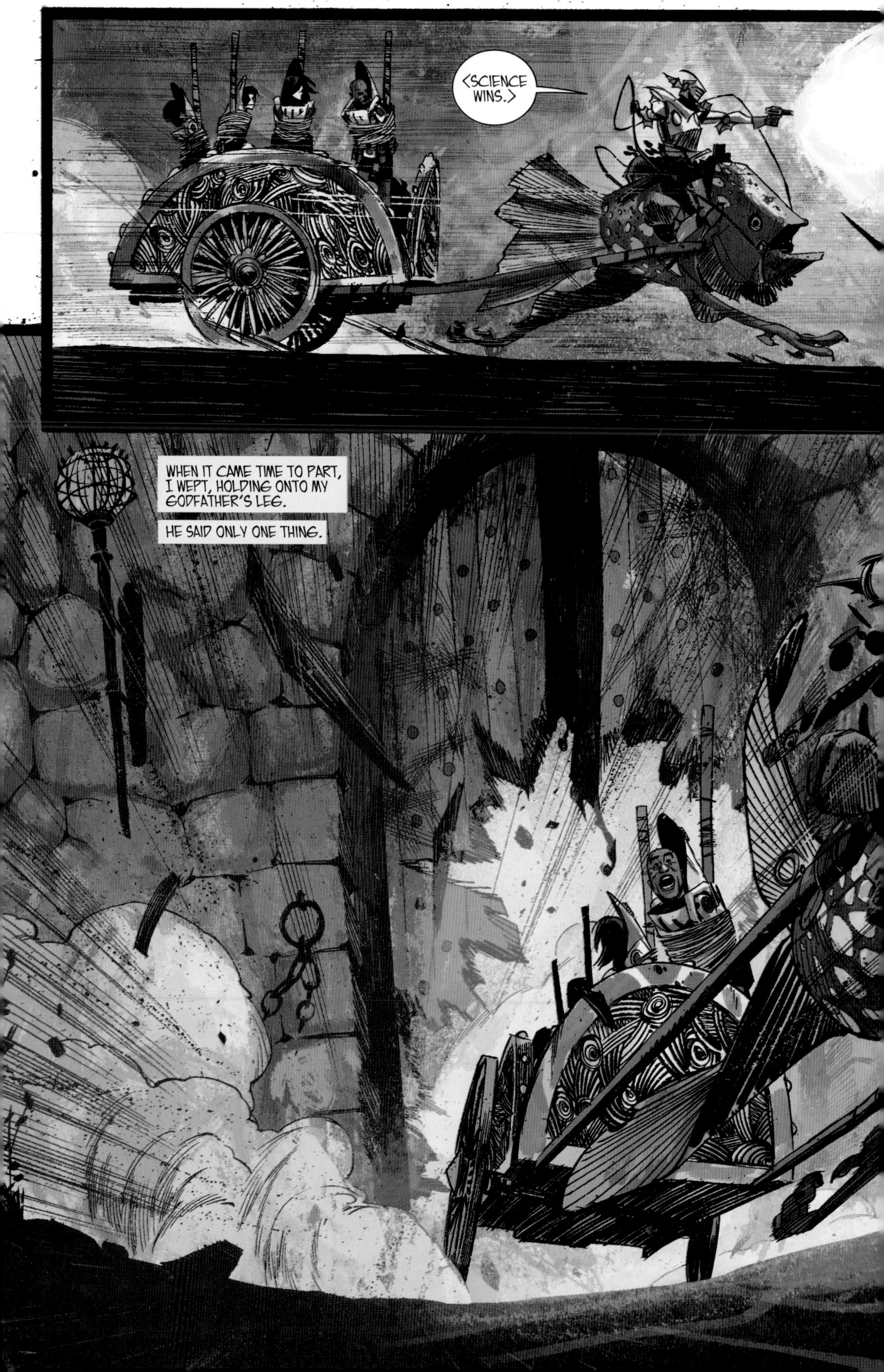
<SCIENCE WINS.>
WHEN IT CAME TIME TO PART, I WEPT, HOLDING ONTO MY GODFATHER'S LEG.
HE SAID ONLY ONE THING.

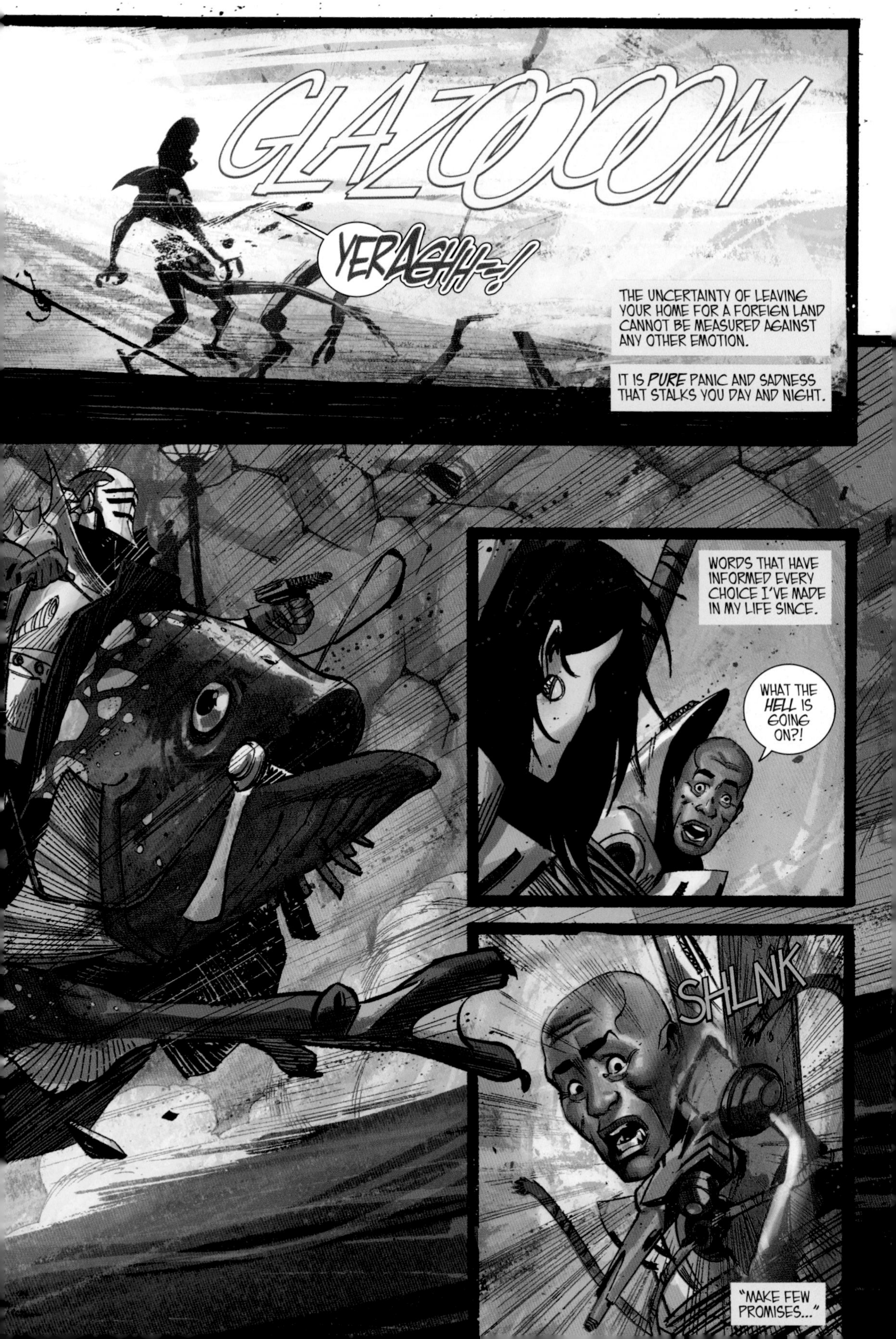
GLAZOOOOM
YERAGHH-!
THE UNCERTAINTY OF LEAVING YOUR HOME FOR A FOREIGN LAND CANNOT BE MEASURED AGAINST ANY OTHER EMOTION.
IT IS PURE PANIC AND SADNESS THAT STALKS YOU DAY AND NIGHT.
WORDS THAT HAVE INFORMED EVERY CHOICE I'VE MADE IN MY LIFE SINCE.
WHAT THE HELL IS GOING ON?!
SHLNK
"MAKE FEW PROMISES..."

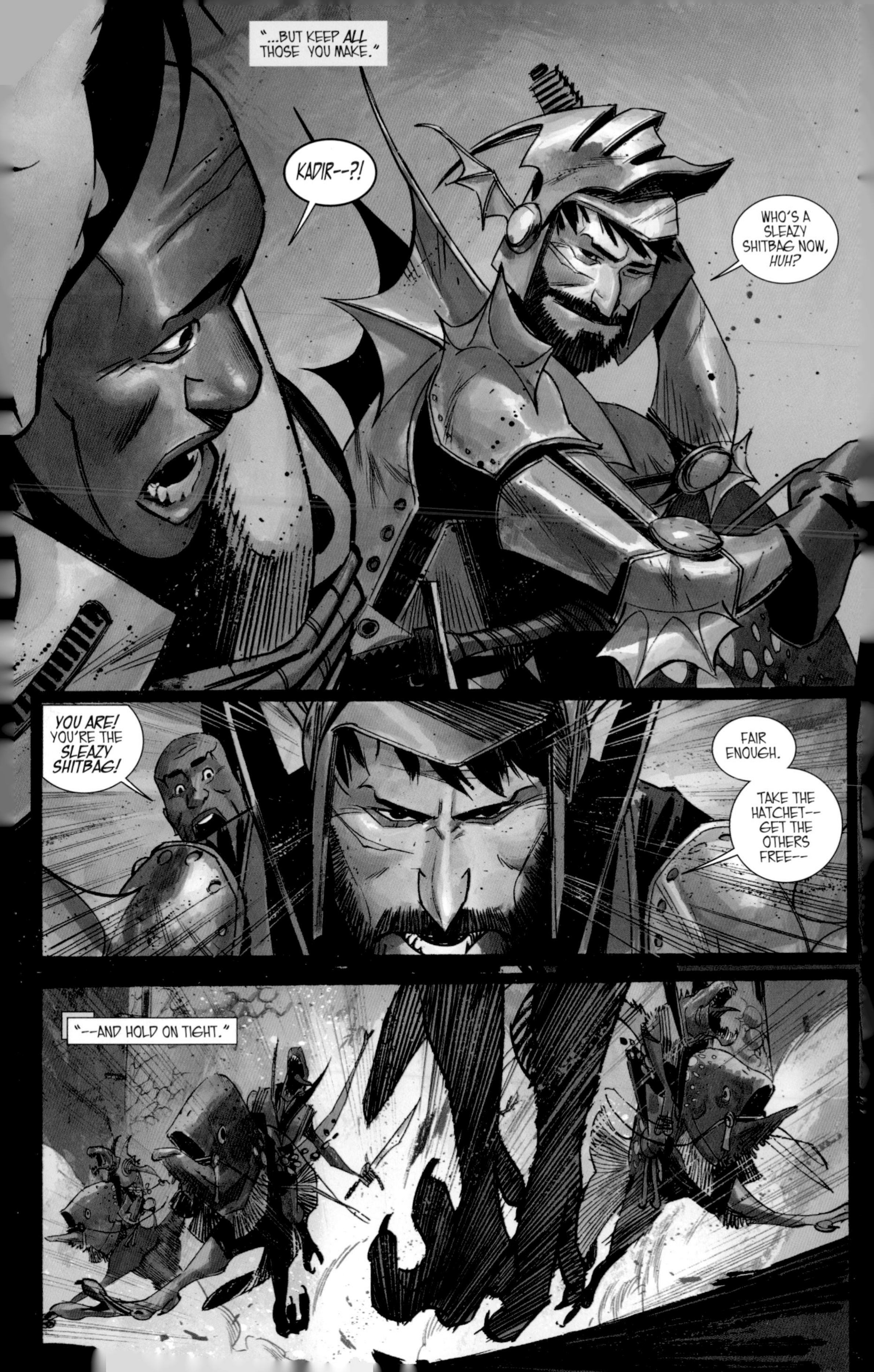
"...BUT KEEP ALL THOSE YOU MAKE."
KADIR--?!
WHO'S A SLEAZY SHITBAG NOW, HUH?
YOU ARE! YOU'RE THE SLEAZY SHITBAG!
FAIR ENOUGH.
TAKE THE HATCHET--GET THE OTHERS FREE--
"--AND HOLD ON TIGHT."

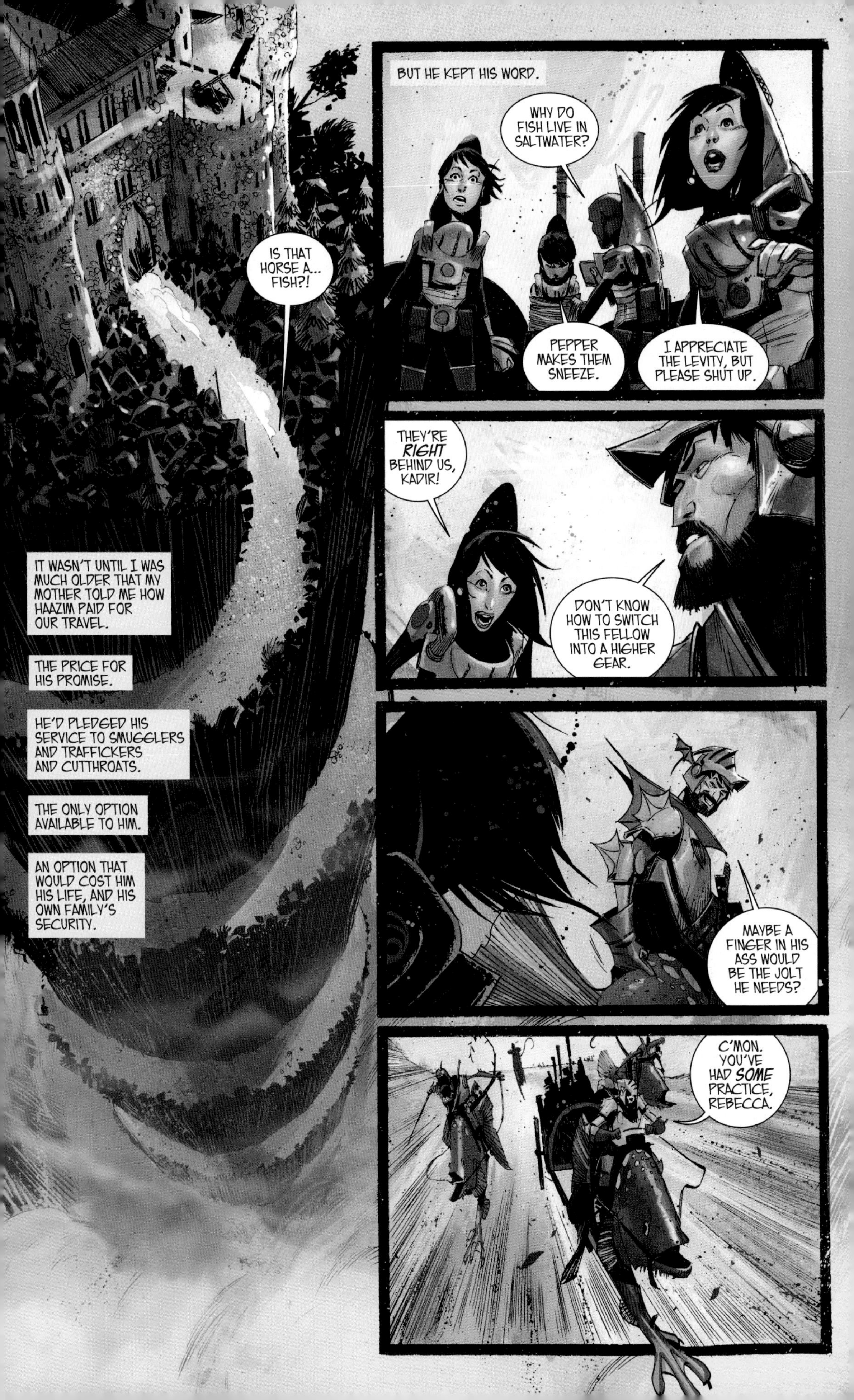
IS THAT HORSE A... FISH?!
BUT HE KEPT HIS WORD.
WHY DO FISH LIVE IN SALTWATER?
PEPPER MAKES THEM SNEEZE.
I APPRECIATE THE LEVITY, BUT PLEASE SHUT UP.
IT WASN'T UNTIL I WAS MUCH OLDER THAT MY MOTHER TOLD ME HOW HAAZIM PAID FOR OUR TRAVEL.
THE PRICE FOR HIS PROMISE.
HE'D PLEDGED HIS SERVICE TO SMUGGLERS AND TRAFFICKERS AND CUTTHROATS.
THE ONLY OPTION AVAILABLE TO HIM.
AN OPTION THAT WOULD COST HIM HIS LIFE, AND HIS OWN FAMILY'S SECURITY.
THEY'RE RIGHT BEHIND US, KADIR!
DON'T KNOW HOW TO SWITCH THIS FELLOW INTO A HIGHER GEAR.
MAYBE A FINGER IN HIS ASS WOULD BE THE JOLT HE NEEDS?
C'MON. YOU'VE HAD SOME PRACTICE, REBECCA.

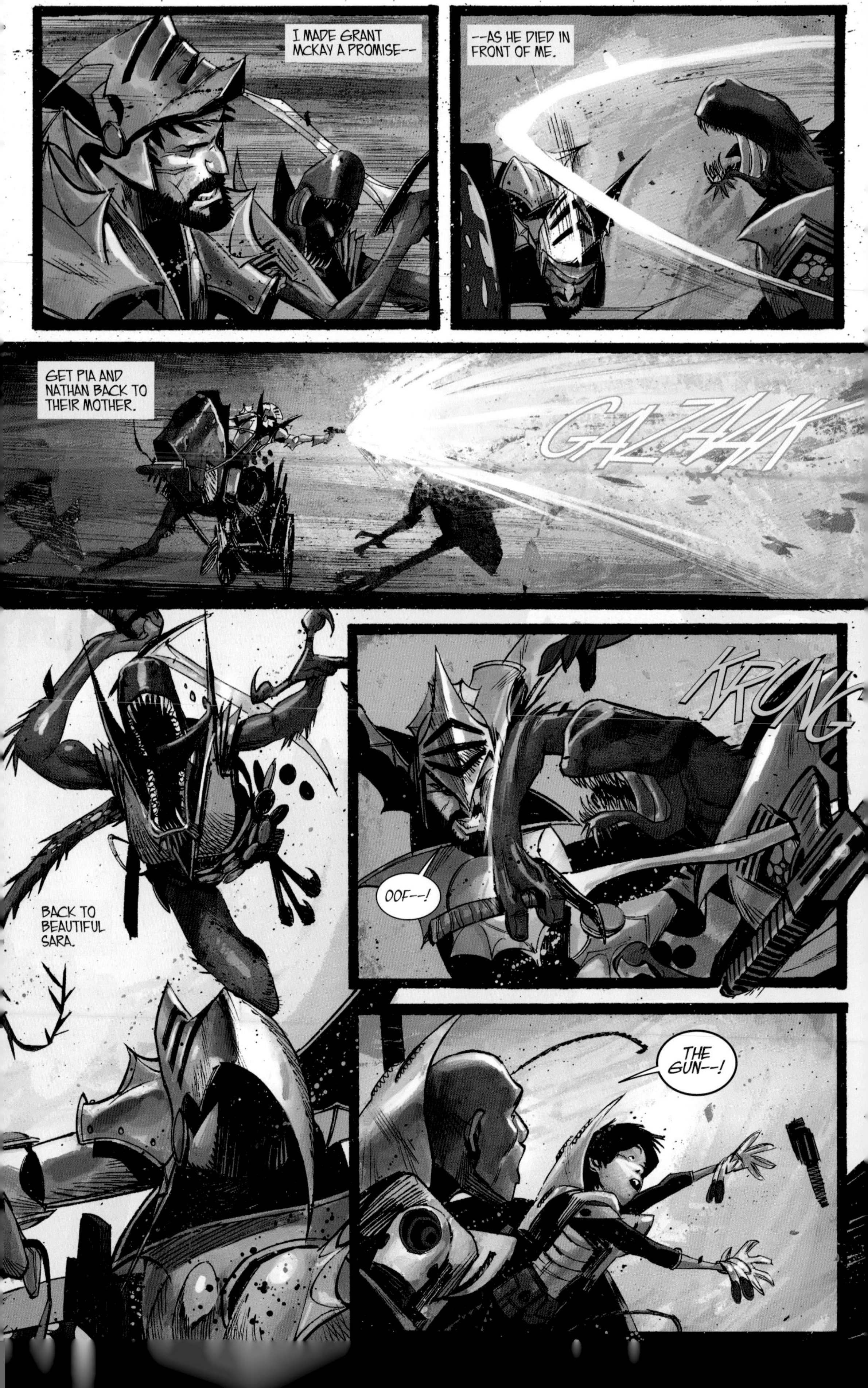
I MADE GRANT MCKAY A PROMISE--
--AS HE DIED IN FRONT OF ME.
GET PIA AND NATHAN BACK TO THEIR MOTHER.
GAZAAK
BACK TO BEAUTIFUL SARA.
KRUNG
OOF--!
THE GUN--!

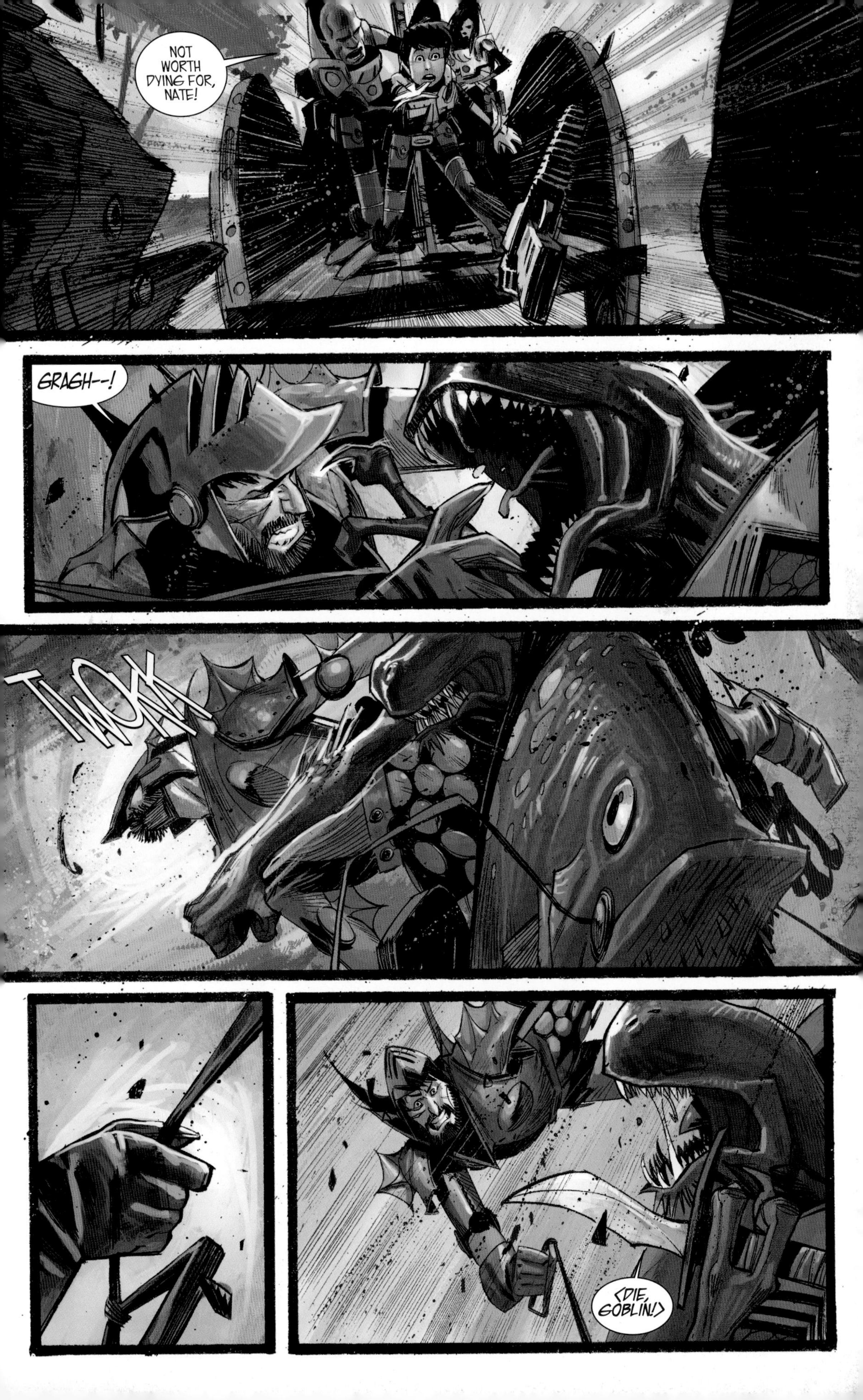
NOT WORTH DYING FOR, NATE!
GRAGH--!
TWOKK
<DIE, GOBLIN!>

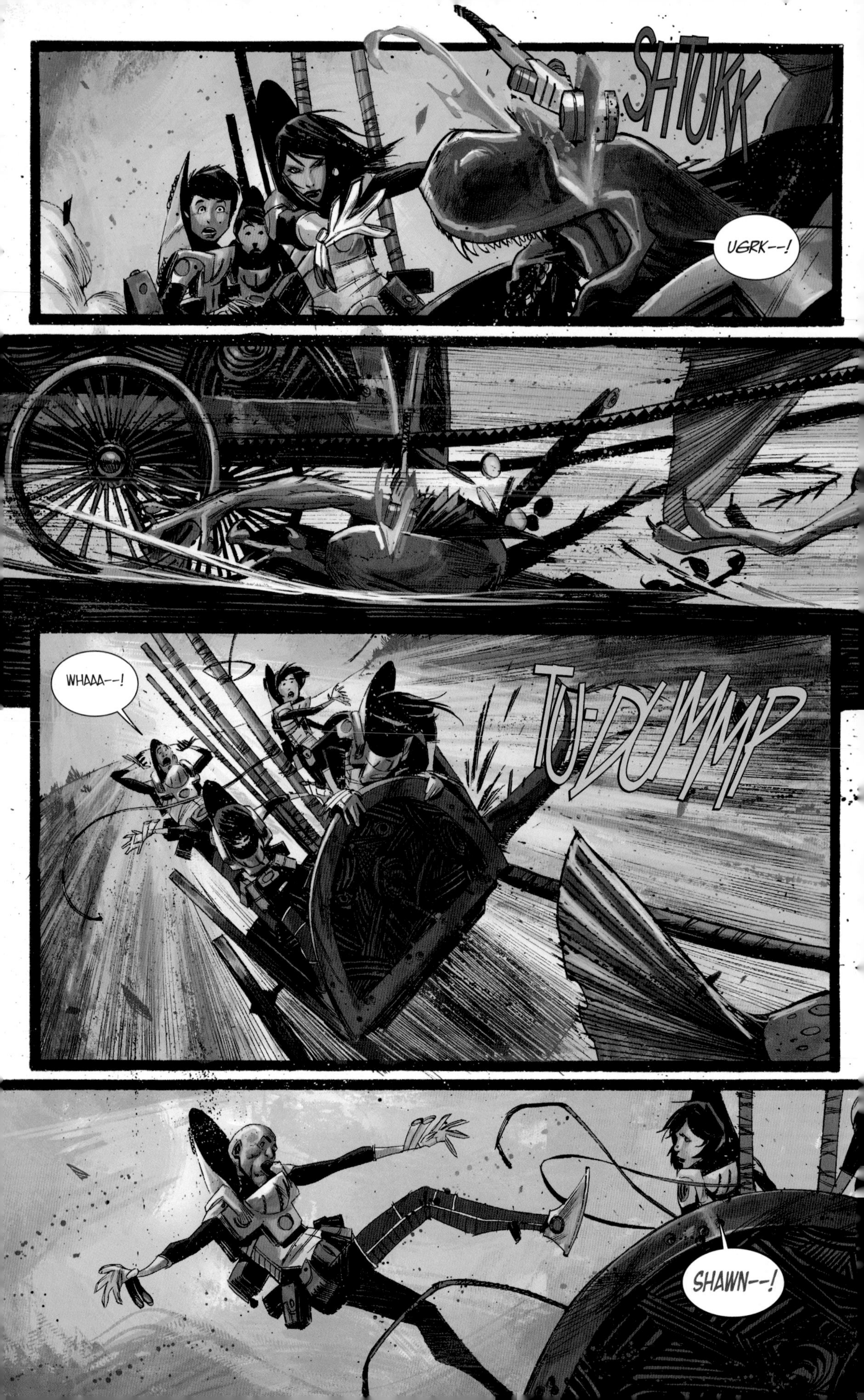
SHTUKK
UGRK--!
WHAAA--!
TU-DUMMP
SHAWN--!

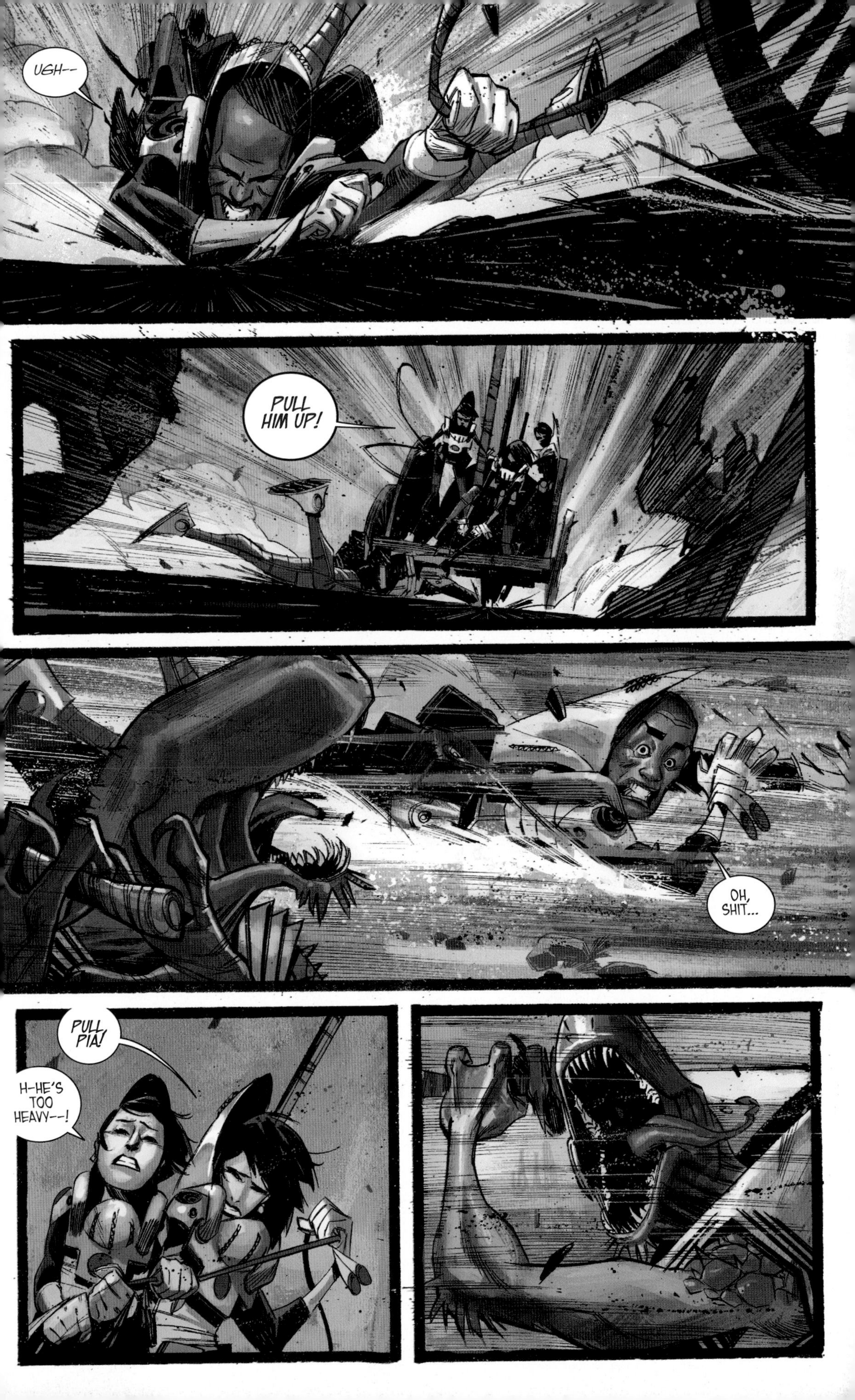
UGH--
PULL HIM UP!
OH, SHIT...
PULL PIA!
H-HE'S TOO HEAVY--!

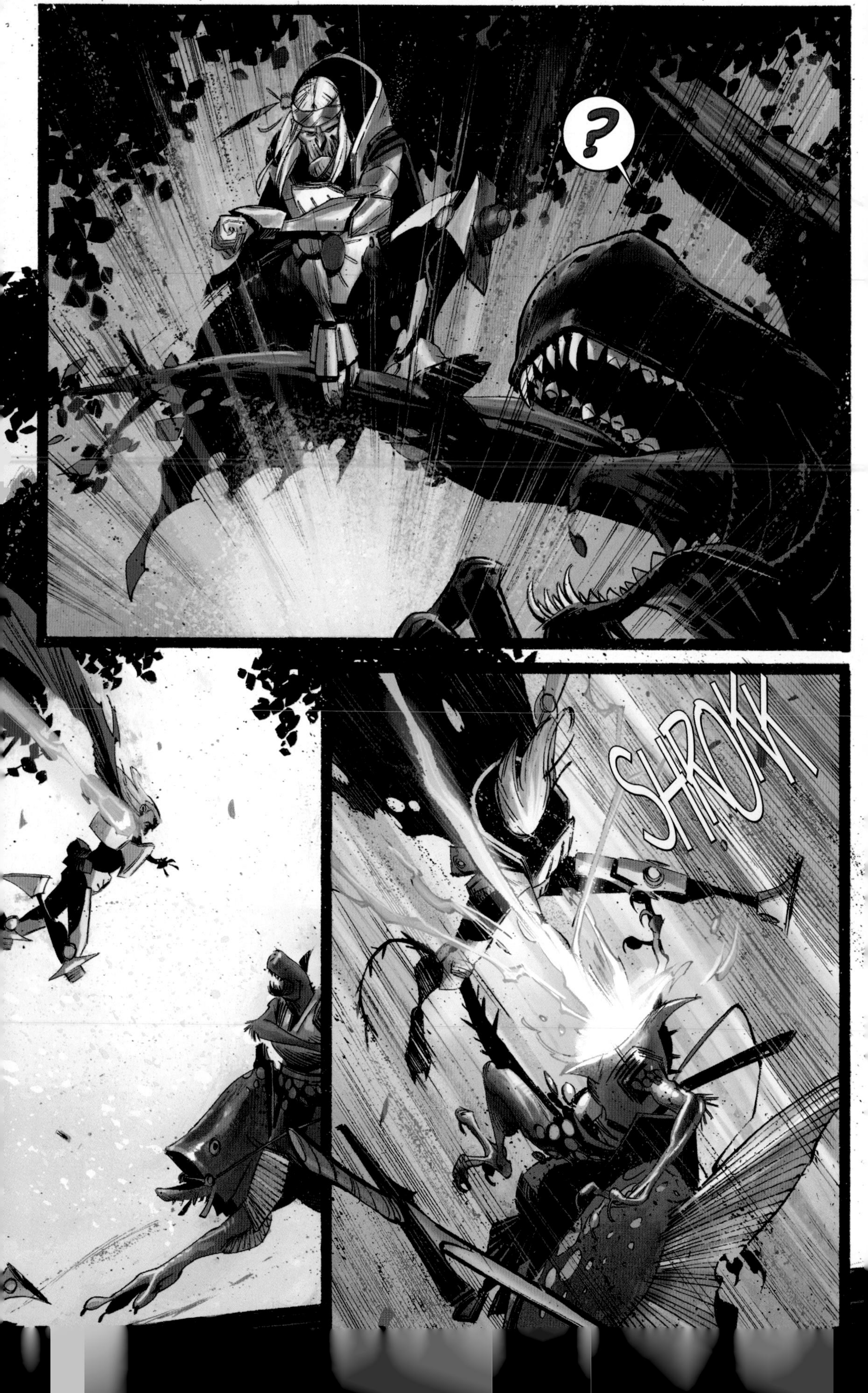
?
SHROKK

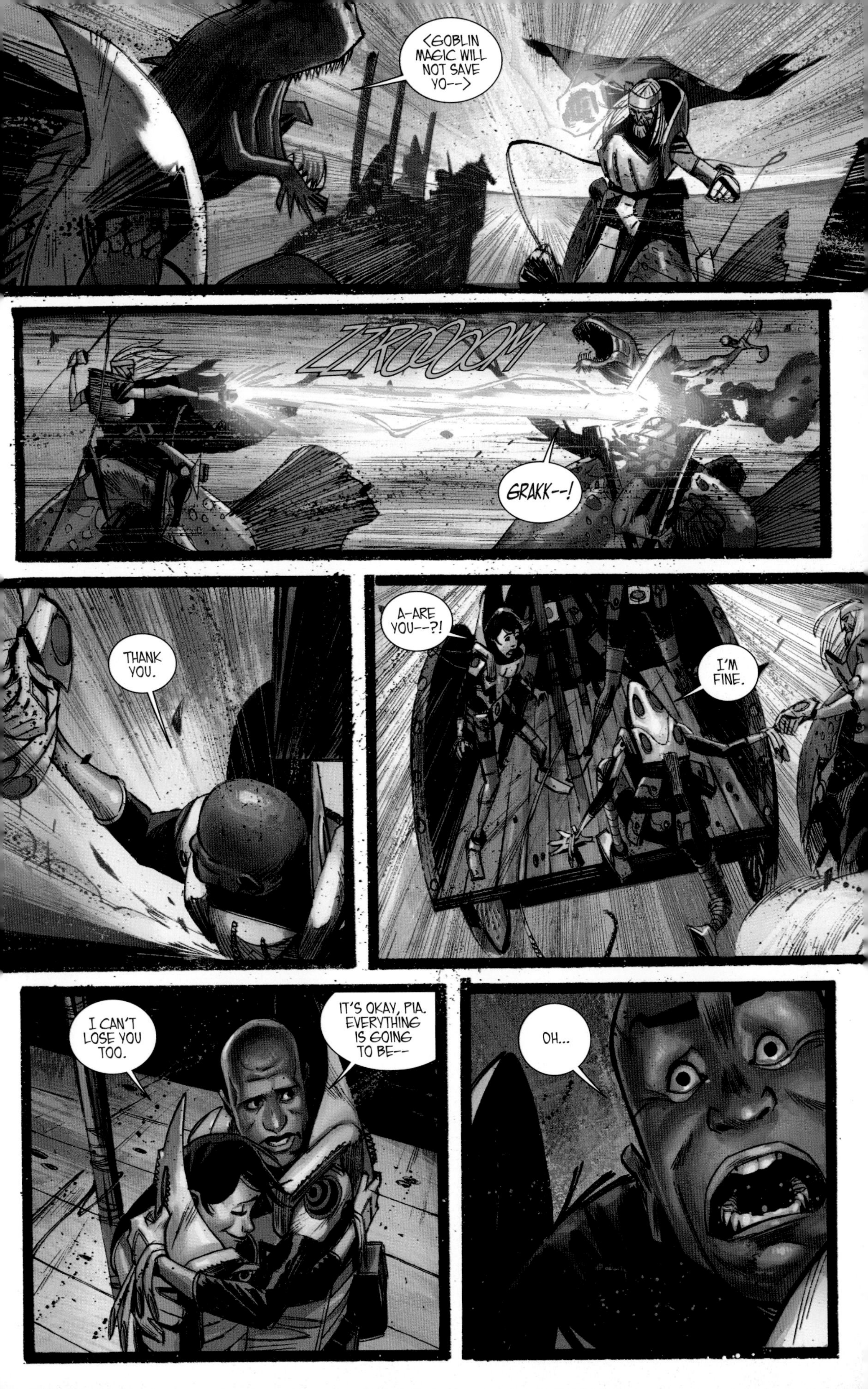
<GOBLIN MAGIC WILL NOT SAVE YO-->
ZZROOOOOM
GRAKK--!
THANK YOU.
A-ARE YOU--?!
I'M FINE.
I CAN'T LOSE YOU TOO.
IT'S OKAY, PIA. EVERYTHING IS GOING TO BE--
OH...

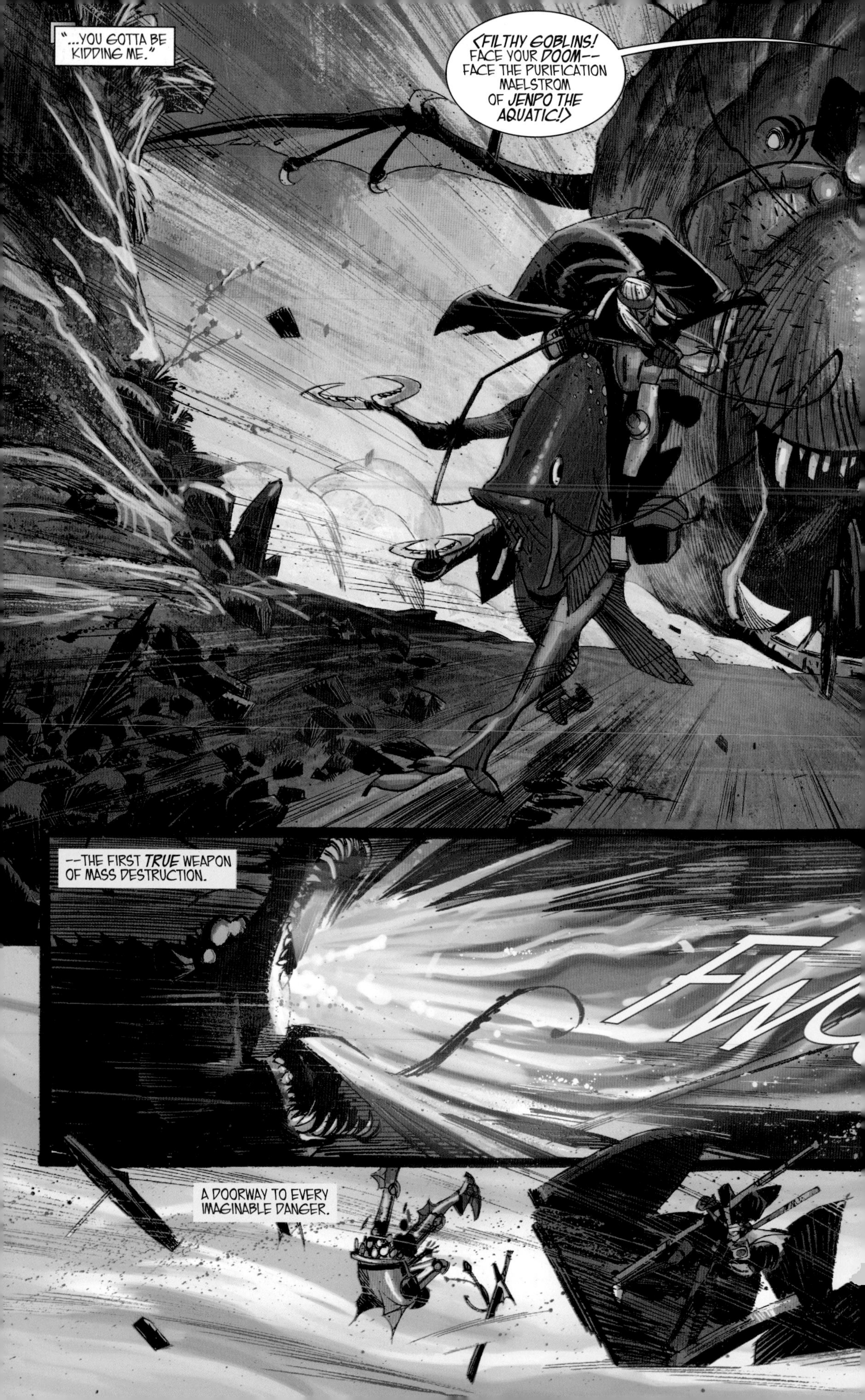
"...YOU GOTTA BE KIDDING ME."
<FILTHY GOBLINS! FACE YOUR DOOM-- FACE THE PURIFICATION MAELSTROM OF JENPO THE AQUATIC!>
--THE FIRST TRUE WEAPON OF MASS DESTRUCTION.
A DOORWAY TO EVERY IMAGINABLE DANGER.

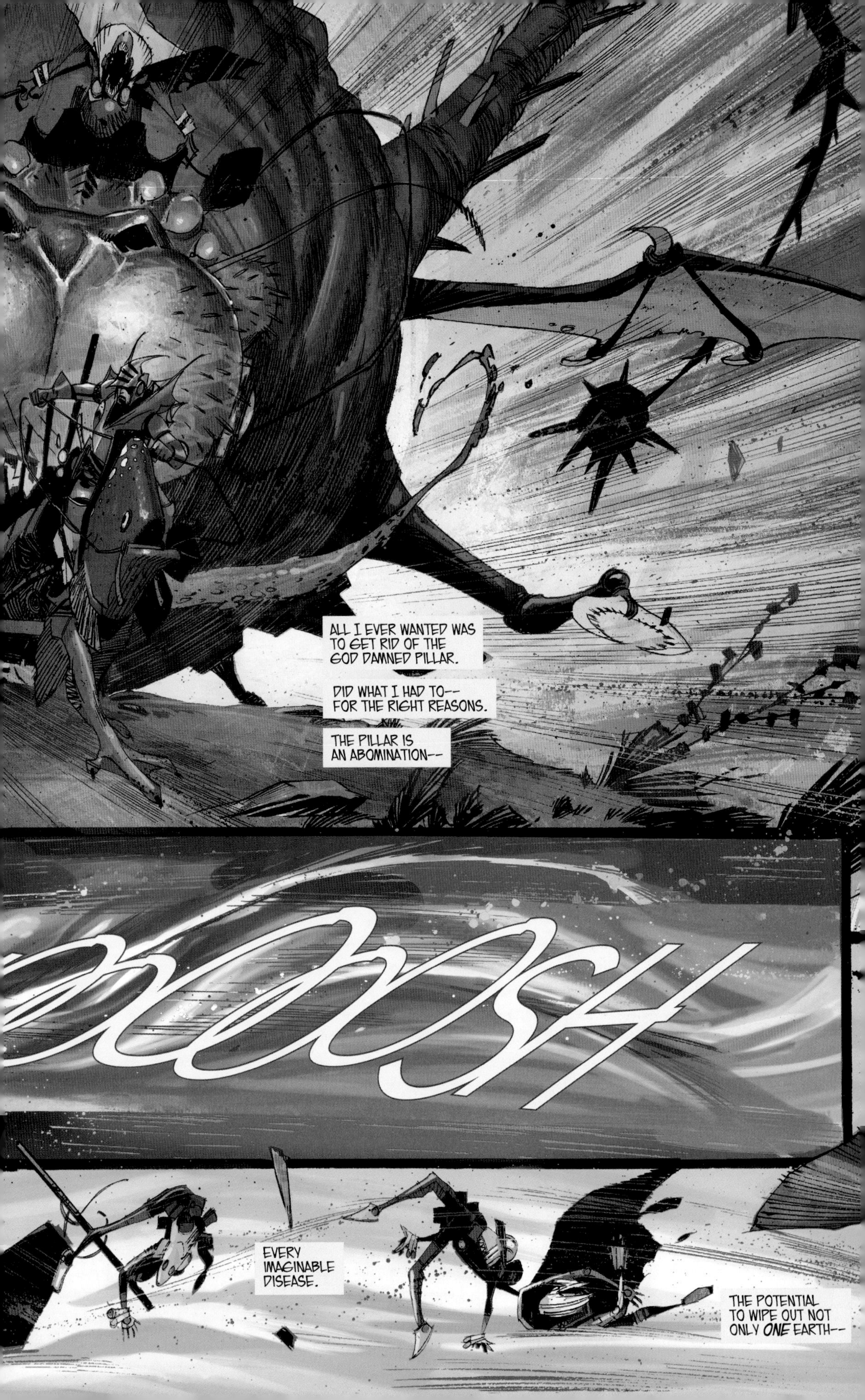
ALL I EVER WANTED WAS TO GET RID OF THE GOD DAMNED PILLAR.
DID WHAT I HAD TO-- FOR THE RIGHT REASONS.
THE PILLAR IS AN ABOMINATION--
EVERY IMAGINABLE DISEASE.
THE POTENTIAL TO WIPE OUT NOT ONLY *ONE* EARTH--

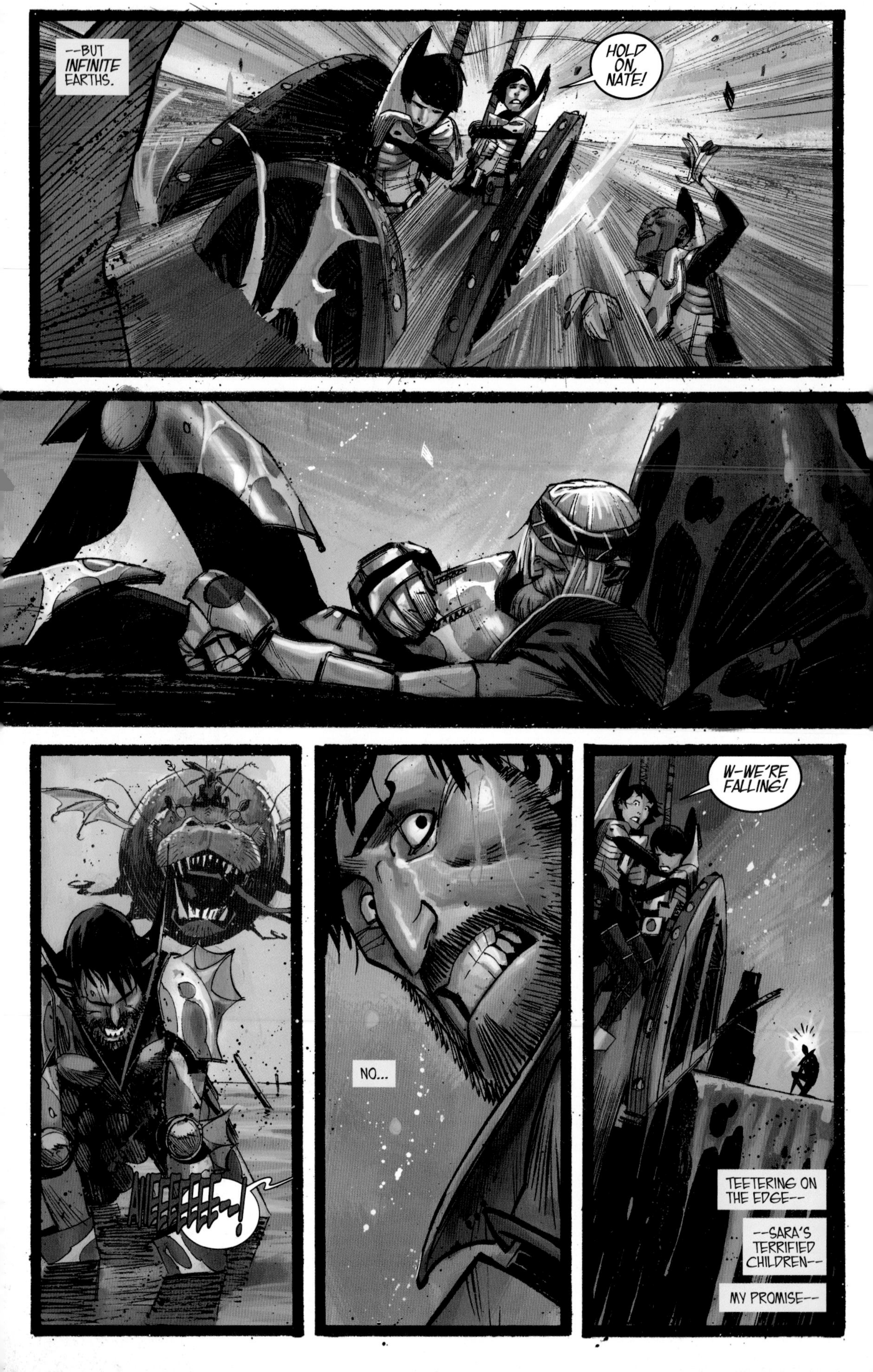
--BUT INFINITE EARTHS.
HOLD ON NATE!
AIIEEEEEEE!
NO...
W-WE'RE FALLING!
TEETERING ON THE EDGE--
--SARA'S TERRIFIED CHILDREN--
MY PROMISE--

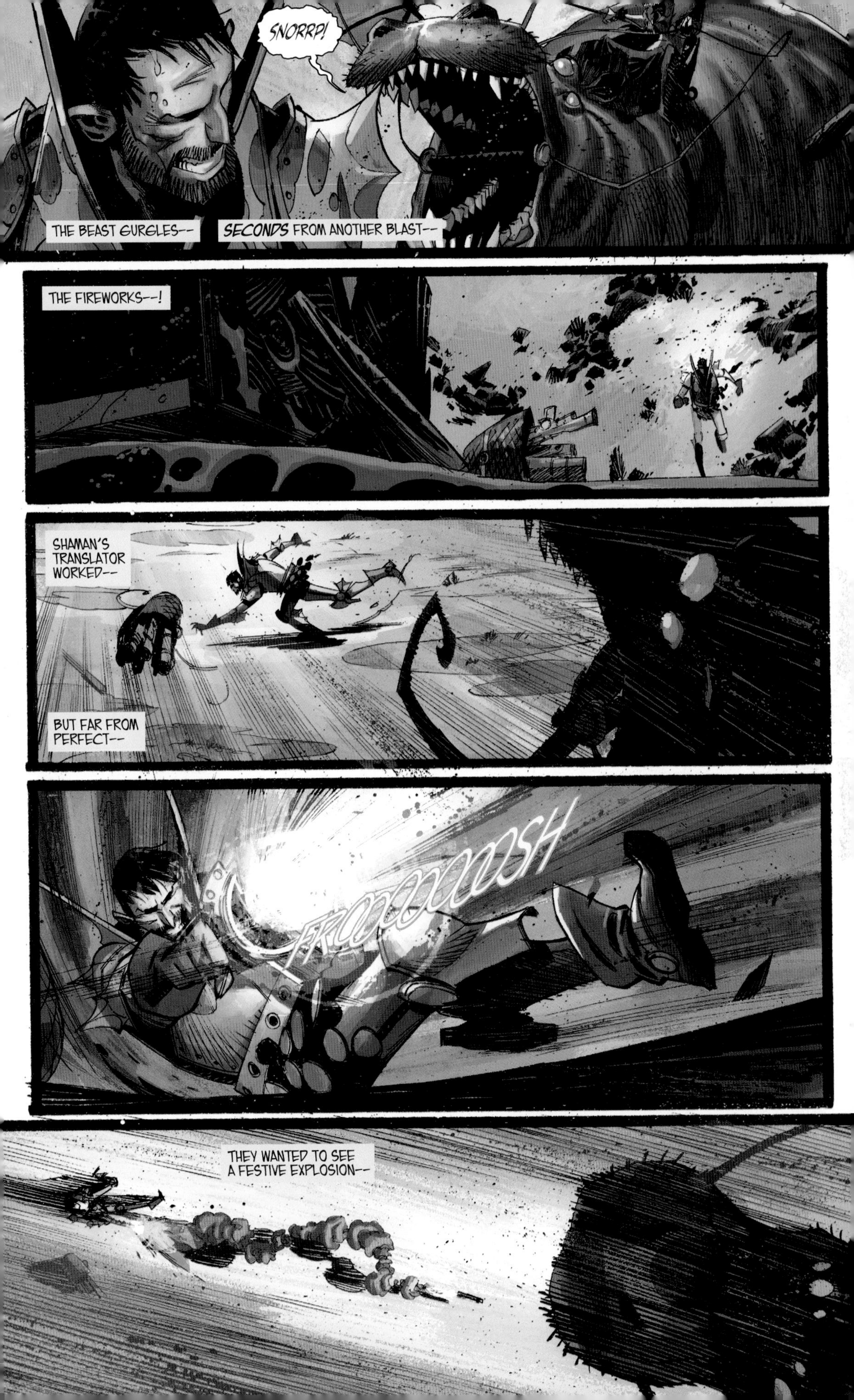
SNORRP!
THE BEAST GURGLES--
SECONDS FROM ANOTHER BLAST--
THE FIREWORKS--!
SHAMAN'S TRANSLATOR WORKED--
BUT FAR FROM PERFECT--
FRROOOOOOOSH
THEY WANTED TO SEE A FESTIVE EXPLOSION--

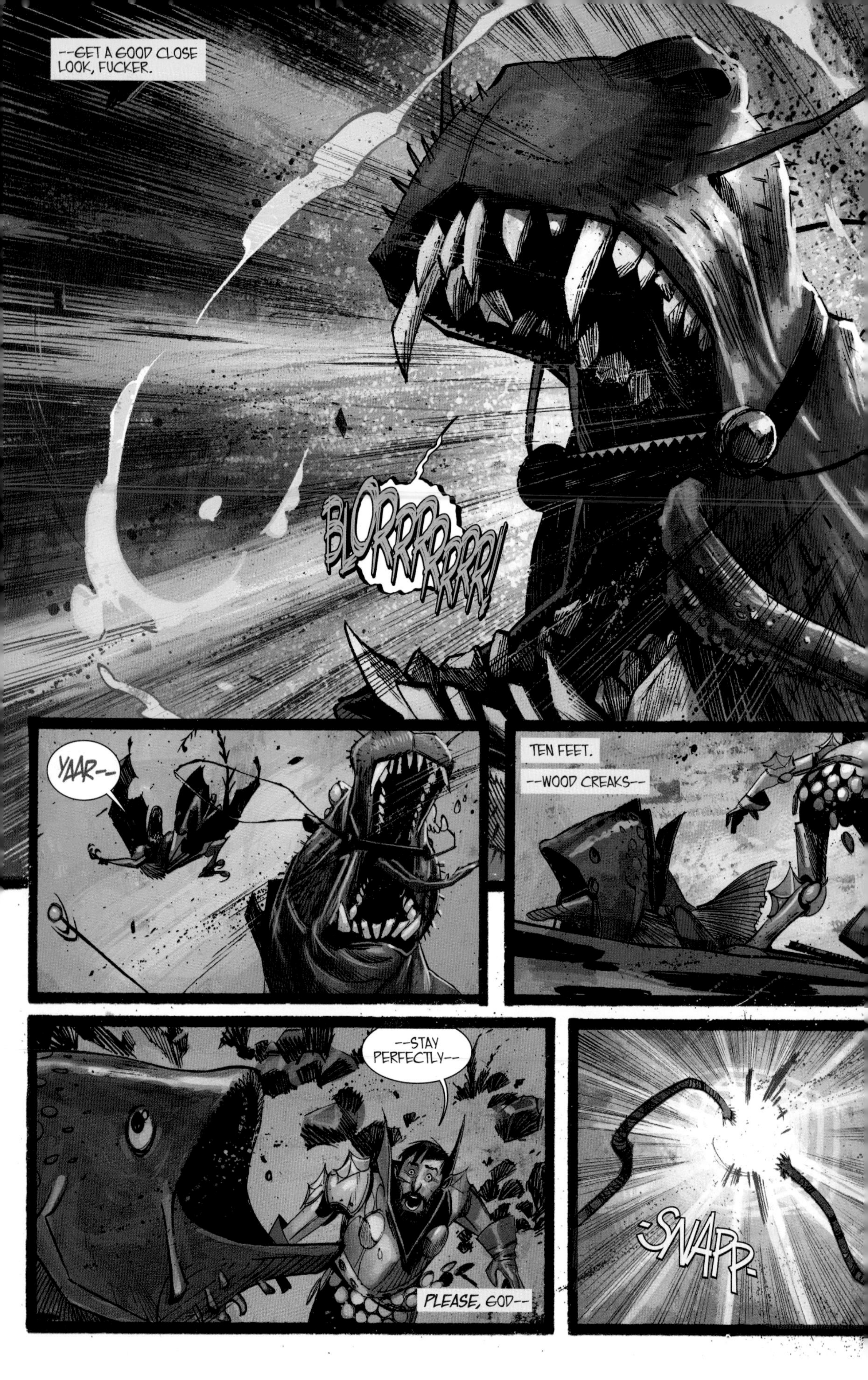
--GET A GOOD CLOSE LOOK, FUCKER.
BLORRRRRRRR!
YAAR--
TEN FEET.
--WOOD CREAKS--
--STAY PERFECTLY--
PLEASE, GOD--
-SNAPP-

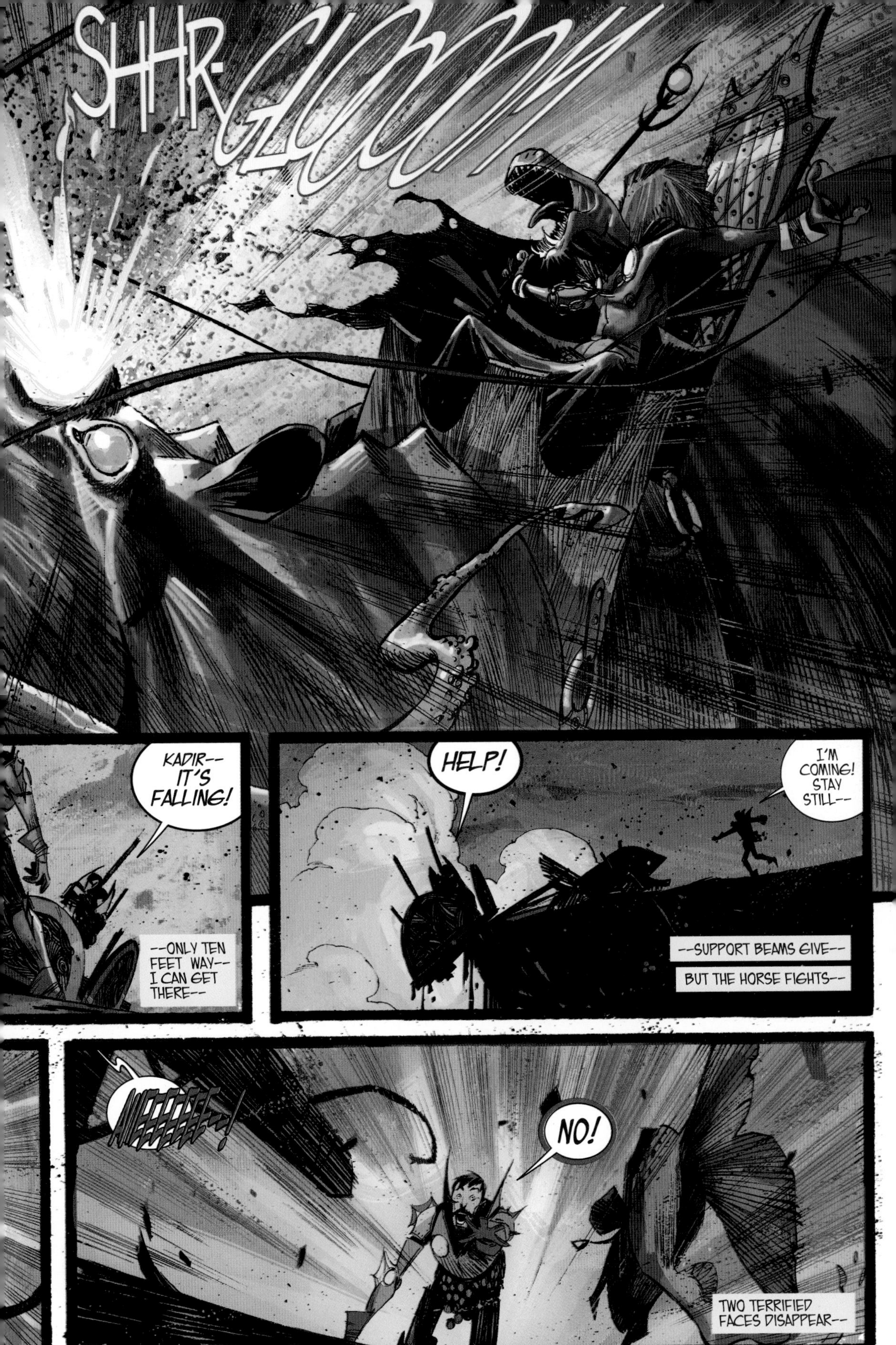
SHHR-GLOOOM
KADIR-- IT'S FALLING!
--ONLY TEN FEET WAY-- I CAN GET THERE--
HELP!
I'M COMING! STAY STILL--
--SUPPORT BEAMS GIVE--
BUT THE HORSE FIGHTS--
AIIEEEEEEEE--!
NO!
TWO TERRIFIED FACES DISAPPEAR--

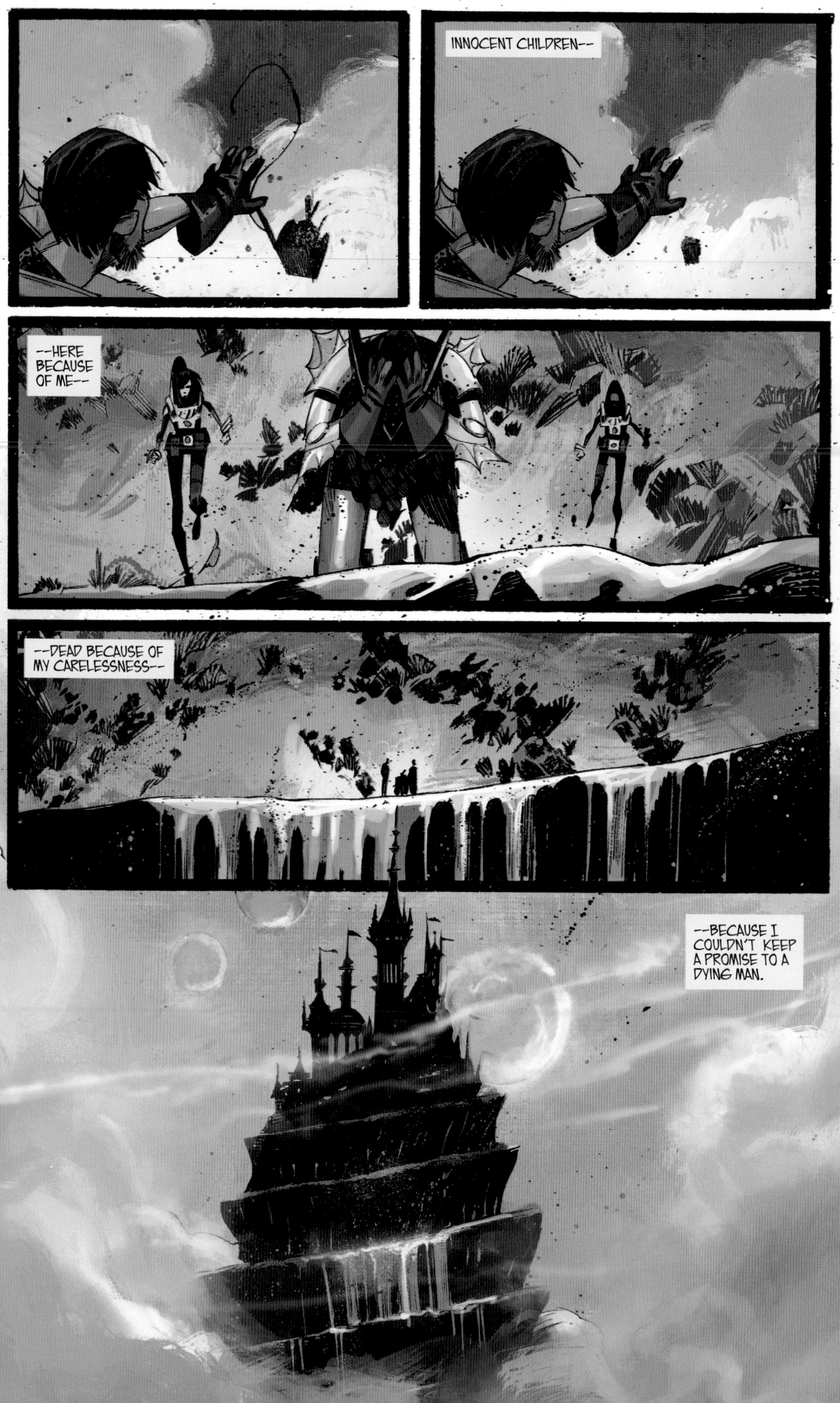
INNOCENT CHILDREN--
--HERE BECAUSE OF ME--
--DEAD BECAUSE OF MY CARELESSNESS--
--BECAUSE I COULDN'T KEEP A PROMISE TO A DYING MAN.

8

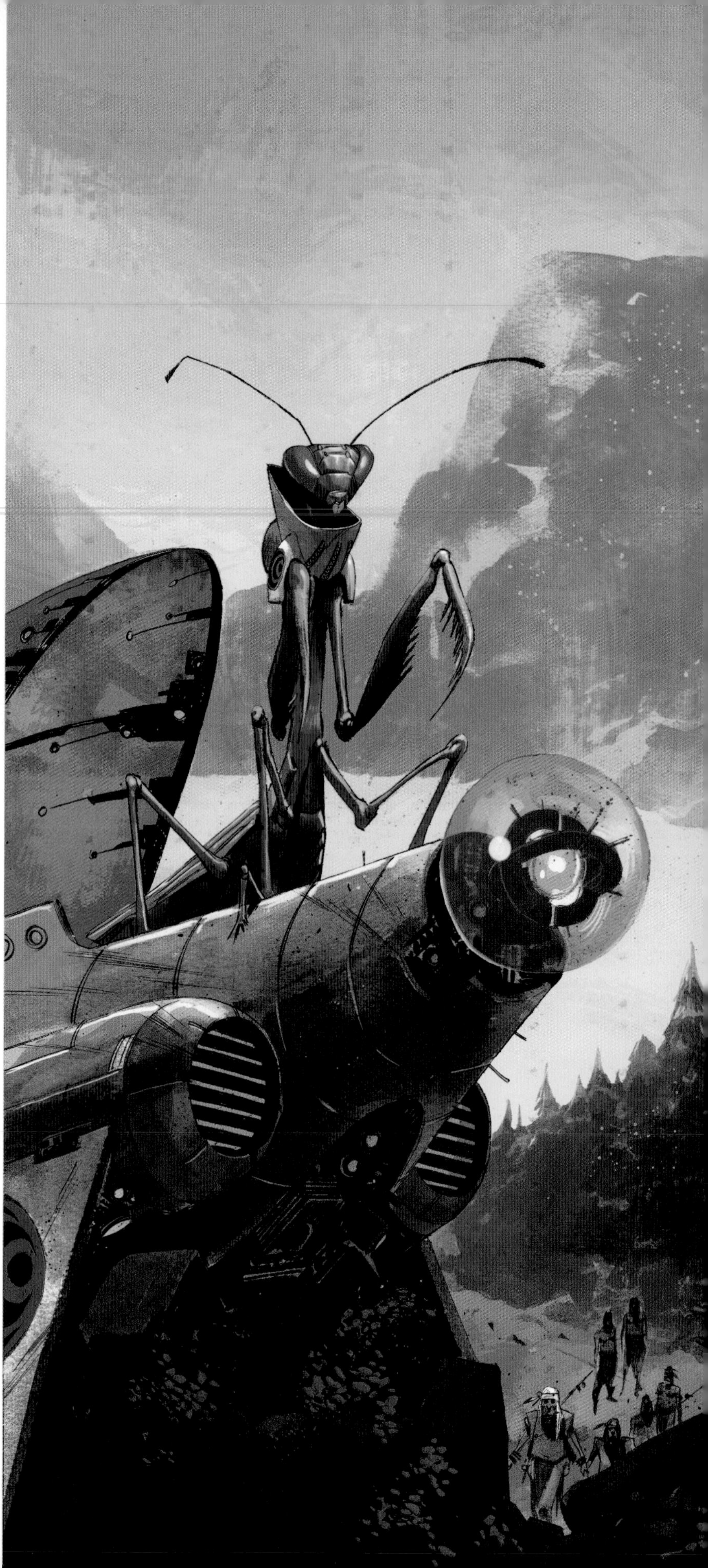

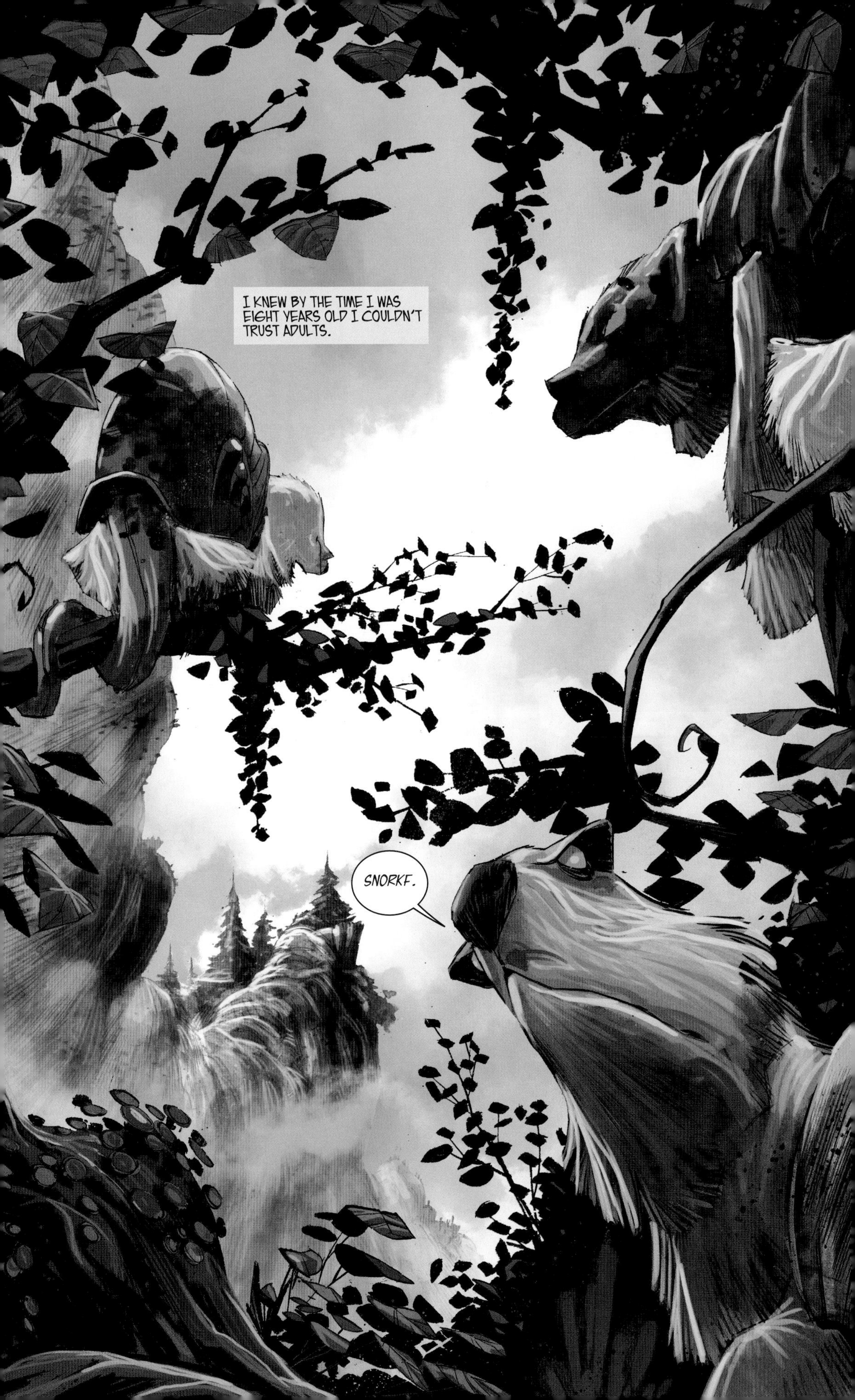
I KNEW BY THE TIME I WAS EIGHT YEARS OLD I COULDN'T TRUST ADULTS.
SNORKF.

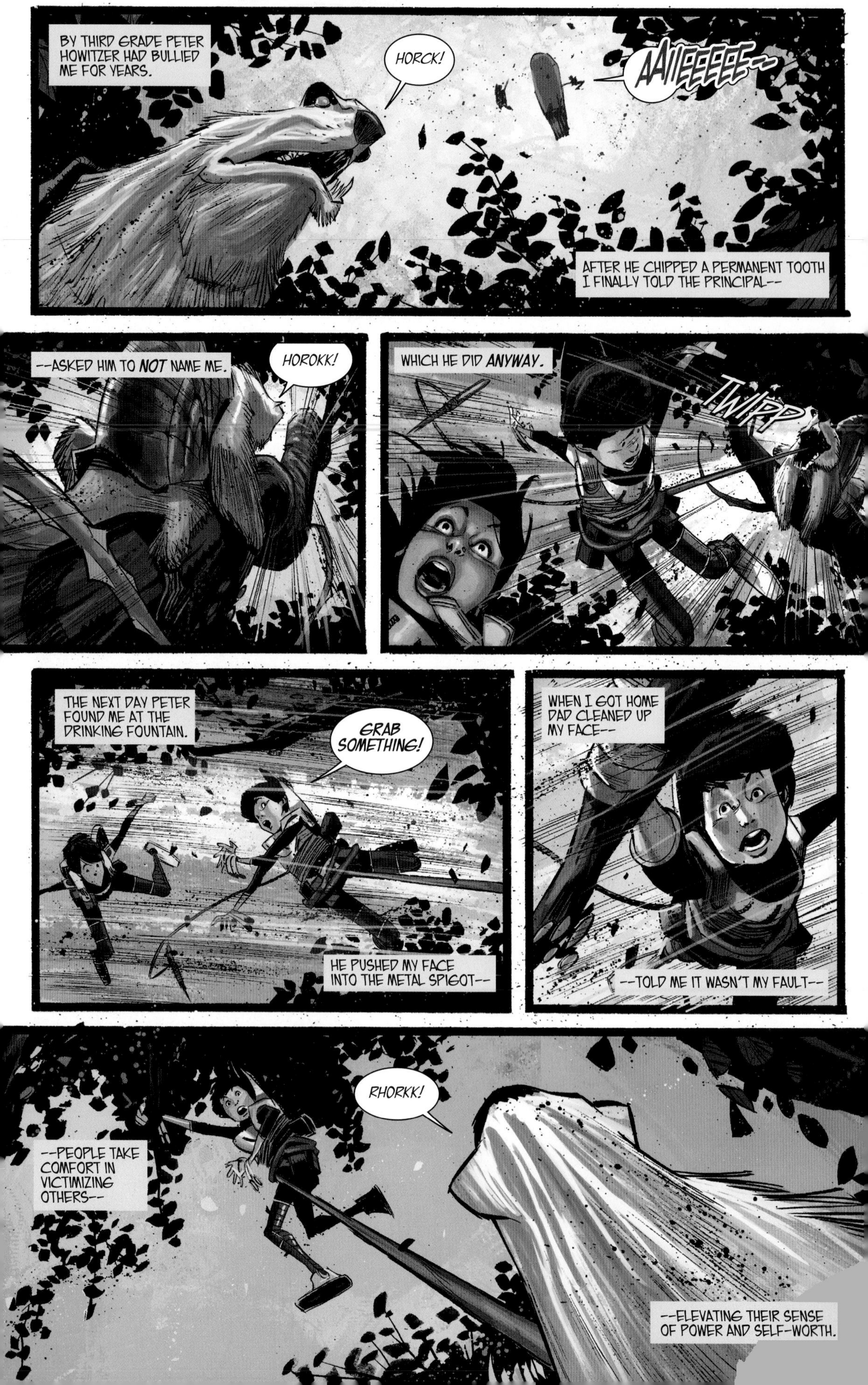
BY THIRD GRADE PETER HOWITZER HAD BULLIED ME FOR YEARS.
HORCK!
AAIIEEEEEE--
AFTER HE CHIPPED A PERMANENT TOOTH I FINALLY TOLD THE PRINCIPAL--
--ASKED HIM TO NOT NAME ME.
HOROKK!
WHICH HE DID ANYWAY.
TWIRP
THE NEXT DAY PETER FOUND ME AT THE DRINKING FOUNTAIN.
GRAB SOMETHING!
HE PUSHED MY FACE INTO THE METAL SPIGOT--
WHEN I GOT HOME DAD CLEANED UP MY FACE--
--TOLD ME IT WASN'T MY FAULT--
RHORKK!
--PEOPLE TAKE COMFORT IN VICTIMIZING OTHERS--
--ELEVATING THEIR SENSE OF POWER AND SELF-WORTH.

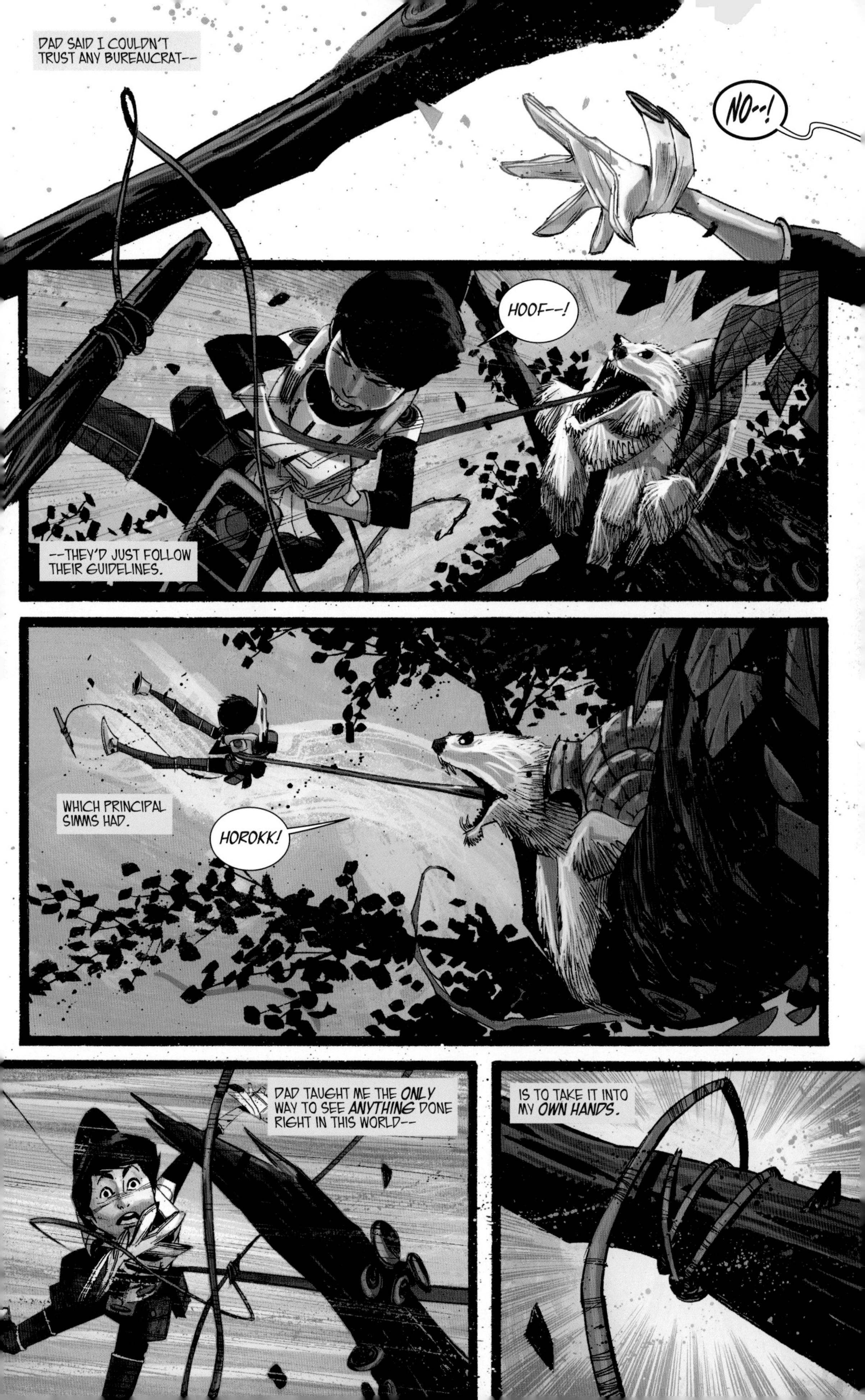

DAD SAID I COULDN'T TRUST ANY BUREAUCRAT--
NO--!
HOOF--!
--THEY'D JUST FOLLOW THEIR GUIDELINES.
WHICH PRINCIPAL SIMMS HAD.
HOROKK!
DAD TAUGHT ME THE ONLY WAY TO SEE ANYTHING DONE RIGHT IN THIS WORLD--
IS TO TAKE IT INTO MY OWN HANDS.

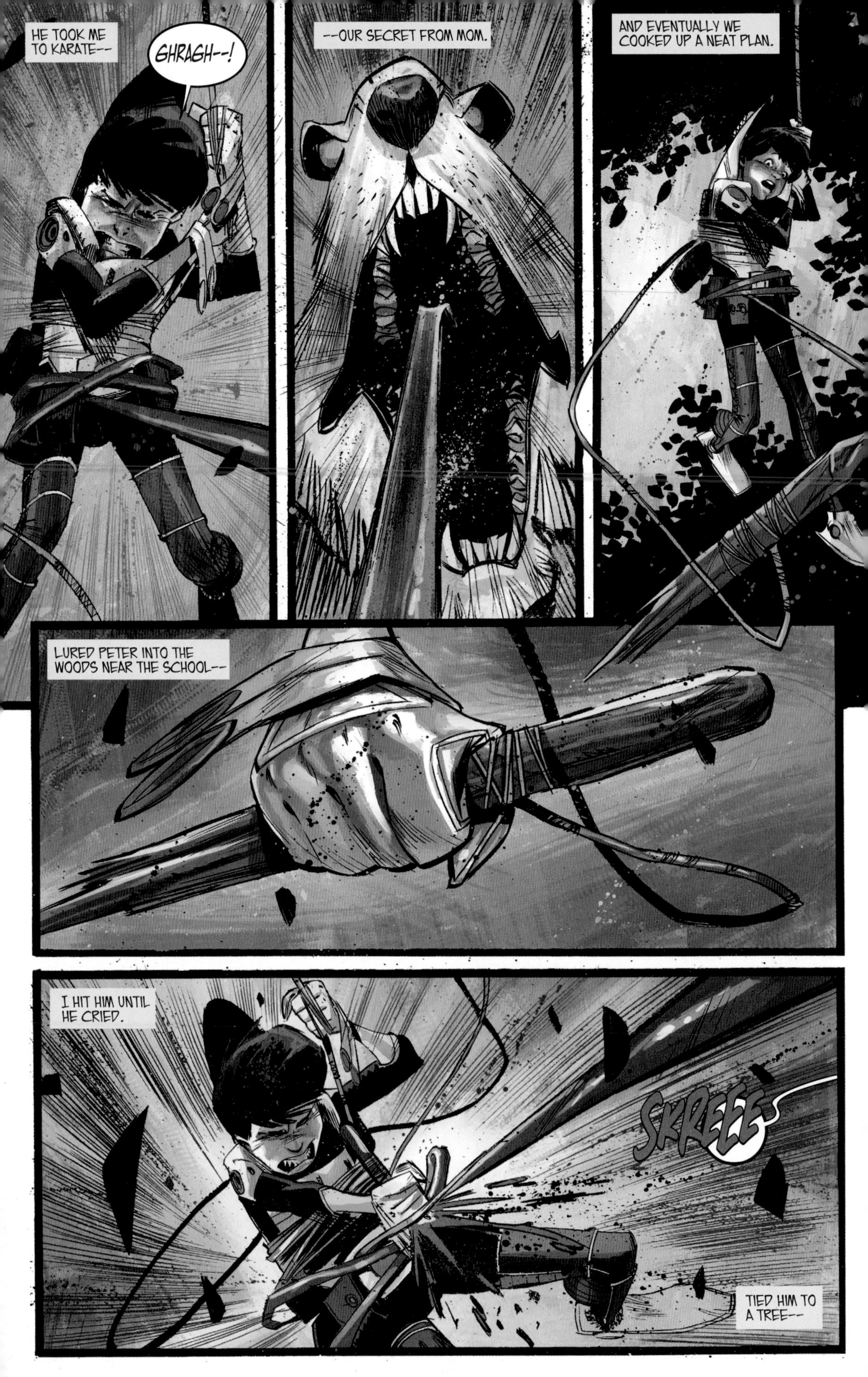
HE TOOK ME TO KARATE--
GHRAGH--!
--OUR SECRET FROM MOM.
AND EVENTUALLY WE COOKED UP A NEAT PLAN.
LURED PETER INTO THE WOODS NEAR THE SCHOOL--
I HIT HIM UNTIL HE CRIED.
SKREEE
TIED HIM TO A TREE--

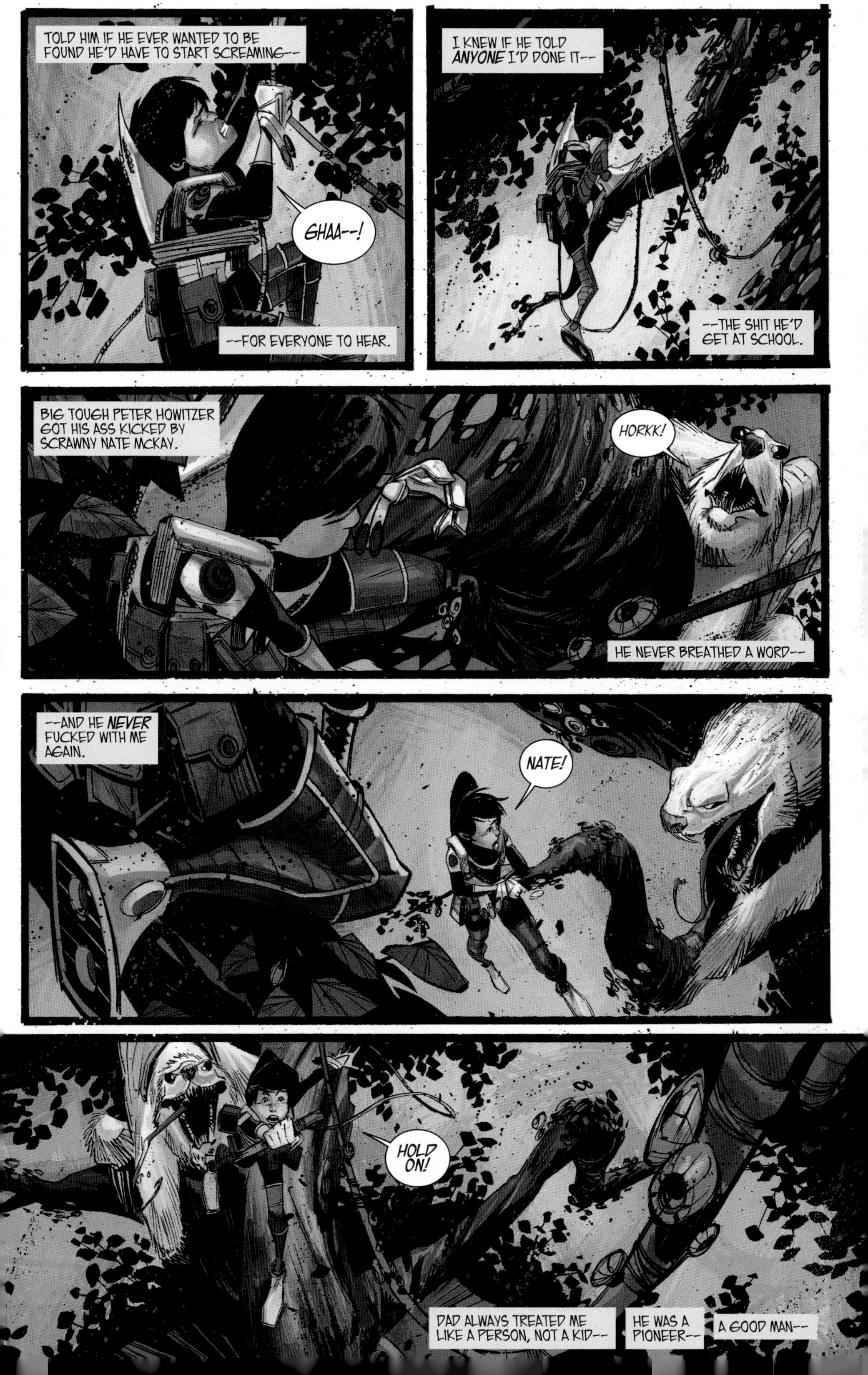
TOLD HIM IF HE EVER WANTED TO BE FOUND HE'D HAVE TO START SCREAMING--
GHAA--!
--FOR EVERYONE TO HEAR.
I KNEW IF HE TOLD *ANYONE* I'D DONE IT--
--THE SHIT HE'D GET AT SCHOOL.
BIG TOUGH PETER HOWITZER GOT HIS ASS KICKED BY SCRAWNY NATE McKAY.
HORKK!
HE NEVER BREATHED A WORD--
--AND HE *NEVER* FUCKED WITH ME AGAIN.
NATE!
HOLD ON!
DAD ALWAYS TREATED ME LIKE A PERSON, NOT A KID--
HE WAS A PIONEER--
A GOOD MAN--

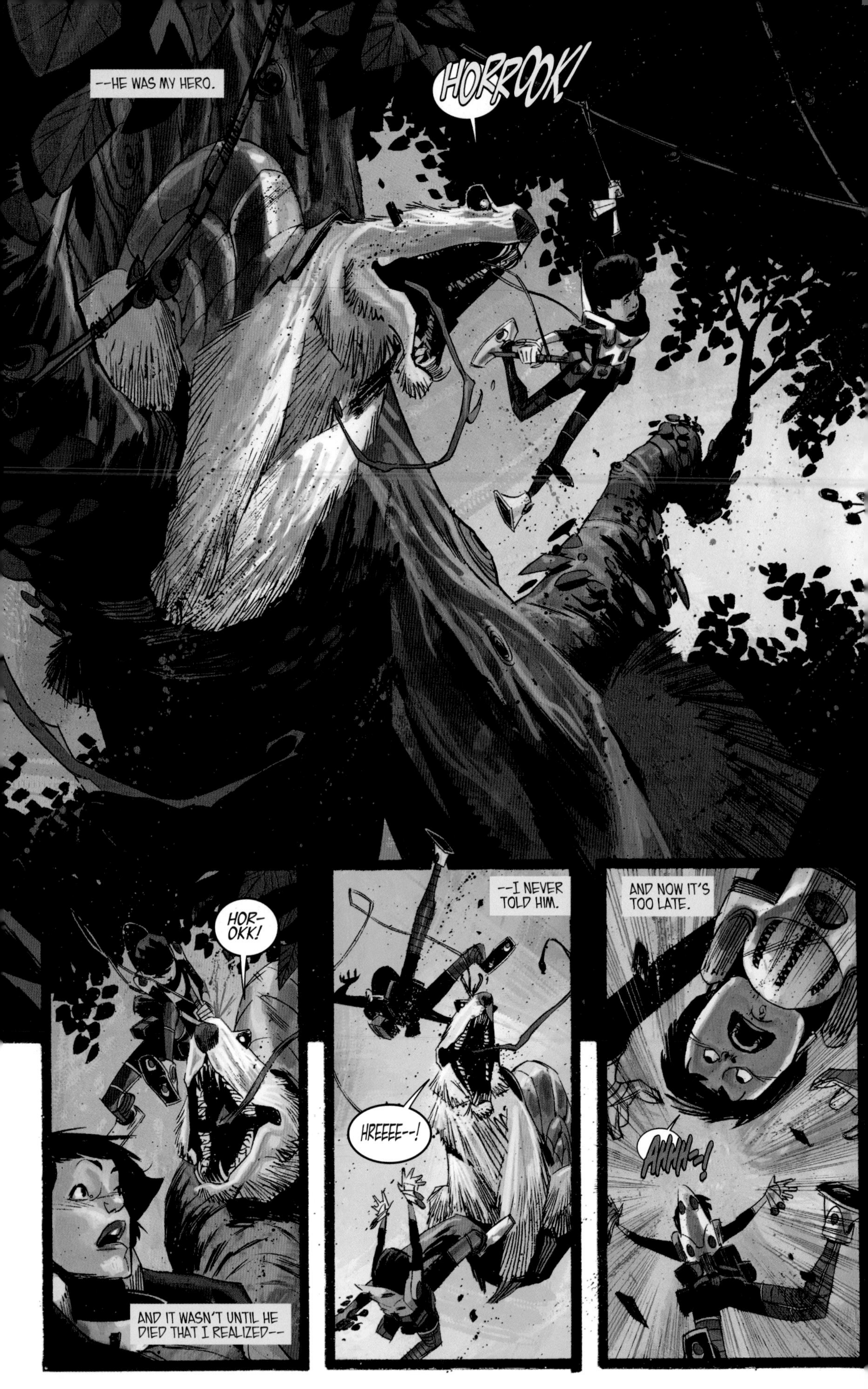
--HE WAS MY HERO.
HORROOK!
HOR-OKK!
AND IT WASN'T UNTIL HE DIED THAT I REALIZED--
--I NEVER TOLD HIM.
HREEEE--!
AND NOW IT'S TOO LATE.
AHHH--!

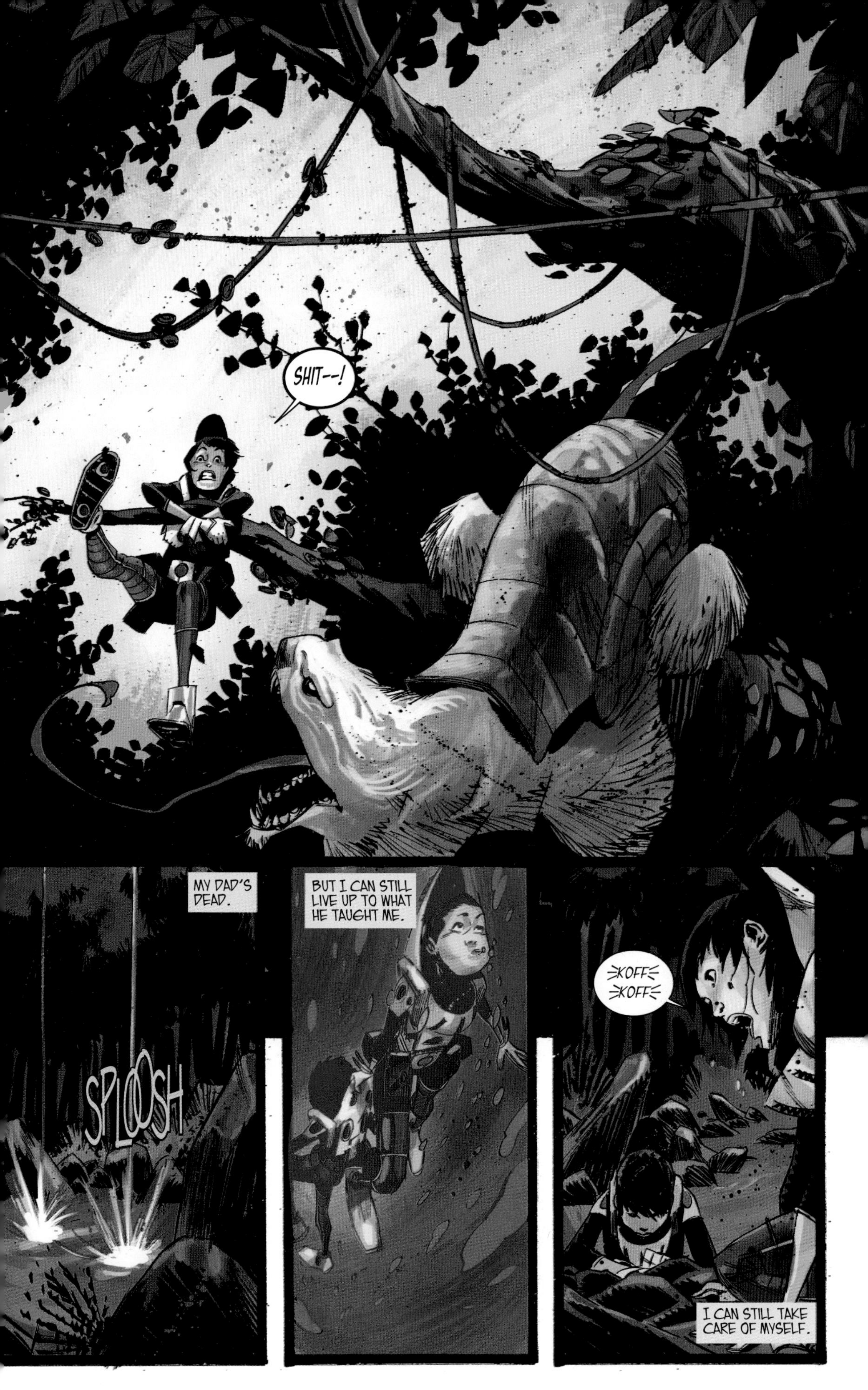

SHIT--!
MY DAD'S DEAD.
SPLOOSH
BUT I CAN STILL LIVE UP TO WHAT HE TAUGHT ME.
KOFF KOFF
I CAN STILL TAKE CARE OF MYSELF.

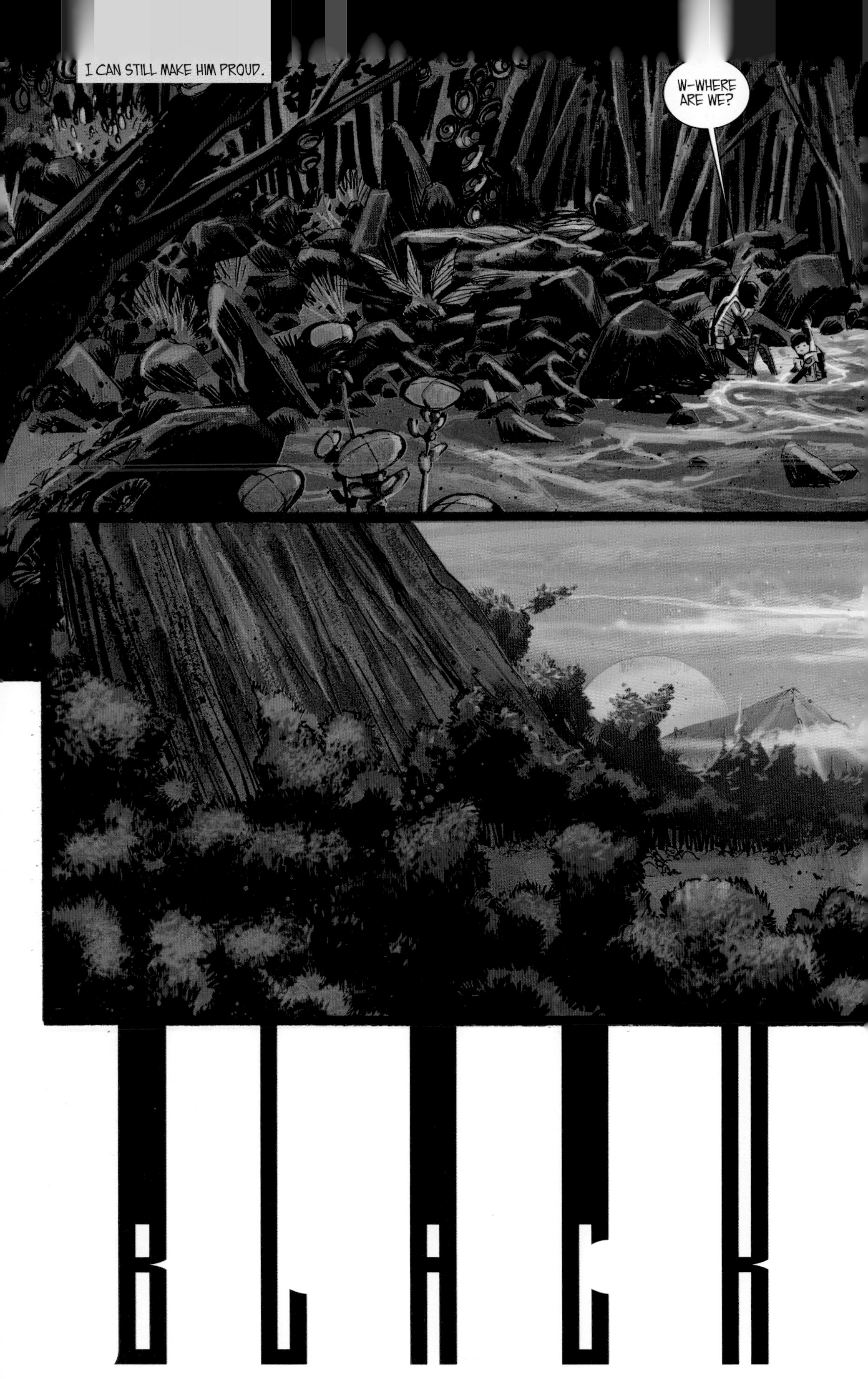

I CAN STILL MAKE HIM PROUD.
W-WHERE ARE WE?
BLACK

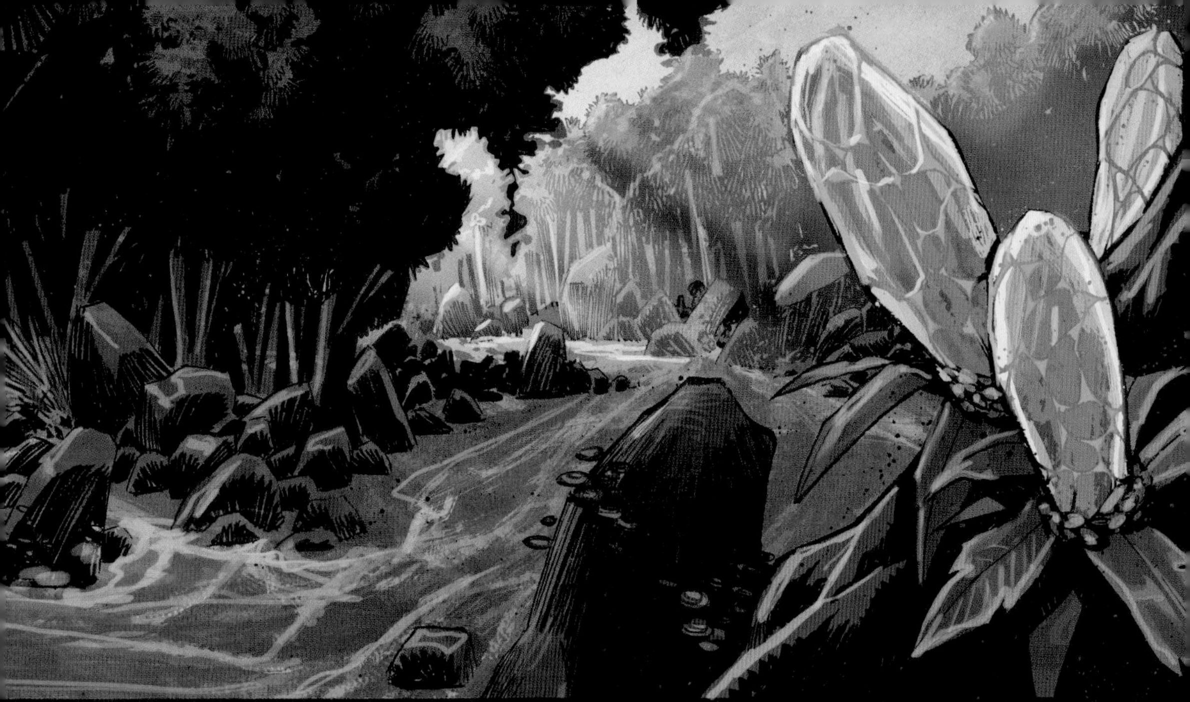

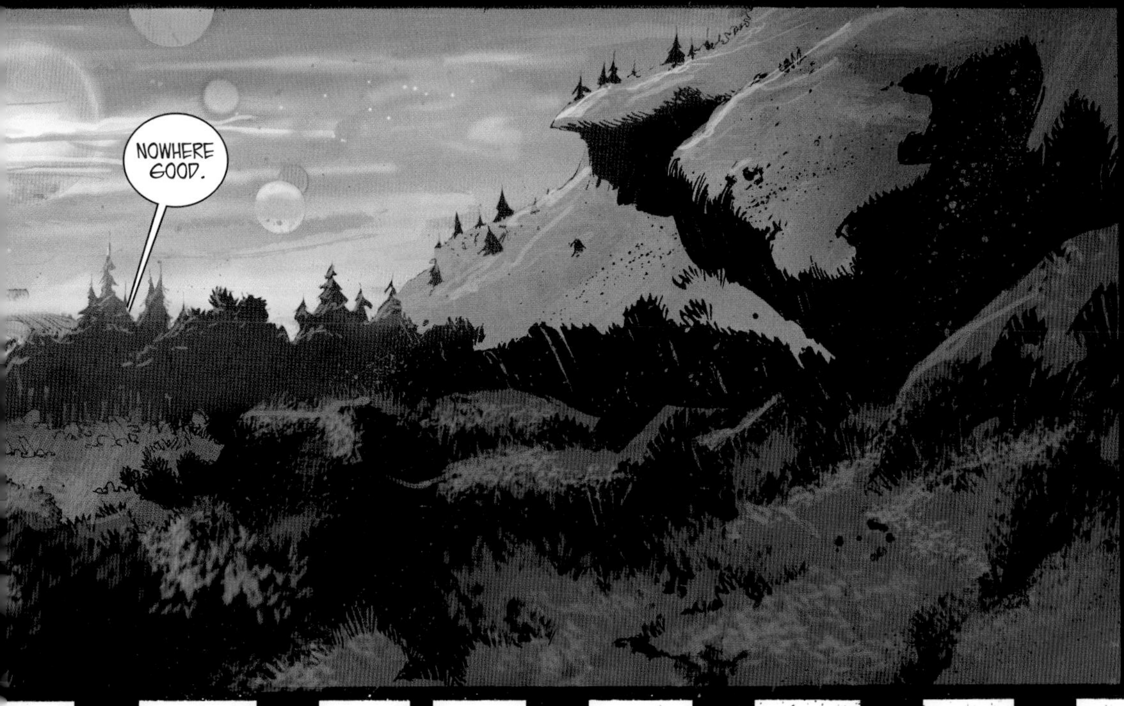
NOWHERE GOOD.

SCIENCE

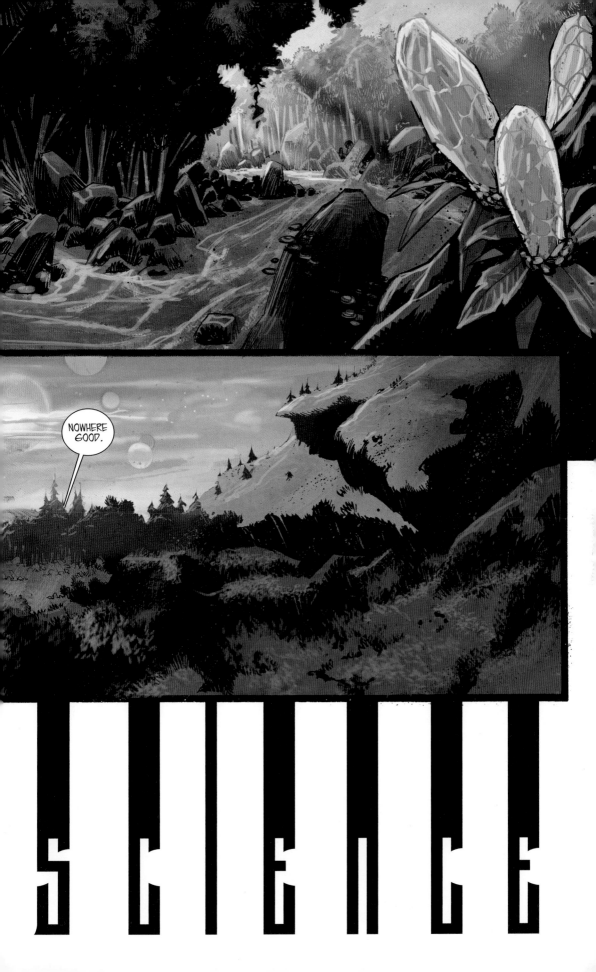

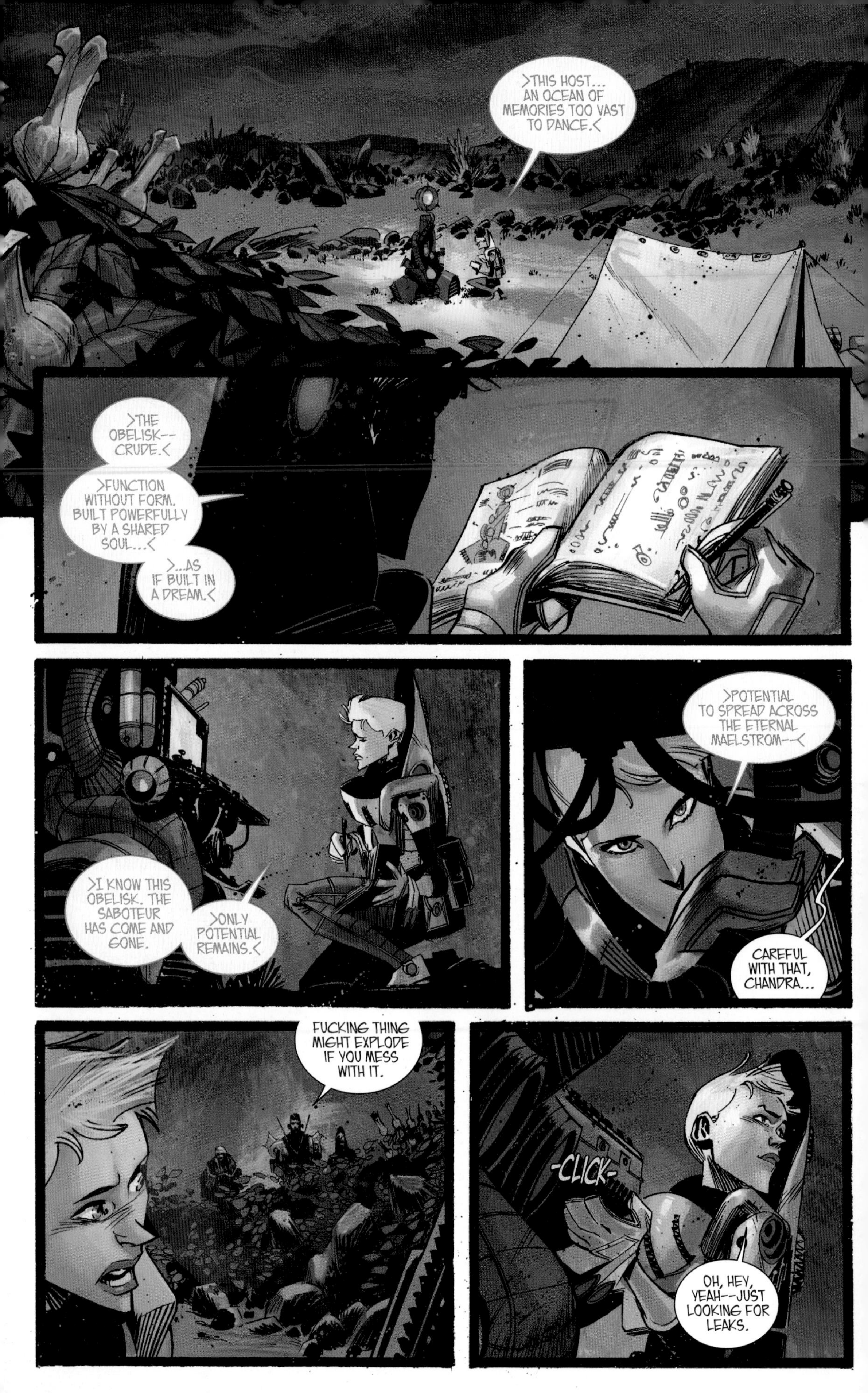
>THIS HOST... AN OCEAN OF MEMORIES TOO VAST TO DANCE.<
>THE OBELISK--CRUDE.<
>FUNCTION WITHOUT FORM. BUILT POWERFULLY BY A SHARED SOUL...<
>...AS IF BUILT IN A DREAM.<
>I KNOW THIS OBELISK. THE SABOTEUR HAS COME AND GONE.
>ONLY POTENTIAL REMAINS.<
>POTENTIAL TO SPREAD ACROSS THE ETERNAL MAELSTROM--<
CAREFUL WITH THAT, CHANDRA...
FUCKING THING MIGHT EXPLODE IF YOU MESS WITH IT.
-CLICK-
OH, HEY, YEAH--JUST LOOKING FOR LEAKS.

WHERE ARE THE KIDS?

KADIR...?

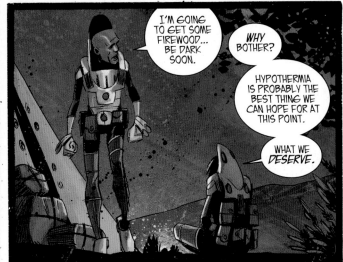

I'M GOING TO GET SOME FIREWOOD... BE DARK SOON.

WHY BOTHER?

HYPOTHERMIA IS PROBABLY THE BEST THING WE CAN HOPE FOR AT THIS POINT.

WHAT WE DESERVE.

I'M NOT READY TO DIE.

THERE'S STILL SOME HOPE, SOME GOOD THAT CAN COME FROM THEIR LOSS.

IF WE CAN GET THE PILLAR BACK AND MAP OUT THE EVERVERSE, THE THINGS WE CAN DO...

EVERYONE WE EVER KNEW CAN HAVE A BETTER LIFE.

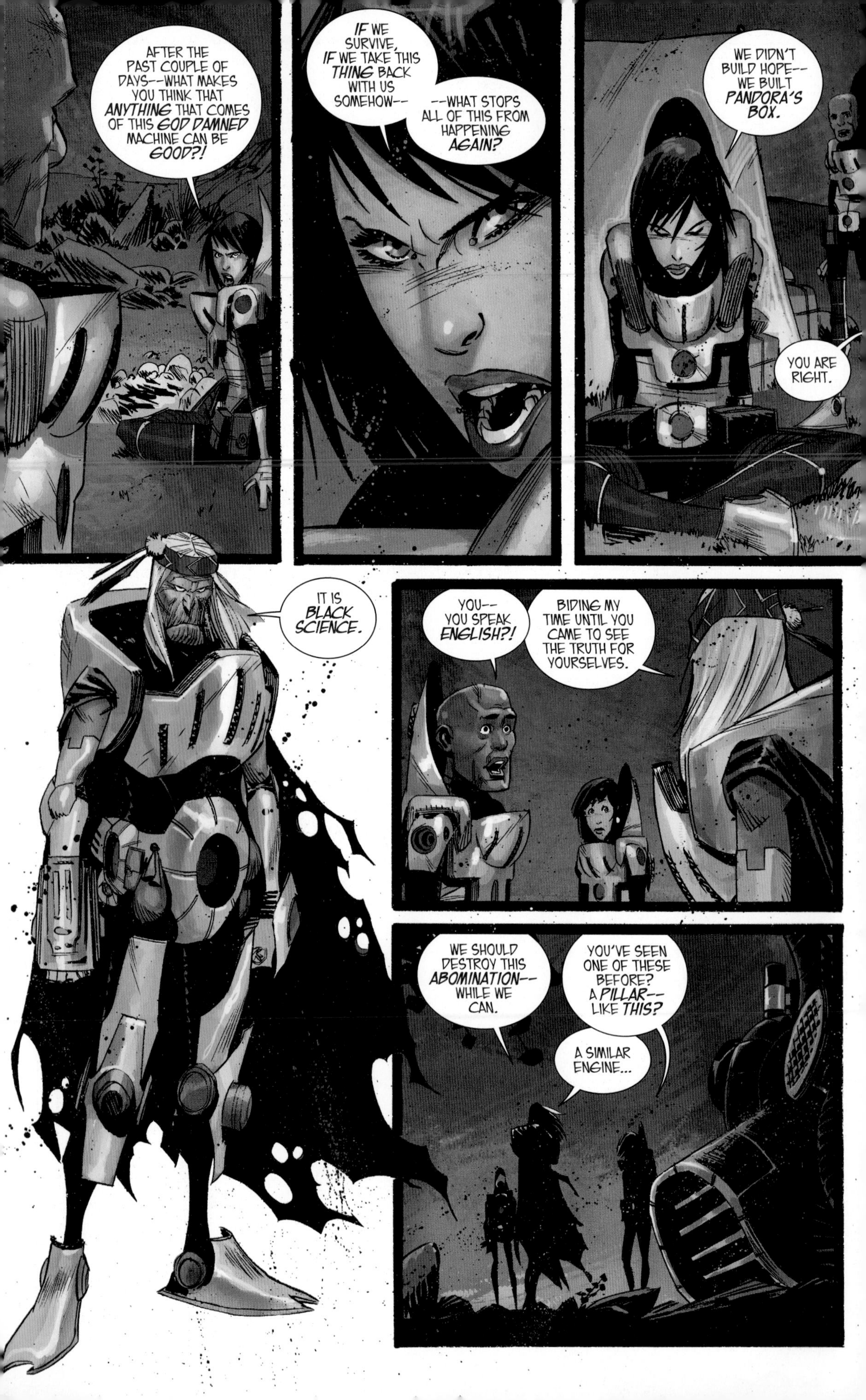
AFTER THE PAST COUPLE OF DAYS--WHAT MAKES YOU THINK THAT ANYTHING THAT COMES OF THIS GOD DAMNED MACHINE CAN BE GOOD?!
IF WE SURVIVE, IF WE TAKE THIS THING BACK WITH US SOMEHOW--
--WHAT STOPS ALL OF THIS FROM HAPPENING AGAIN?
WE DIDN'T BUILD HOPE--WE BUILT PANDORA'S BOX.
YOU ARE RIGHT.
IT IS BLACK SCIENCE.
YOU--YOU SPEAK ENGLISH?!
BIDING MY TIME UNTIL YOU CAME TO SEE THE TRUTH FOR YOURSELVES.
WE SHOULD DESTROY THIS ABOMINATION--WHILE WE CAN.
YOU'VE SEEN ONE OF THESE BEFORE? A PILLAR--LIKE THIS?
A SIMILAR ENGINE...

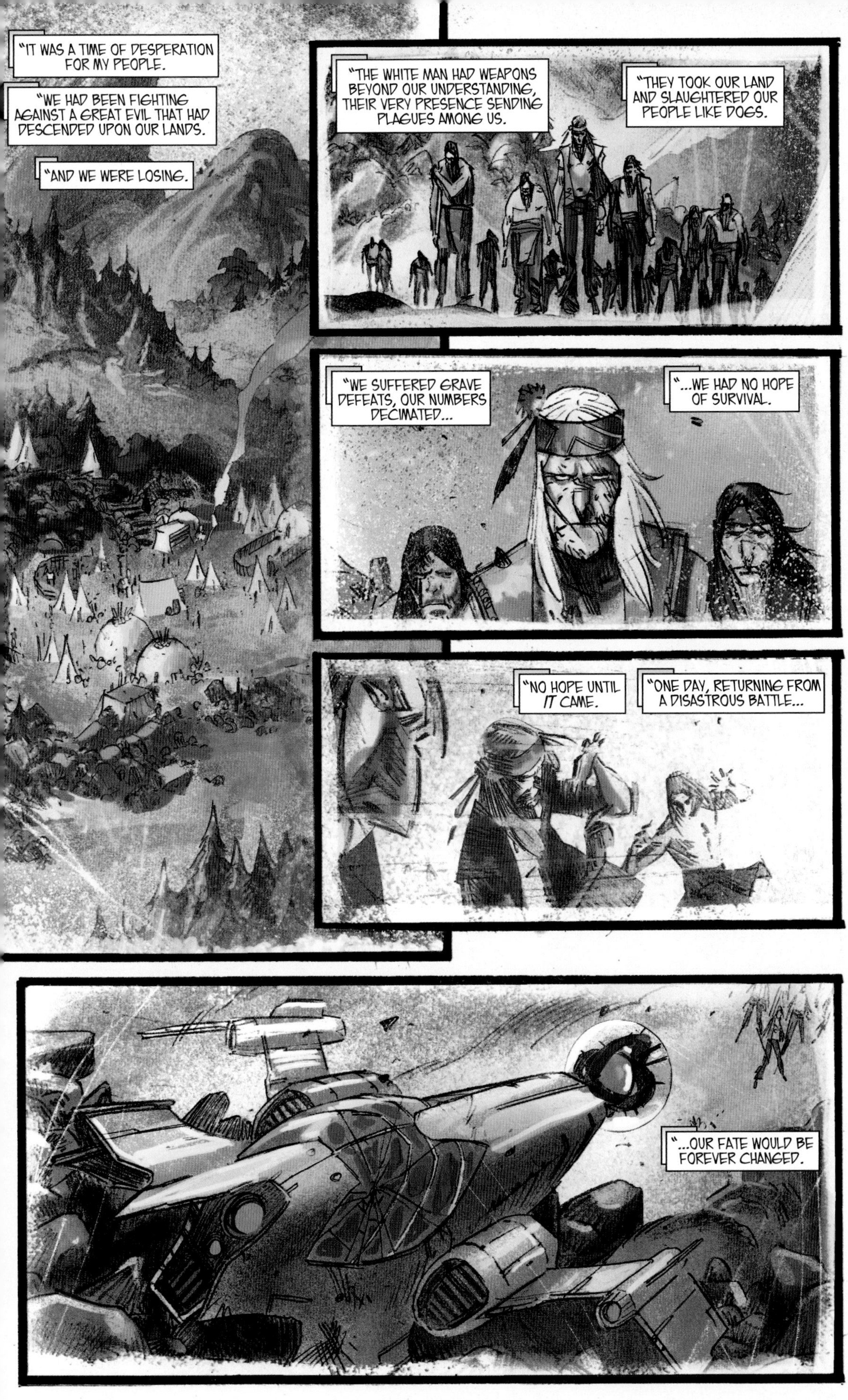
"IT WAS A TIME OF DESPERATION FOR MY PEOPLE.
"WE HAD BEEN FIGHTING AGAINST A GREAT EVIL THAT HAD DESCENDED UPON OUR LANDS.
"AND WE WERE LOSING.
"THE WHITE MAN HAD WEAPONS BEYOND OUR UNDERSTANDING, THEIR VERY PRESENCE SENDING PLAGUES AMONG US.
"THEY TOOK OUR LAND AND SLAUGHTERED OUR PEOPLE LIKE DOGS.
"WE SUFFERED GRAVE DEFEATS, OUR NUMBERS DECIMATED...
"...WE HAD NO HOPE OF SURVIVAL.
"NO HOPE UNTIL IT CAME.
"ONE DAY, RETURNING FROM A DISASTROUS BATTLE...
"...OUR FATE WOULD BE FOREVER CHANGED.

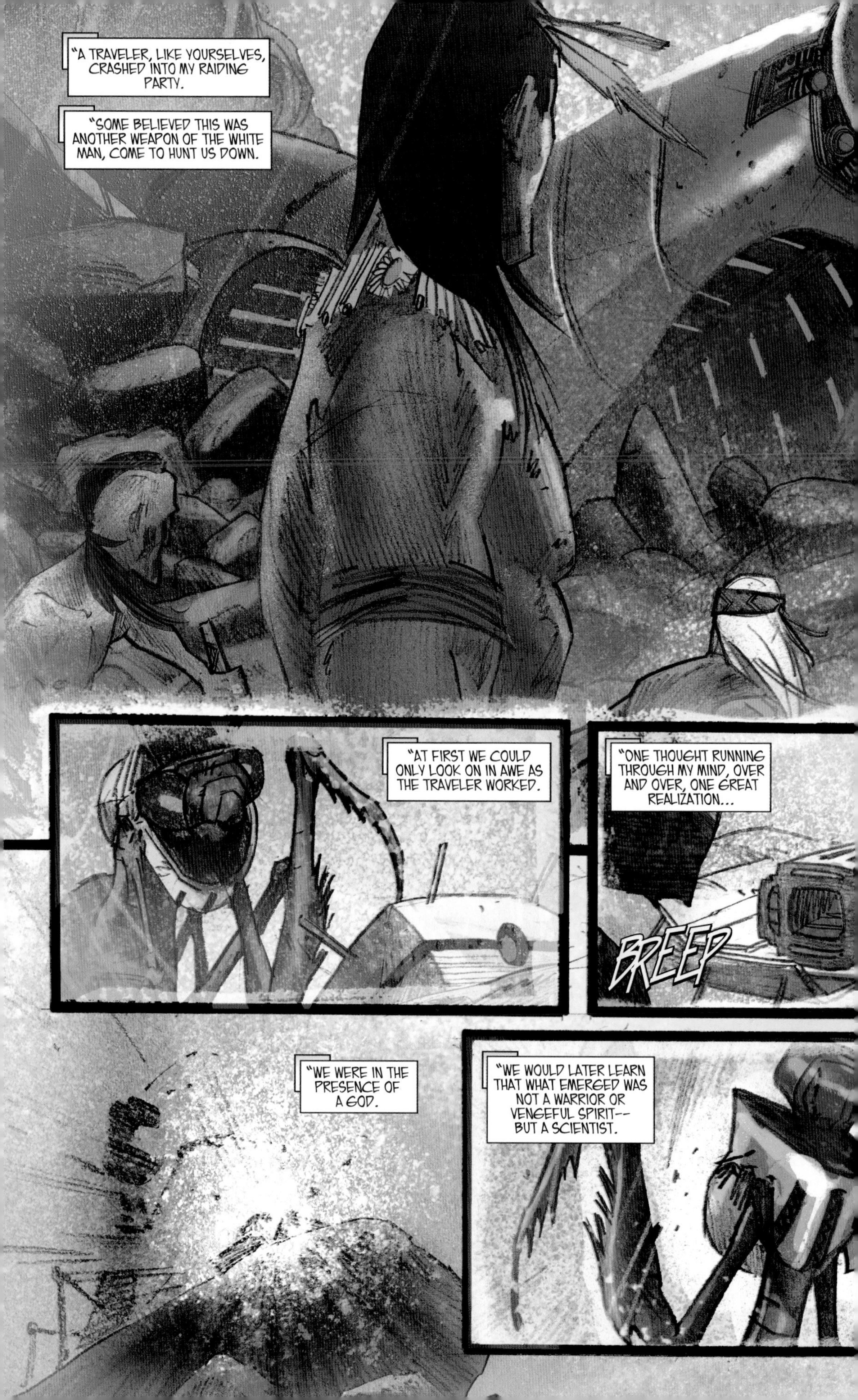
"A TRAVELER, LIKE YOURSELVES, CRASHED INTO MY RAIDING PARTY.
"SOME BELIEVED THIS WAS ANOTHER WEAPON OF THE WHITE MAN, COME TO HUNT US DOWN.
"AT FIRST WE COULD ONLY LOOK ON IN AWE AS THE TRAVELER WORKED.
"ONE THOUGHT RUNNING THROUGH MY MIND, OVER AND OVER, ONE GREAT REALIZATION...
BREEP
"WE WERE IN THE PRESENCE OF A GOD.
"WE WOULD LATER LEARN THAT WHAT EMERGED WAS NOT A WARRIOR OR VENGEFUL SPIRIT-- BUT A SCIENTIST.

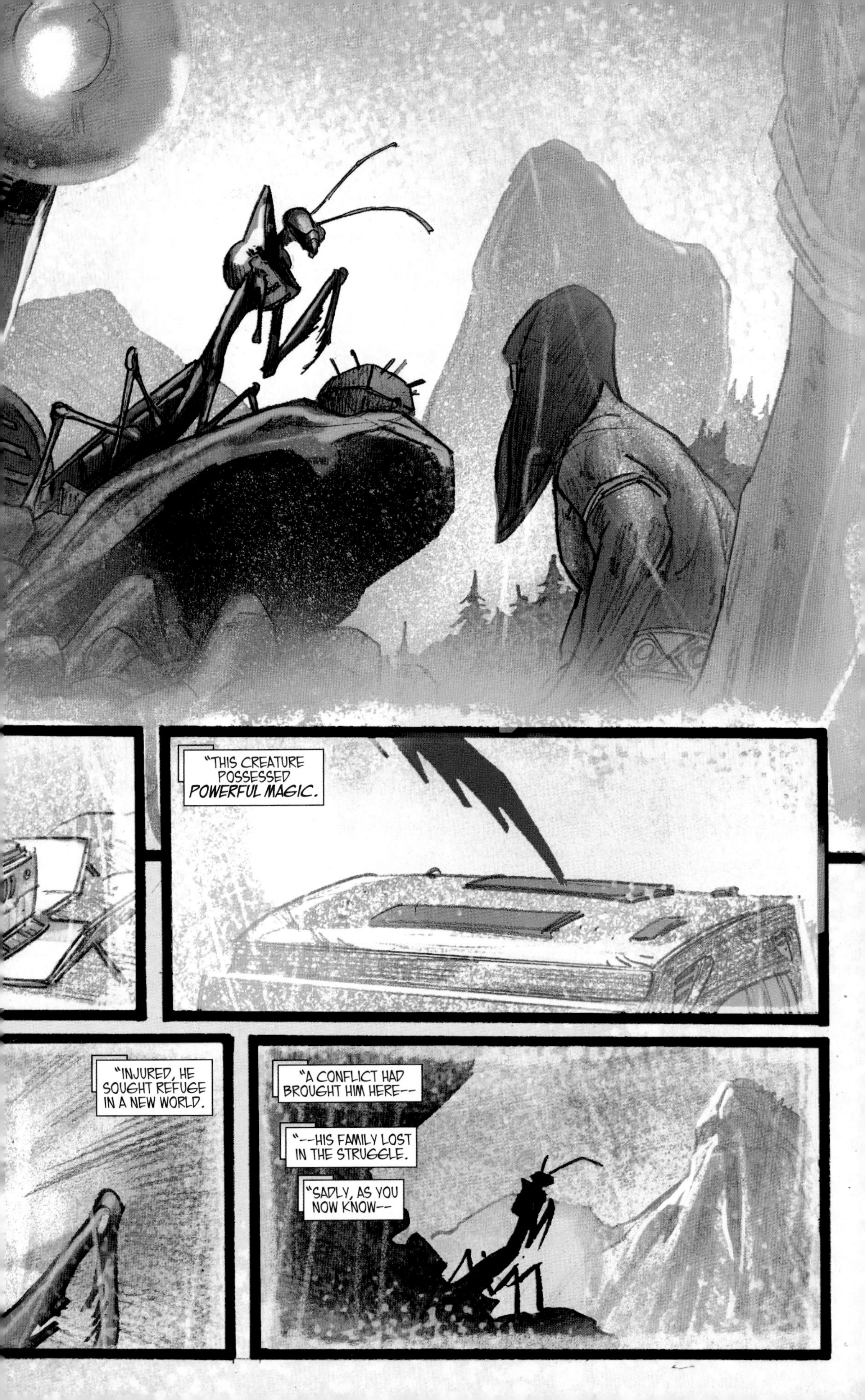
"THIS CREATURE POSSESSED *POWERFUL MAGIC*.
"INJURED, HE SOUGHT REFUGE IN A NEW WORLD.
"A CONFLICT HAD BROUGHT HIM HERE--
"--HIS FAMILY LOST IN THE STRUGGLE.
"SADLY, AS YOU NOW KNOW--

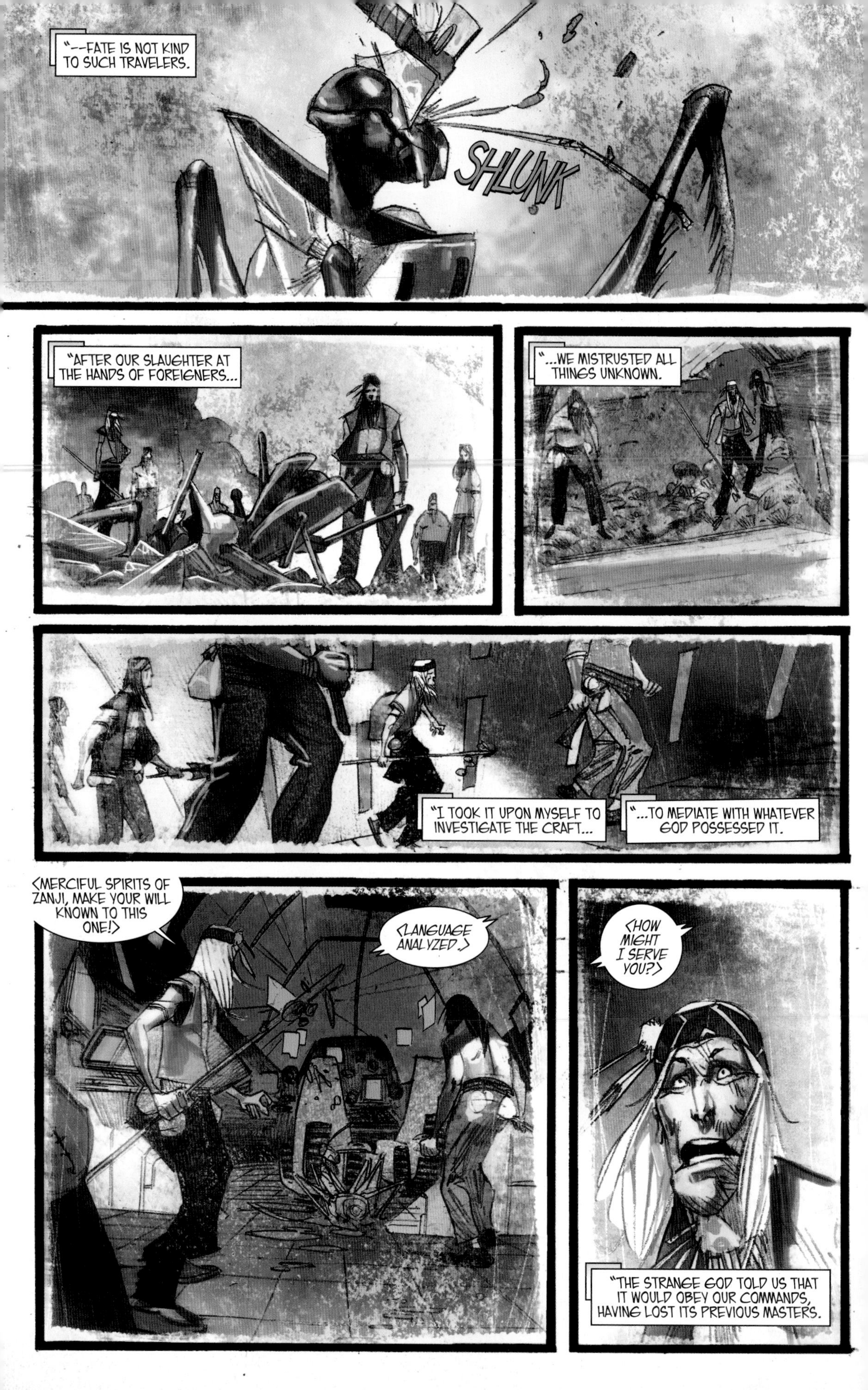
"--FATE IS NOT KIND TO SUCH TRAVELERS.
SHLUNK
"AFTER OUR SLAUGHTER AT THE HANDS OF FOREIGNERS...
"...WE MISTRUSTED ALL THINGS UNKNOWN.
"I TOOK IT UPON MYSELF TO INVESTIGATE THE CRAFT...
"...TO MEDIATE WITH WHATEVER GOD POSSESSED IT.
<MERCIFUL SPIRITS OF ZANJI, MAKE YOUR WILL KNOWN TO THIS ONE!>
<LANGUAGE ANALYZED.>
<HOW MIGHT I SERVE YOU?>
"THE STRANGE GOD TOLD US THAT IT WOULD OBEY OUR COMMANDS, HAVING LOST ITS PREVIOUS MASTERS.

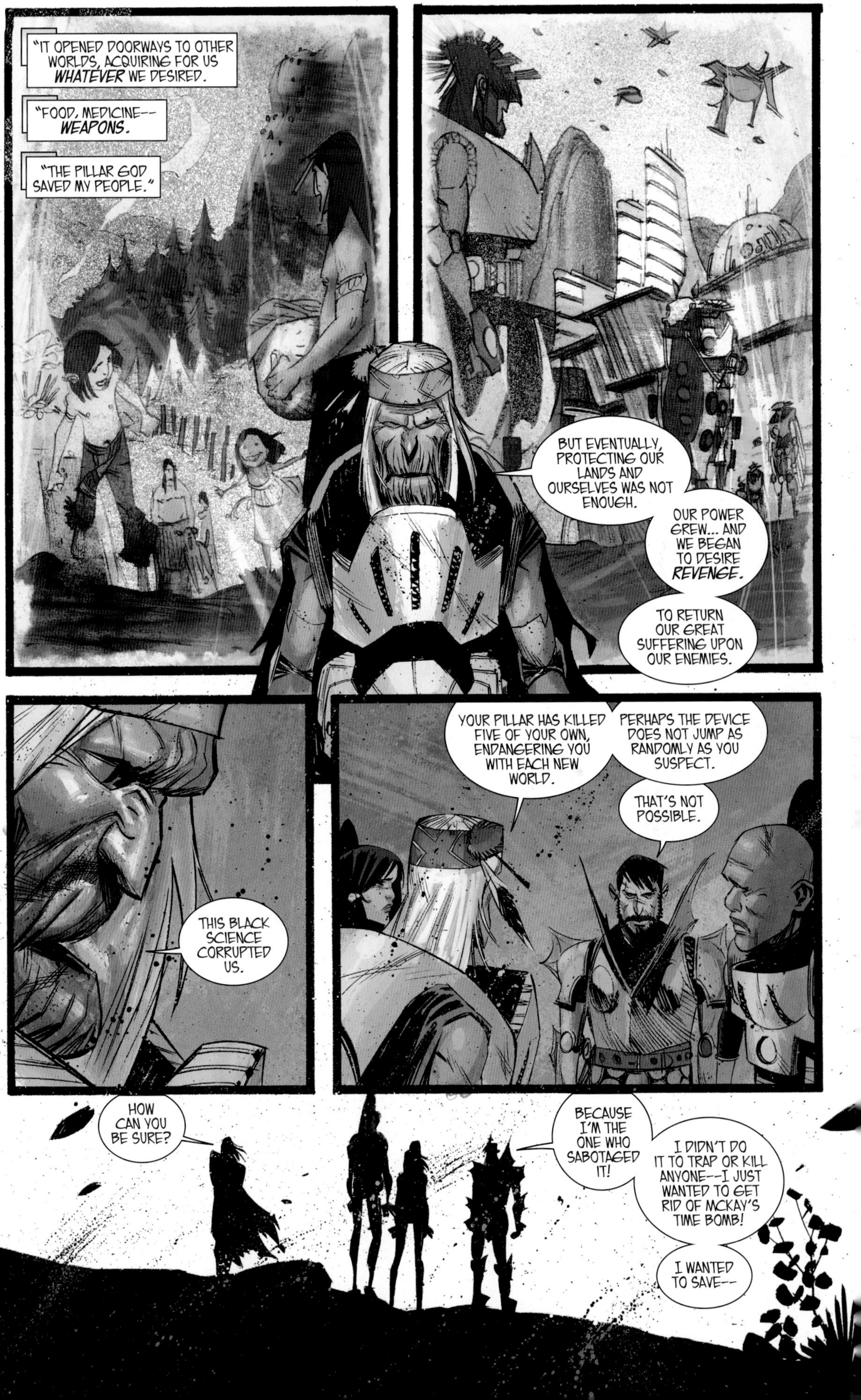
"IT OPENED DOORWAYS TO OTHER WORLDS, ACQUIRING FOR US *WHATEVER* WE DESIRED.
"FOOD, MEDICINE-- *WEAPONS.*
"THE PILLAR GOD SAVED MY PEOPLE."
BUT EVENTUALLY, PROTECTING OUR LANDS AND OURSELVES WAS NOT ENOUGH.
OUR POWER GREW... AND WE BEGAN TO DESIRE *REVENGE.*
TO RETURN OUR GREAT SUFFERING UPON OUR ENEMIES.
THIS BLACK SCIENCE CORRUPTED US.
YOUR PILLAR HAS KILLED FIVE OF YOUR OWN, ENDANGERING YOU WITH EACH NEW WORLD.
PERHAPS THE DEVICE DOES NOT JUMP AS RANDOMLY AS YOU SUSPECT.
THAT'S NOT POSSIBLE.
HOW CAN YOU BE SURE?
BECAUSE I'M THE ONE WHO SABOTAGED IT!
I DIDN'T DO IT TO TRAP OR KILL ANYONE--I JUST WANTED TO GET RID OF MCKAY'S TIME BOMB!
I WANTED TO SAVE--

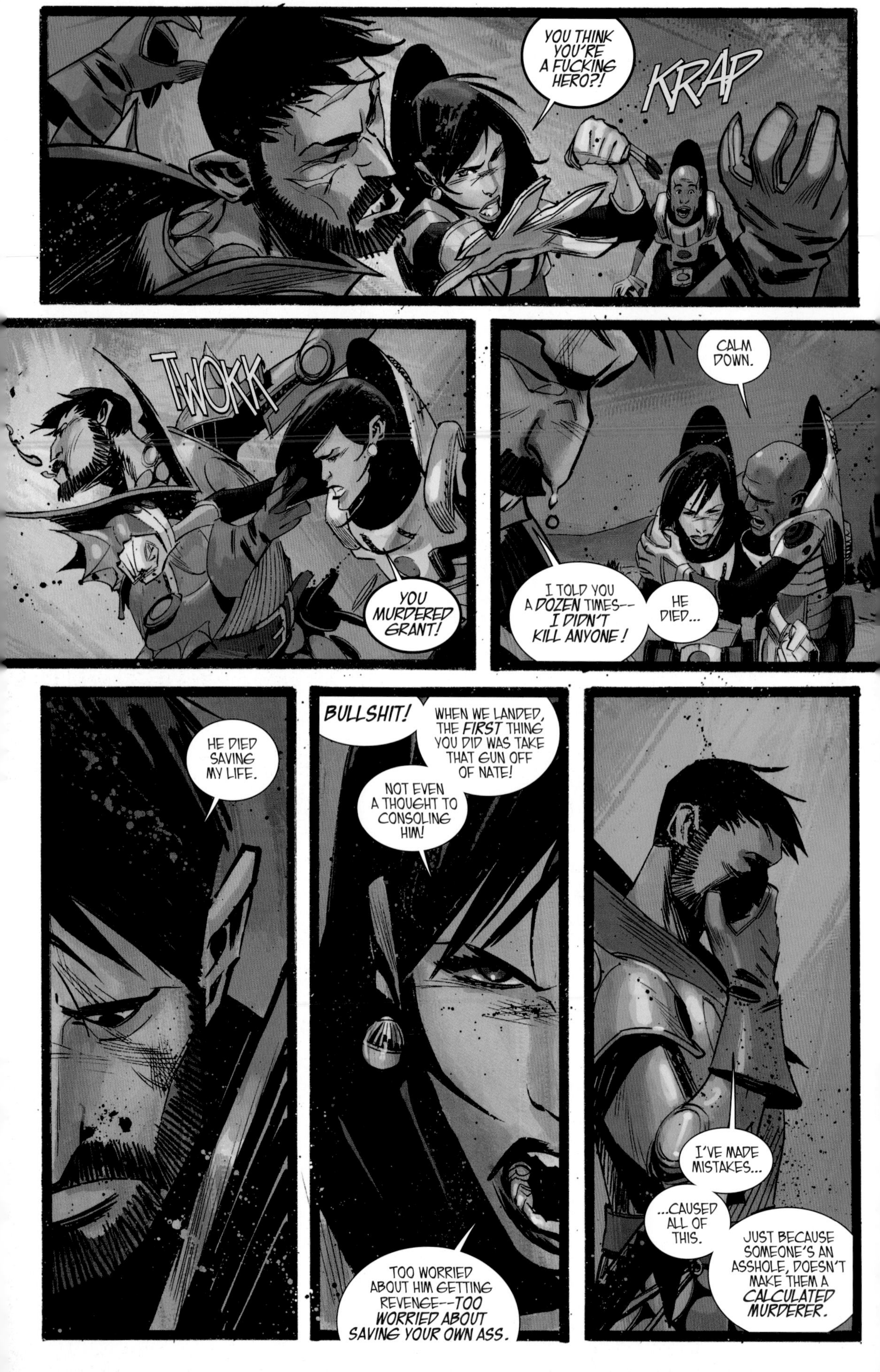
YOU THINK YOU'RE A FUCKING HERO?!
KRAP
TWOKK
YOU MURDERED GRANT!
CALM DOWN.
I TOLD YOU A DOZEN TIMES-- I DIDN'T KILL ANYONE!
HE DIED...
HE DIED SAVING MY LIFE.
BULLSHIT!
WHEN WE LANDED, THE FIRST THING YOU DID WAS TAKE THAT GUN OFF OF NATE!
NOT EVEN A THOUGHT TO CONSOLING HIM!
TOO WORRIED ABOUT HIM GETTING REVENGE--TOO WORRIED ABOUT SAVING YOUR OWN ASS.
I'VE MADE MISTAKES...
...CAUSED ALL OF THIS.
JUST BECAUSE SOMEONE'S AN ASSHOLE, DOESN'T MAKE THEM A CALCULATED MURDERER.

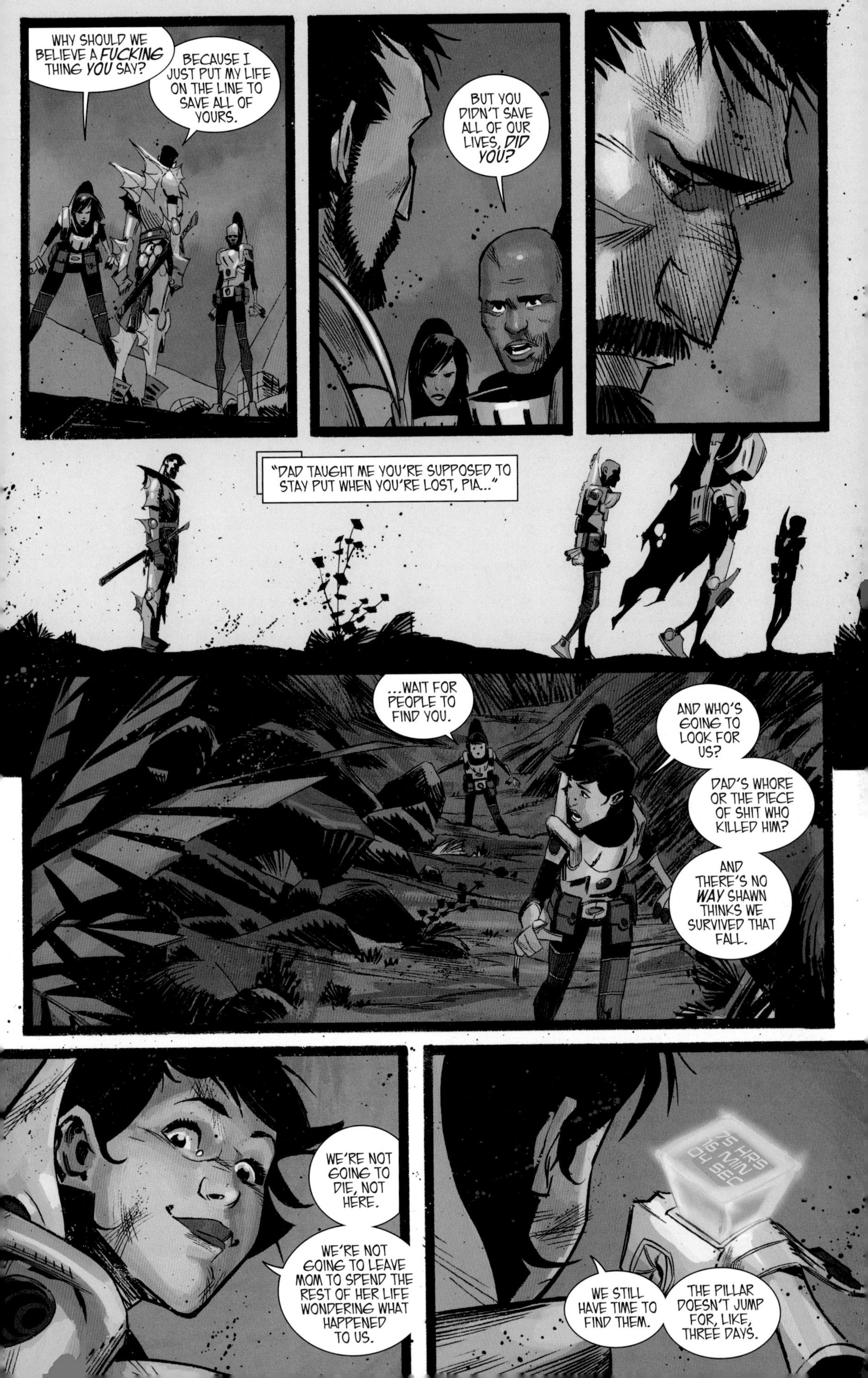
WHY SHOULD WE BELIEVE A *FUCKING* THING *YOU* SAY?
BECAUSE I JUST PUT MY LIFE ON THE LINE TO SAVE ALL OF YOURS.
BUT YOU DIDN'T SAVE ALL OF OUR LIVES, *DID YOU?*
"DAD TAUGHT ME YOU'RE SUPPOSED TO STAY PUT WHEN YOU'RE LOST, PIA..."
...WAIT FOR PEOPLE TO FIND YOU.
AND WHO'S GOING TO LOOK FOR US?
DAD'S WHORE OR THE PIECE OF SHIT WHO KILLED HIM?
AND THERE'S NO *WAY* SHAWN THINKS WE SURVIVED THAT FALL.
WE'RE NOT GOING TO DIE, NOT HERE.
WE'RE NOT GOING TO LEAVE MOM TO SPEND THE REST OF HER LIFE WONDERING WHAT HAPPENED TO US.
75 HRS 16 MIN 04 SEC
WE STILL HAVE TIME TO FIND THEM.
THE PILLAR DOESN'T JUMP FOR, LIKE, THREE DAYS.

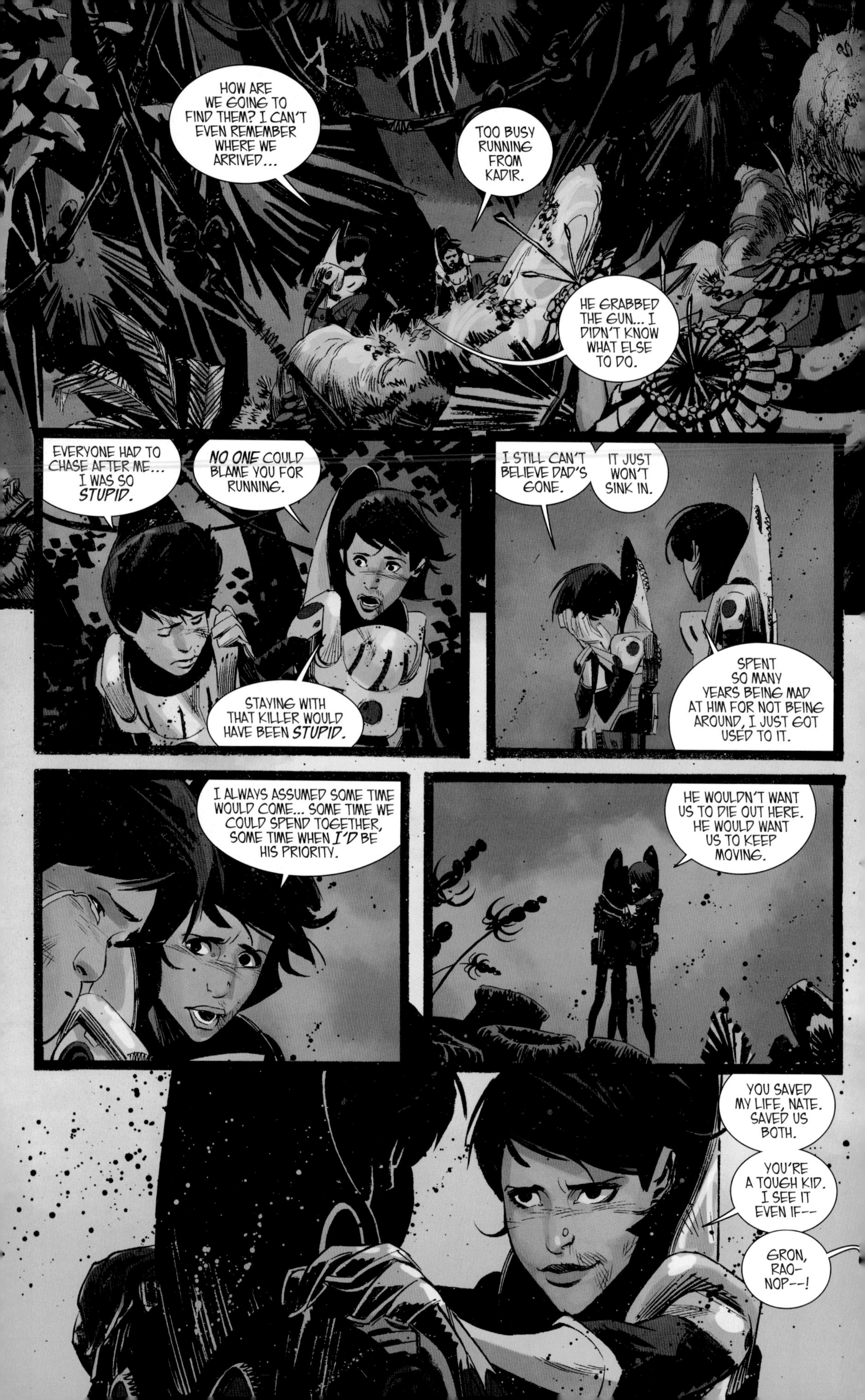
HOW ARE WE GOING TO FIND THEM? I CAN'T EVEN REMEMBER WHERE WE ARRIVED...
TOO BUSY RUNNING FROM KADIR.
HE GRABBED THE GUN... I DIDN'T KNOW WHAT ELSE TO DO.
EVERYONE HAD TO CHASE AFTER ME... I WAS SO STUPID.
NO ONE COULD BLAME YOU FOR RUNNING.
STAYING WITH THAT KILLER WOULD HAVE BEEN STUPID.
I STILL CAN'T BELIEVE DAD'S GONE.
IT JUST WON'T SINK IN.
SPENT SO MANY YEARS BEING MAD AT HIM FOR NOT BEING AROUND, I JUST GOT USED TO IT.
I ALWAYS ASSUMED SOME TIME WOULD COME... SOME TIME WE COULD SPEND TOGETHER, SOME TIME WHEN I'D BE HIS PRIORITY.
HE WOULDN'T WANT US TO DIE OUT HERE. HE WOULD WANT US TO KEEP MOVING.
YOU SAVED MY LIFE, NATE. SAVED US BOTH.
YOU'RE A TOUGH KID. I SEE IT EVEN IF--
GRON, RAO-NOP--!

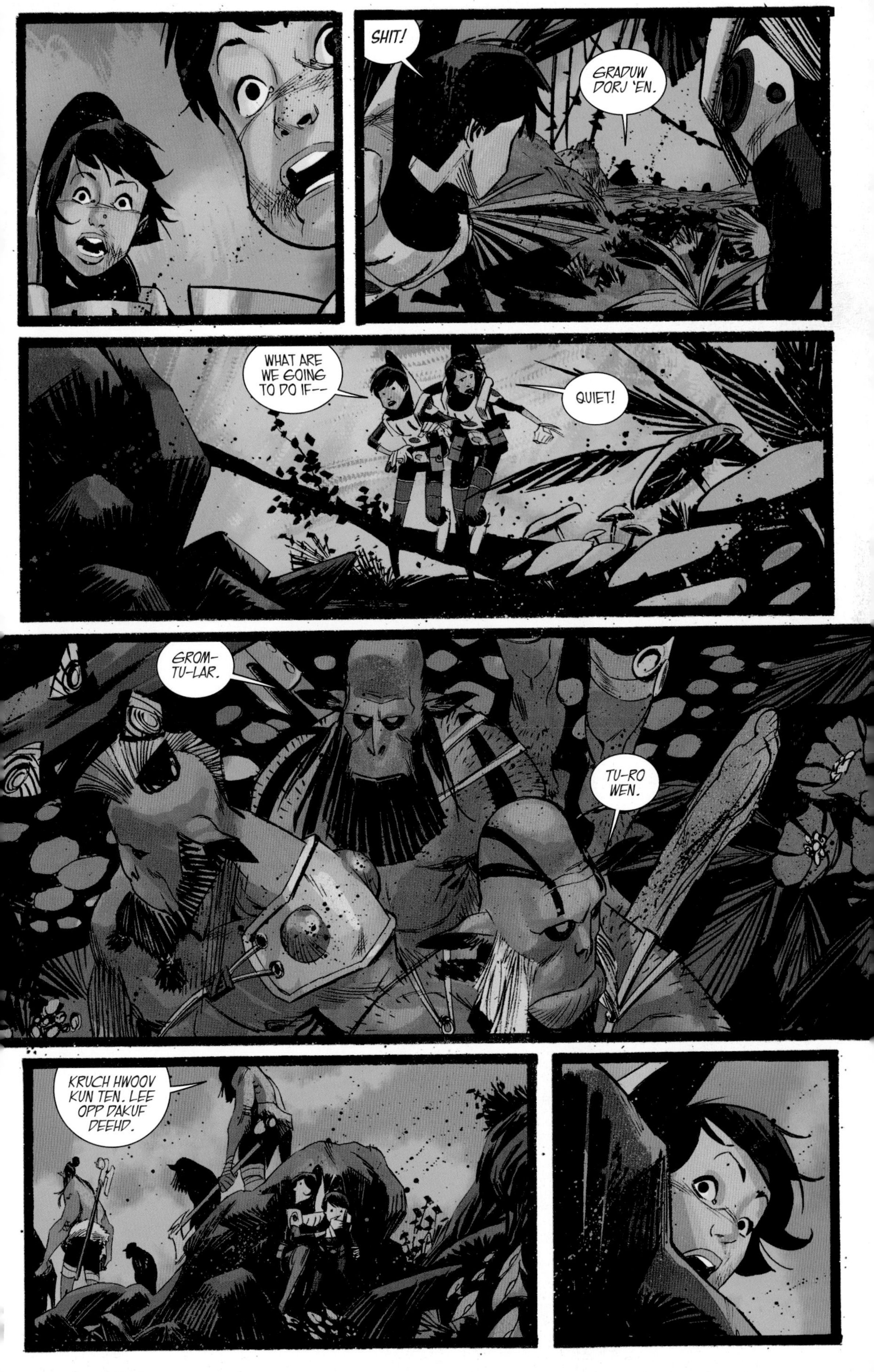
SHIT!
GRADUW DORJ 'EN.
WHAT ARE WE GOING TO DO IF--
QUIET!
GROM-TU-LAR.
TU-RO WEN.
KRUCH HWOOV KUN TEN. LEE OPP DAKUF DEEHD.

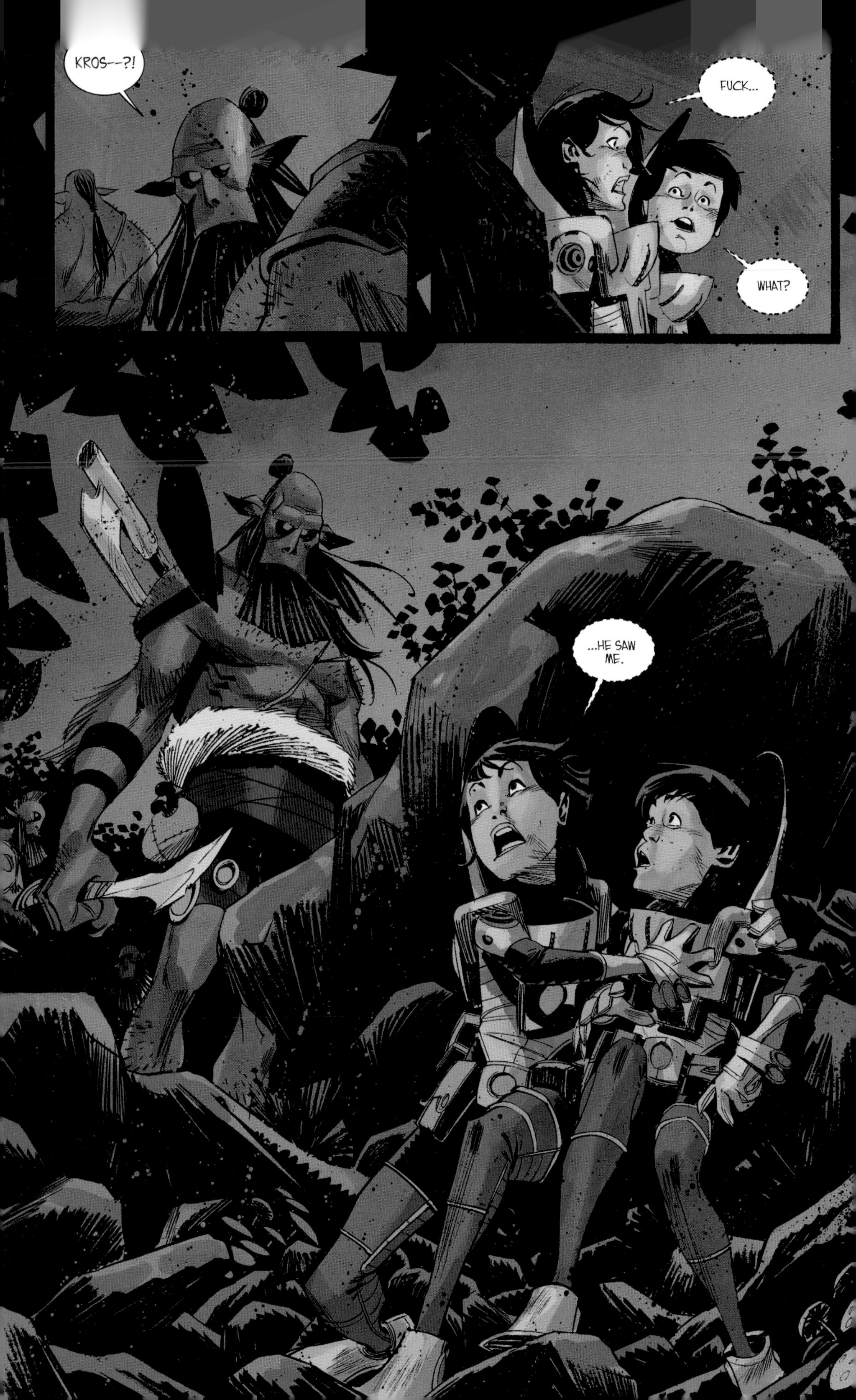
KROS--?!
FUCK...
WHAT?
...HE SAW ME.

9

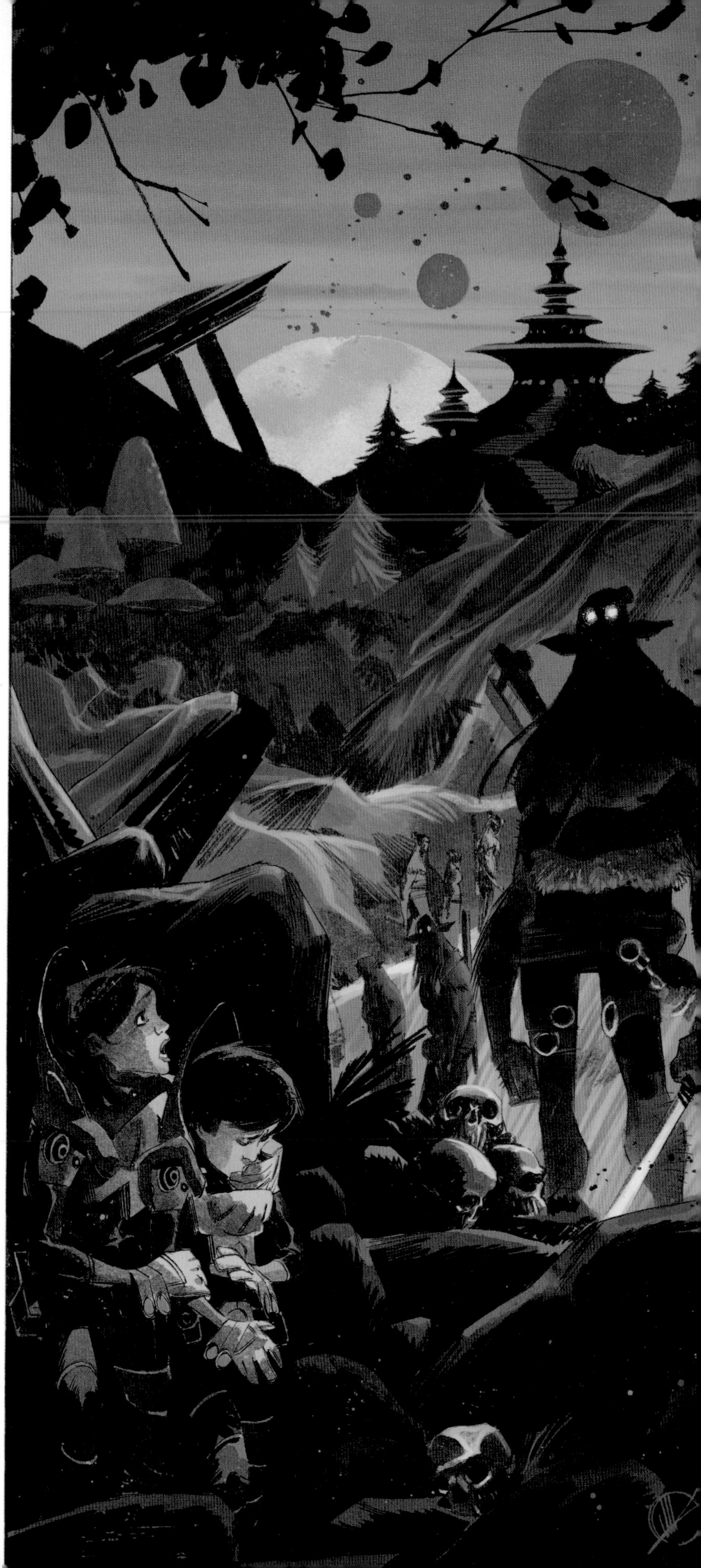

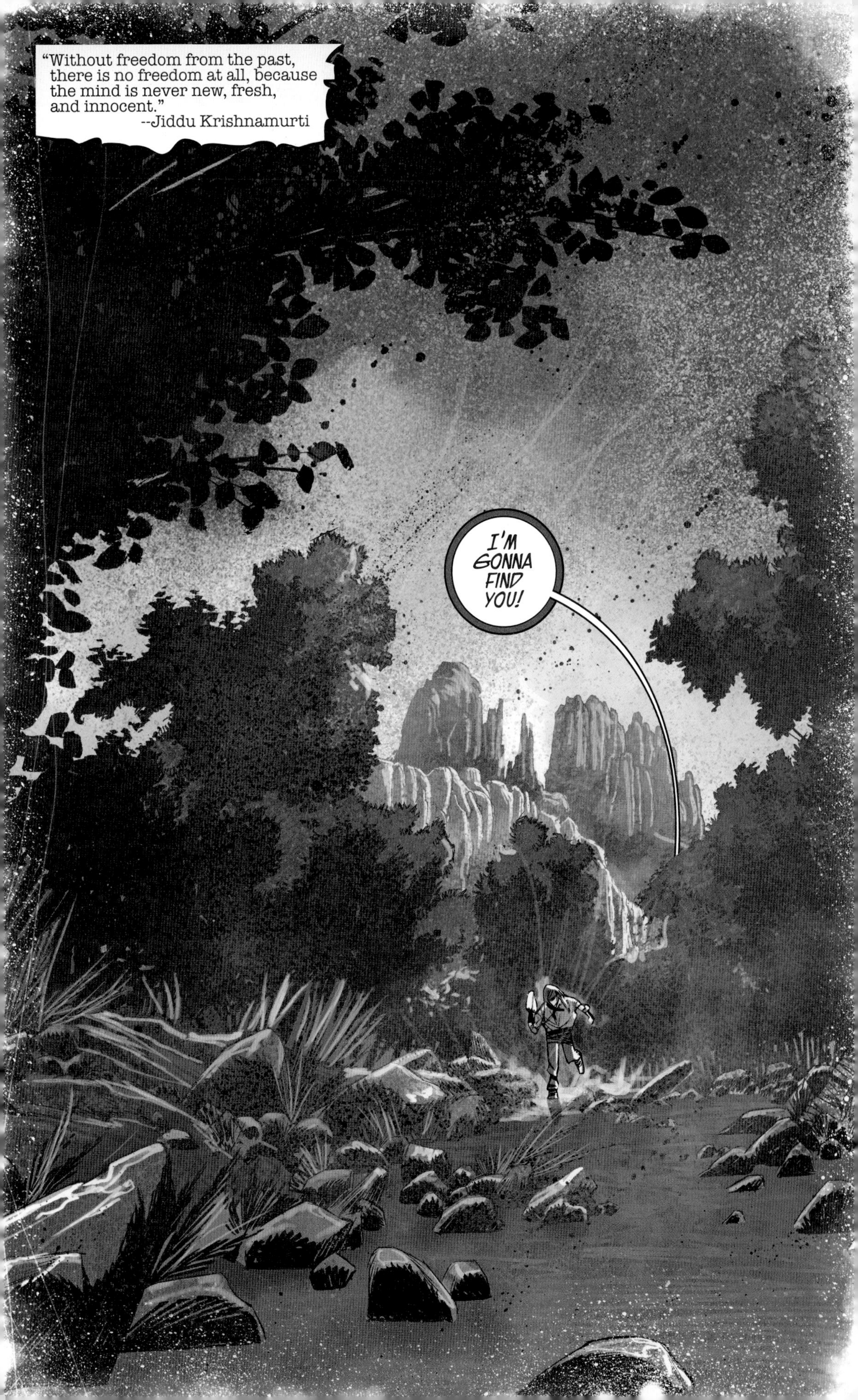
"Without freedom from the past, there is no freedom at all, because the mind is never new, fresh, and innocent."
--Jiddu Krishnamurti
I'M GONNA FIND YOU!

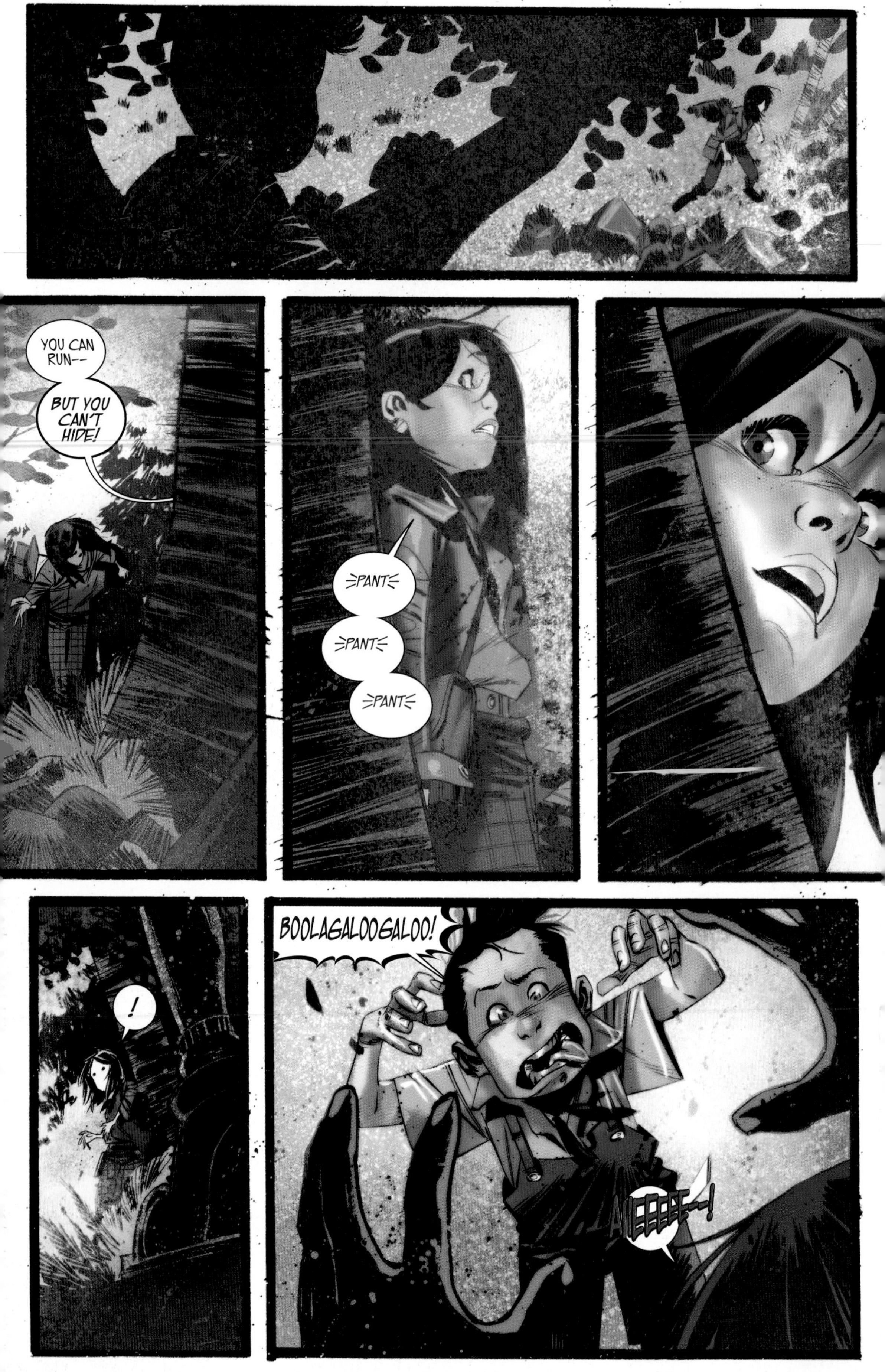
YOU CAN RUN--
BUT YOU CAN'T HIDE!
PANT
PANT
PANT
!
BOOLAGALOOGALOO!
AIEEEEEE--!

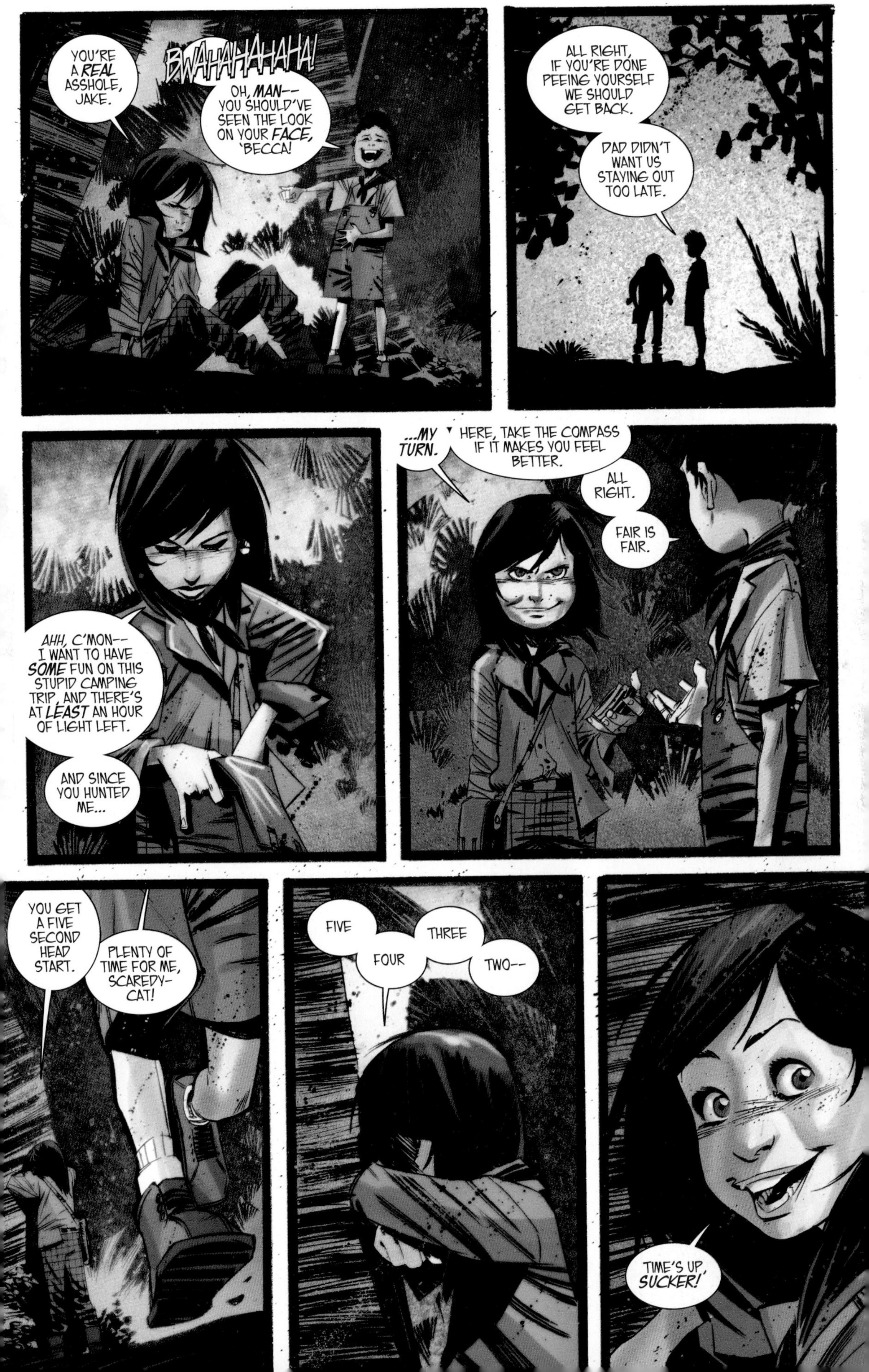
YOU'RE A REAL ASSHOLE, JAKE.
BWAHAHAHAHA!
OH, MAN-- YOU SHOULD'VE SEEN THE LOOK ON YOUR FACE, 'BECCA!
ALL RIGHT, IF YOU'RE DONE PEEING YOURSELF WE SHOULD GET BACK.
DAD DIDN'T WANT US STAYING OUT TOO LATE.
AHH, C'MON-- I WANT TO HAVE SOME FUN ON THIS STUPID CAMPING TRIP, AND THERE'S AT LEAST AN HOUR OF LIGHT LEFT.
AND SINCE YOU HUNTED ME...
...MY TURN.
HERE, TAKE THE COMPASS IF IT MAKES YOU FEEL BETTER.
ALL RIGHT.
FAIR IS FAIR.
YOU GET A FIVE SECOND HEAD START.
PLENTY OF TIME FOR ME, SCAREDY-CAT!
FIVE
FOUR
THREE
TWO--
TIME'S UP, SUCKER!

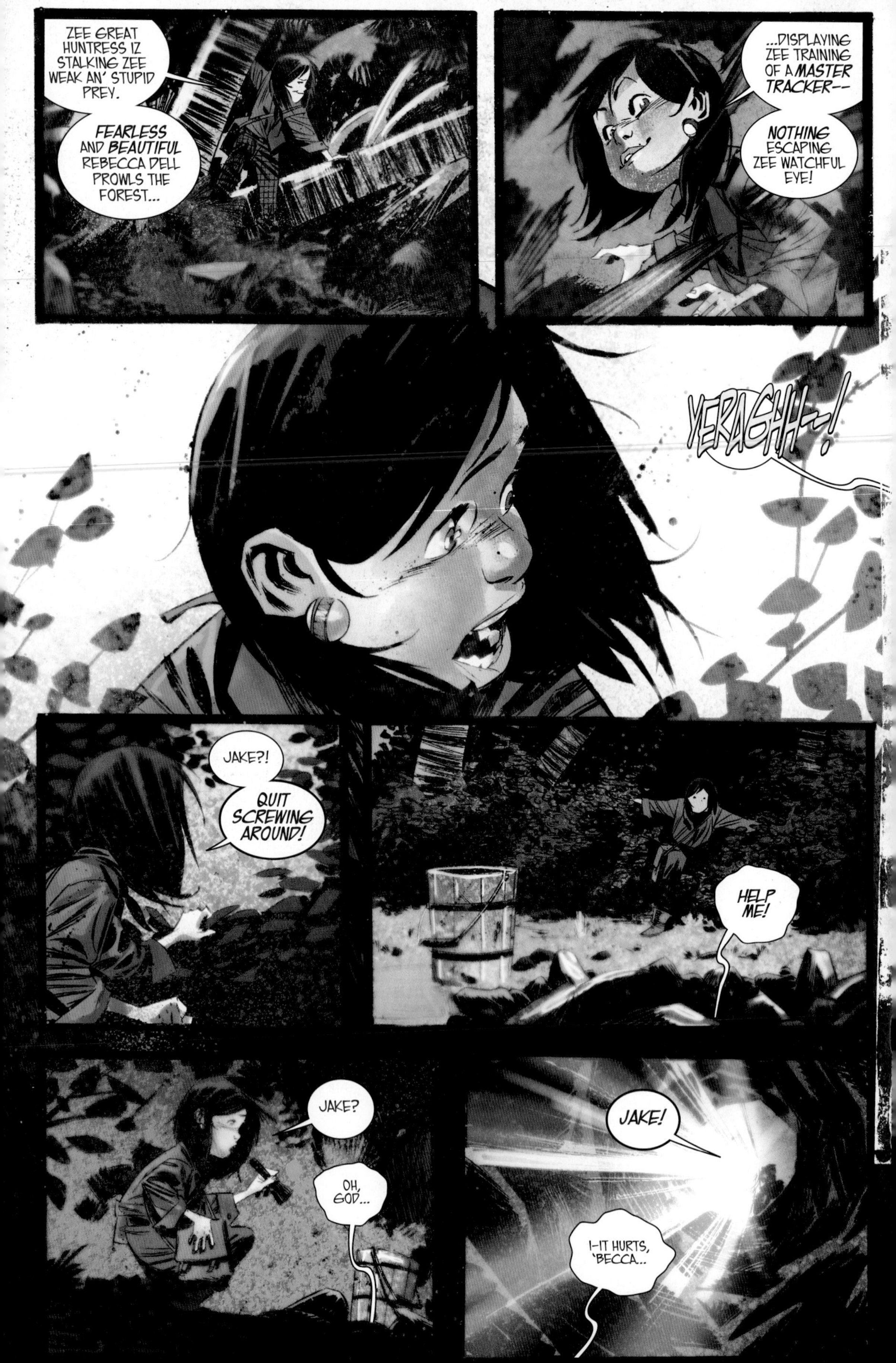
ZEE GREAT HUNTRESS IZ STALKING ZEE WEAK AN' STUPID PREY.
FEARLESS AND BEAUTIFUL REBECCA DELL PROWLS THE FOREST...
...DISPLAYING ZEE TRAINING OF A MASTER TRACKER--
NOTHING ESCAPING ZEE WATCHFUL EYE!
YERAGHH--!
JAKE?!
QUIT SCREWING AROUND!
HELP ME!
JAKE?
OH, GOD...
JAKE!
I-IT HURTS, 'BECCA...

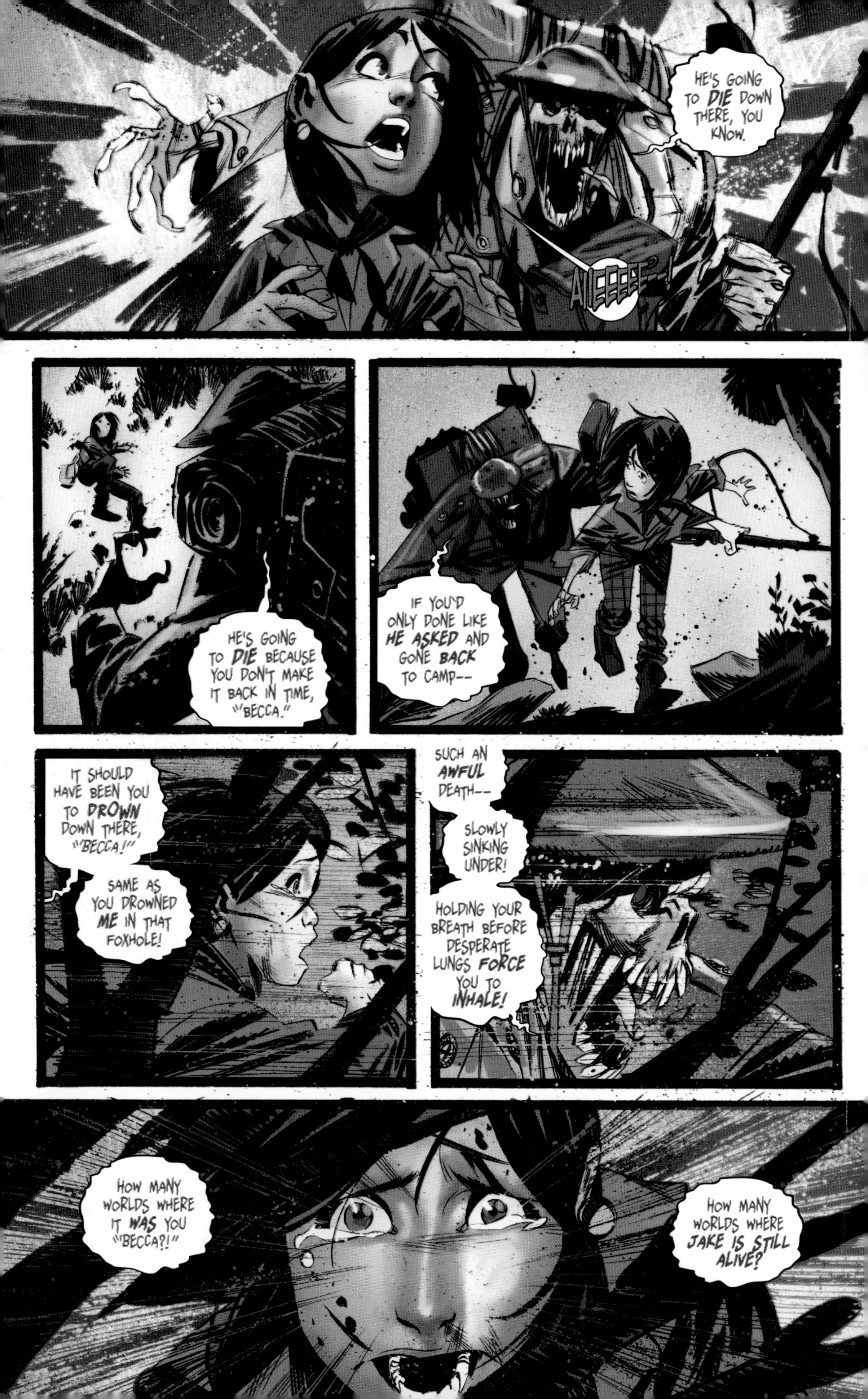
HE'S GOING TO DIE DOWN THERE, YOU KNOW.
AIIEEEEE--!
HE'S GOING TO DIE BECAUSE YOU DON'T MAKE IT BACK IN TIME, "BECCA."
IF YOU'D ONLY DONE LIKE HE ASKED AND GONE BACK TO CAMP--
IT SHOULD HAVE BEEN YOU TO DROWN DOWN THERE, "BECCA!"
SAME AS YOU DROWNED ME IN THAT FOXHOLE!
SUCH AN AWFUL DEATH--
SLOWLY SINKING UNDER!
HOLDING YOUR BREATH BEFORE DESPERATE LUNGS FORCE YOU TO INHALE!
HOW MANY WORLDS WHERE IT WAS YOU "BECCA?!"
HOW MANY WORLDS WHERE JAKE IS STILL ALIVE?

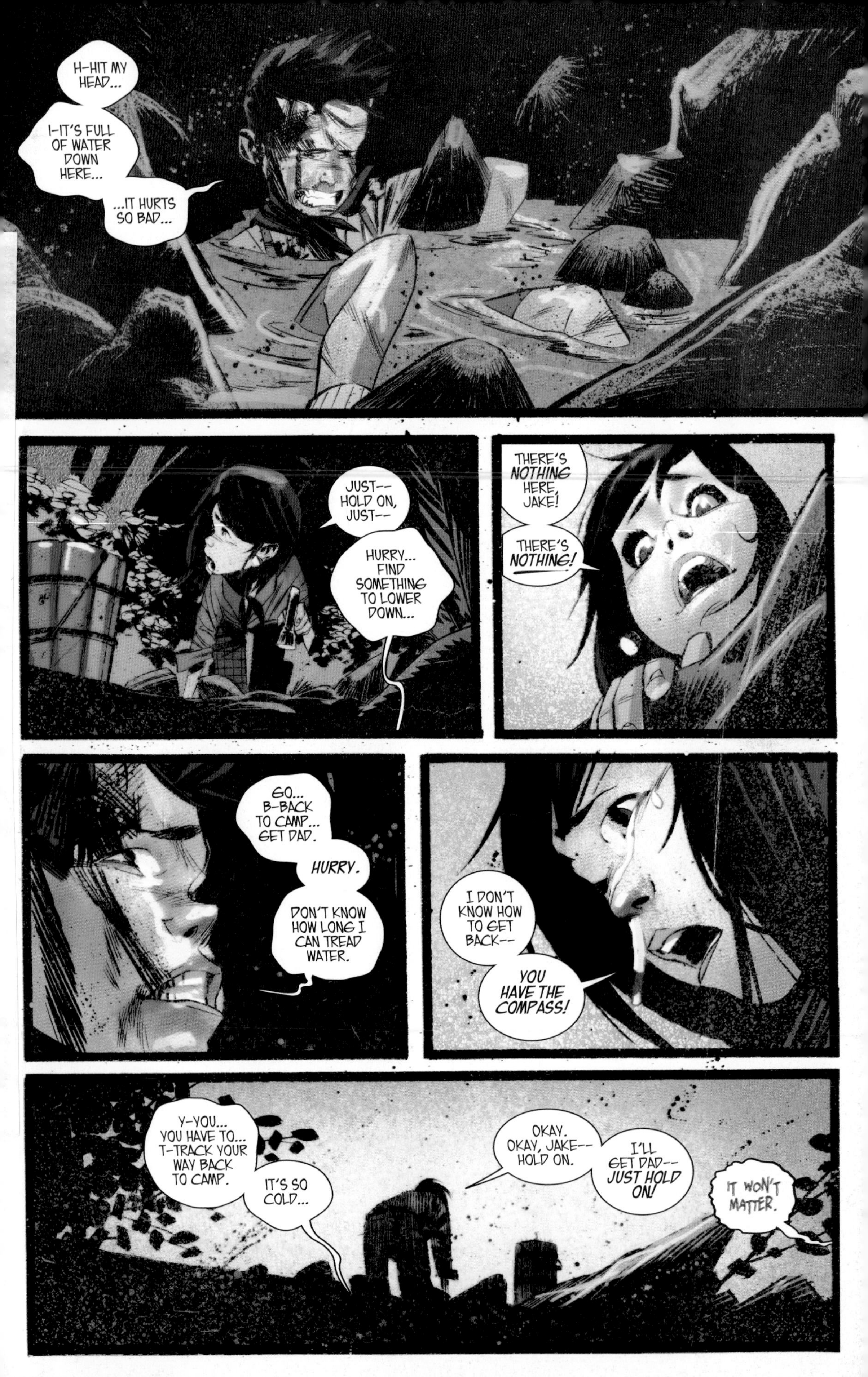
H-HIT MY HEAD...
I-IT'S FULL OF WATER DOWN HERE...
...IT HURTS SO BAD...
JUST-- HOLD ON, JUST--
HURRY... FIND SOMETHING TO LOWER DOWN...
THERE'S NOTHING HERE, JAKE!
THERE'S NOTHING!
GO... B-BACK TO CAMP... GET DAD.
HURRY.
DON'T KNOW HOW LONG I CAN TREAD WATER.
I DON'T KNOW HOW TO GET BACK--
YOU HAVE THE COMPASS!
Y-YOU... YOU HAVE TO... T-TRACK YOUR WAY BACK TO CAMP.
IT'S SO COLD...
OKAY. OKAY, JAKE-- HOLD ON.
I'LL GET DAD-- JUST HOLD ON!
IT WON'T MATTER.

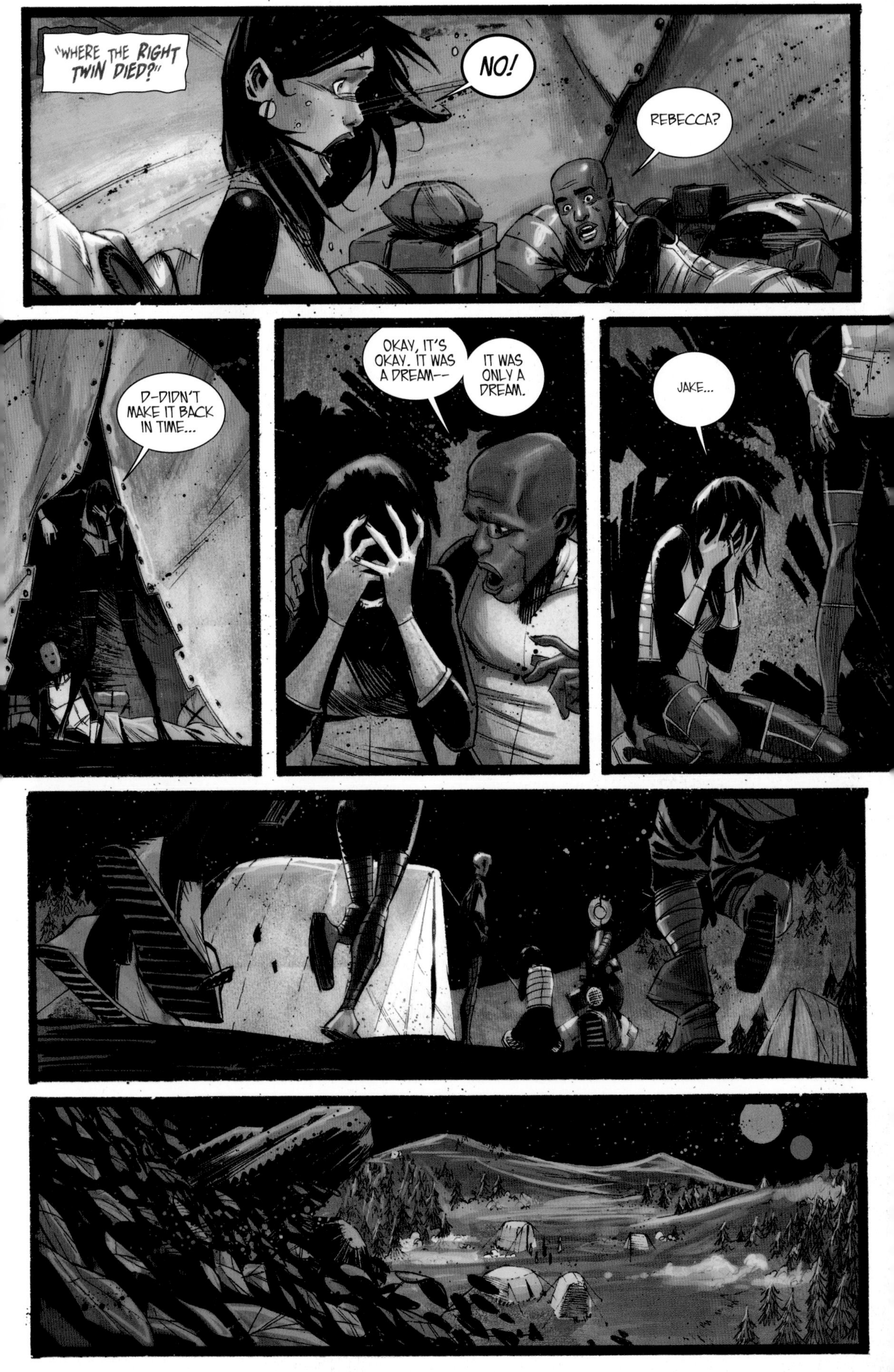
"WHERE THE RIGHT TWIN DIED?"
NO!
REBECCA?
D-DIDN'T MAKE IT BACK IN TIME...
OKAY, IT'S OKAY. IT WAS A DREAM--
IT WAS ONLY A DREAM.
JAKE...

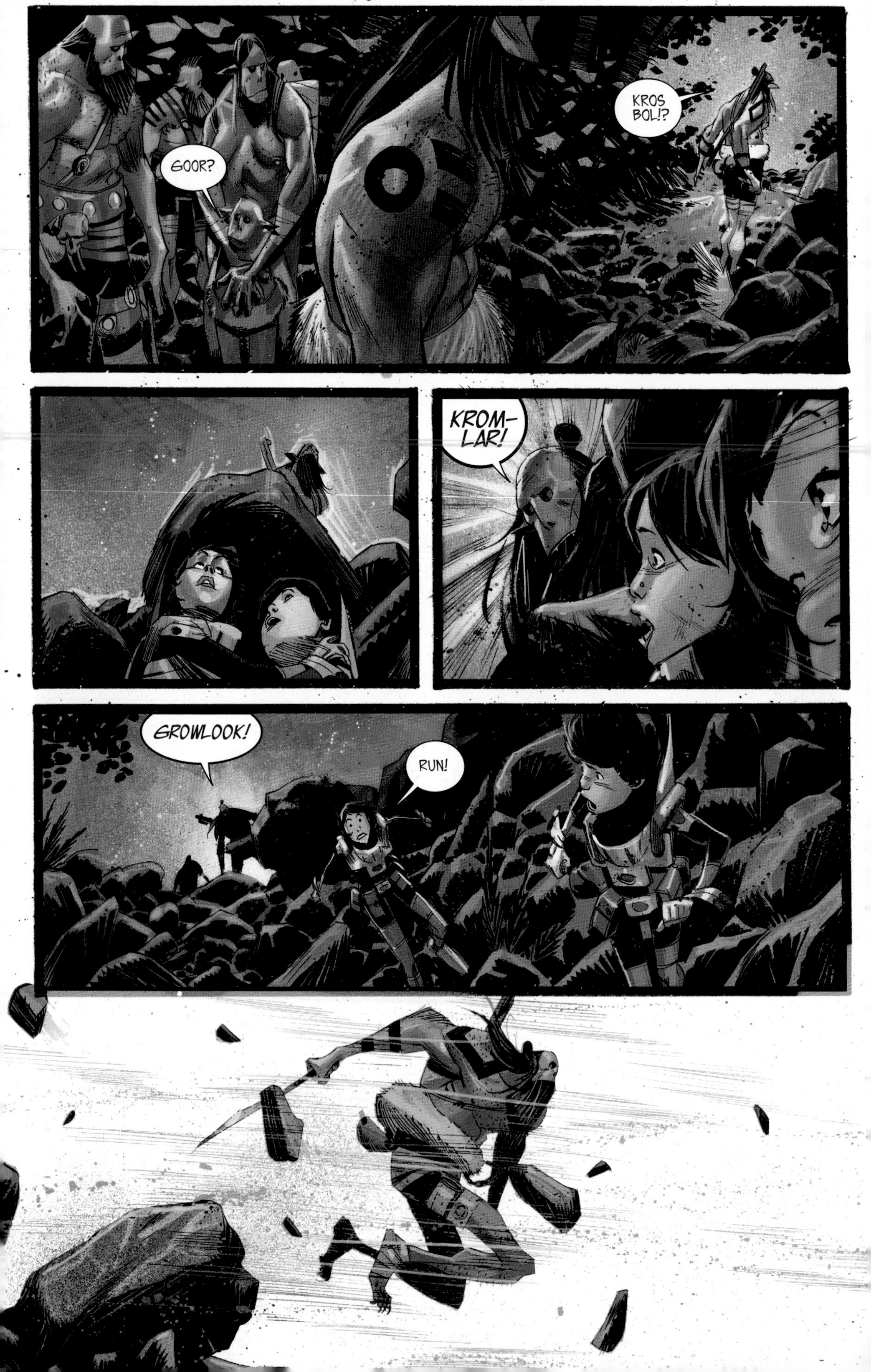
GOOR?
KROS BOL!?
KROM-LAR!
GROWLOOK!
RUN!

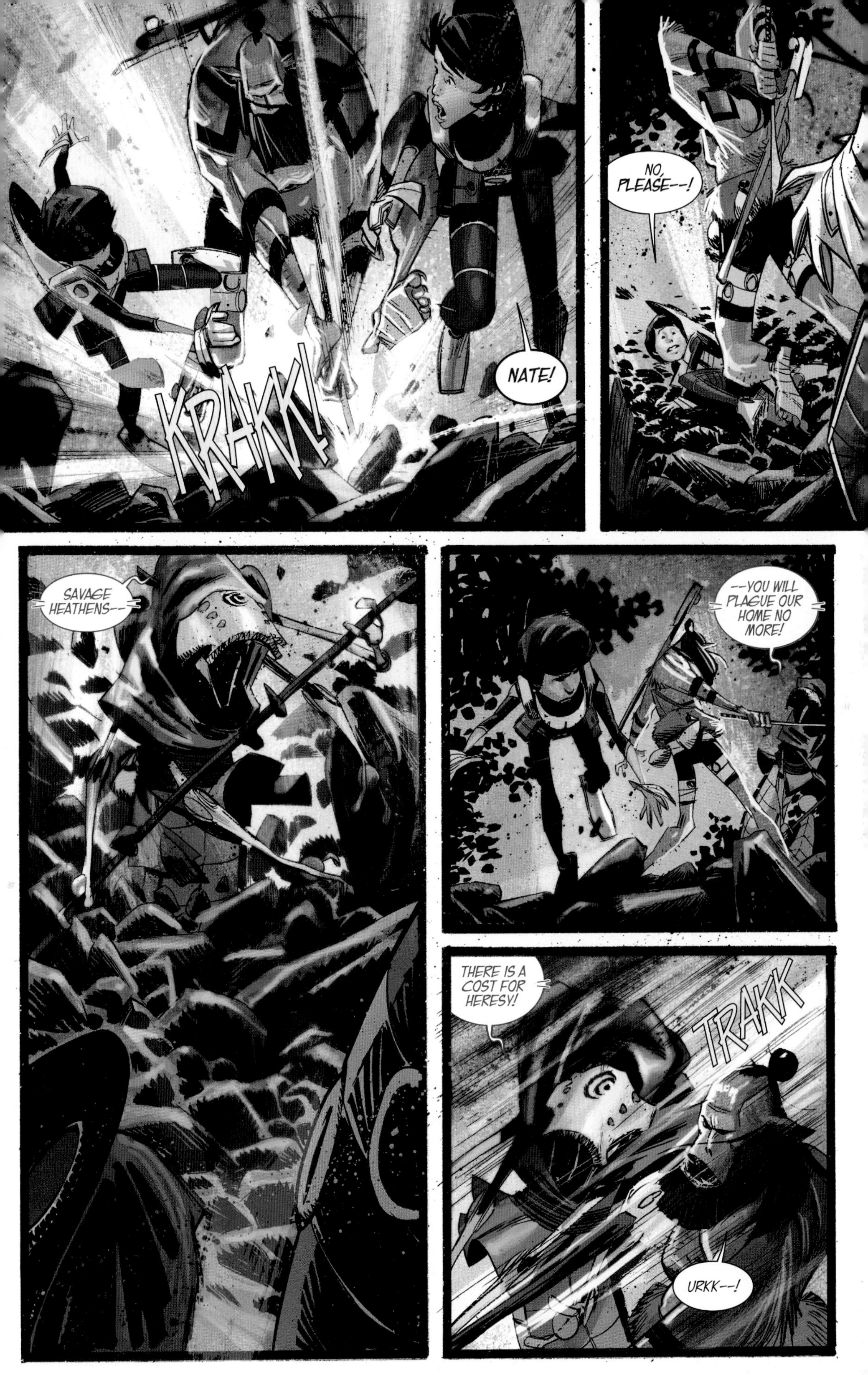
KRAKK!
NATE!
NO, PLEASE--!
SAVAGE HEATHENS--
--YOU WILL PLAGUE OUR HOME NO MORE!
THERE IS A COST FOR HERESY!
TRAKK
URKK--!

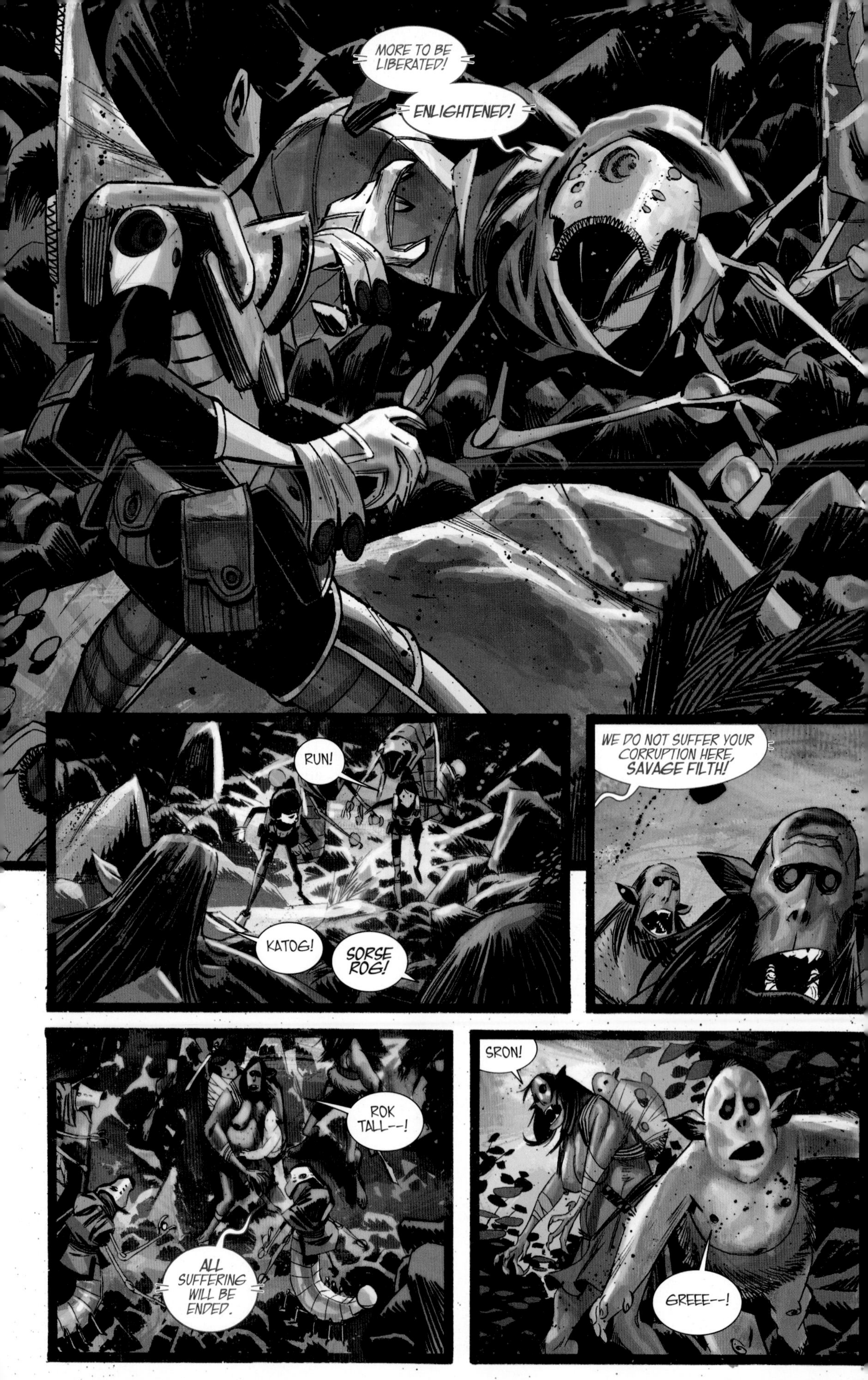
MORE TO BE LIBERATED!
ENLIGHTENED!
RUN!
KATOG!
SORSE ROG!
WE DO NOT SUFFER YOUR CORRUPTION HERE, SAVAGE FILTH!
ROK TALL--!
ALL SUFFERING WILL BE ENDED.
SRON!
GREEE--!

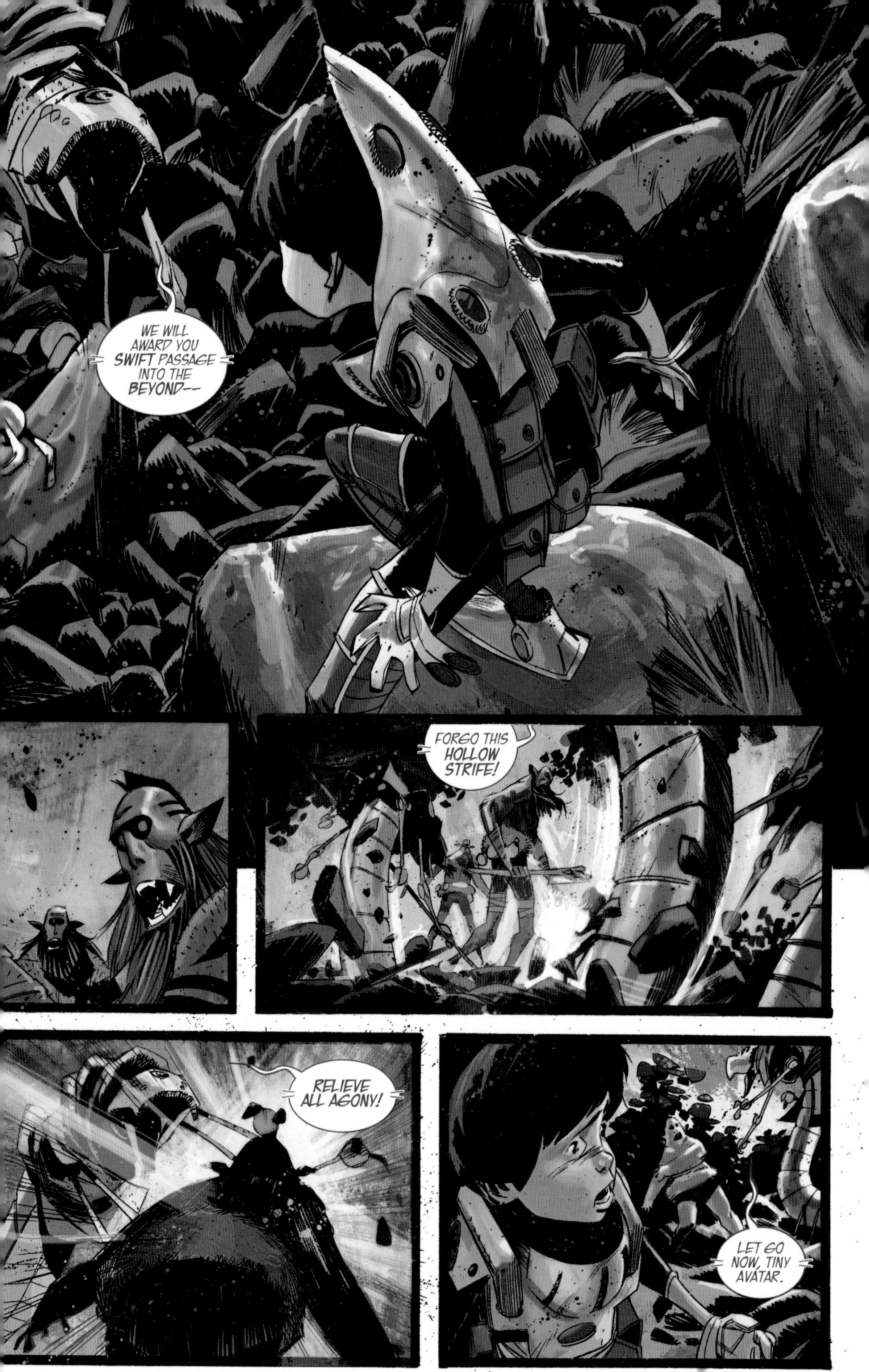
WE WILL AWARD YOU SWIFT PASSAGE INTO THE BEYOND--
FORGO THIS HOLLOW STRIFE!
RELIEVE ALL AGONY!
LET GO NOW, TINY AVATAR.

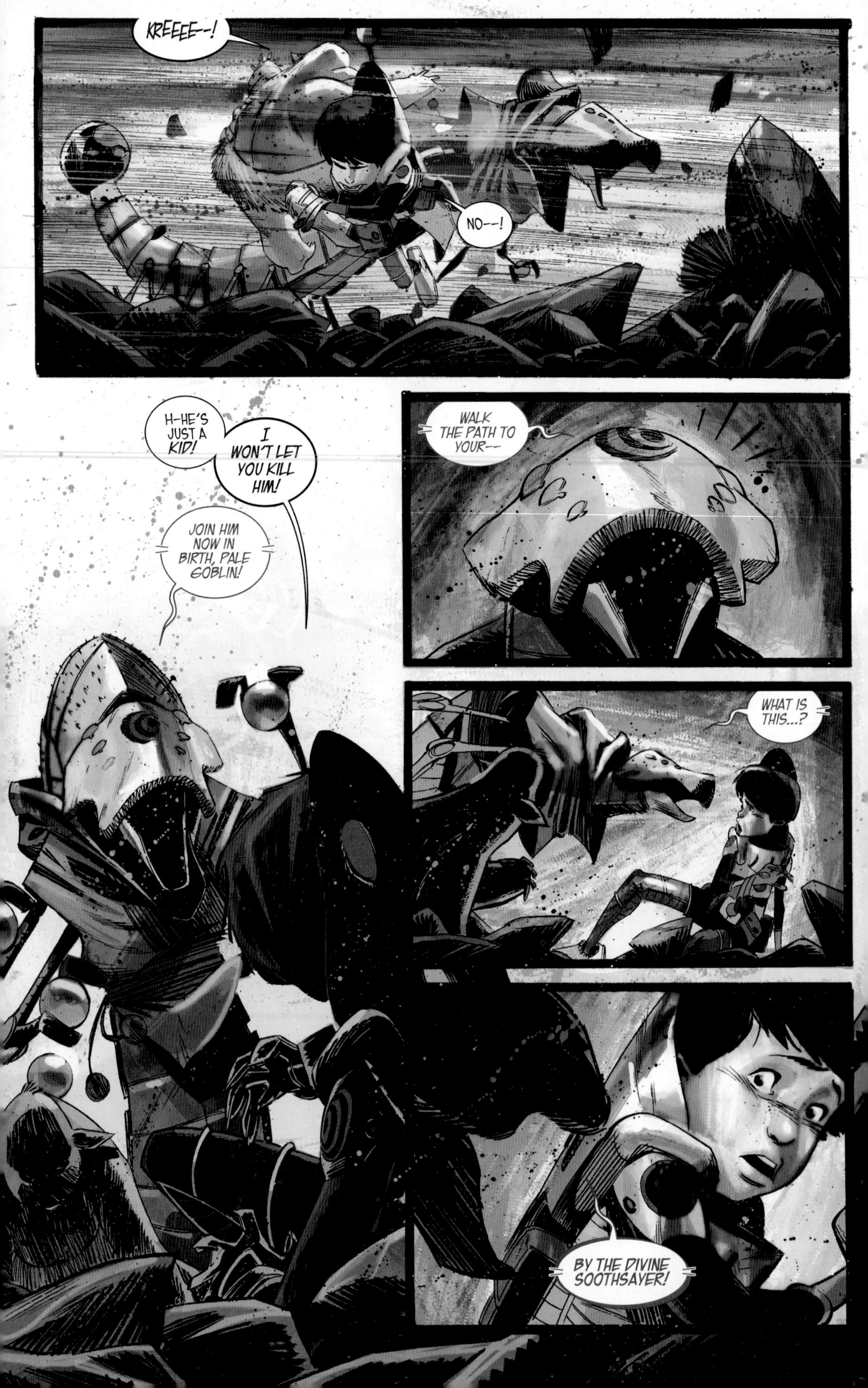
KREEEE--!
NO--!
H-HE'S JUST A KID!
I WON'T LET YOU KILL HIM!
JOIN HIM NOW IN BIRTH, PALE GOBLIN!
WALK THE PATH TO YOUR--
WHAT IS THIS...?
BY THE DIVINE SOOTHSAYER!

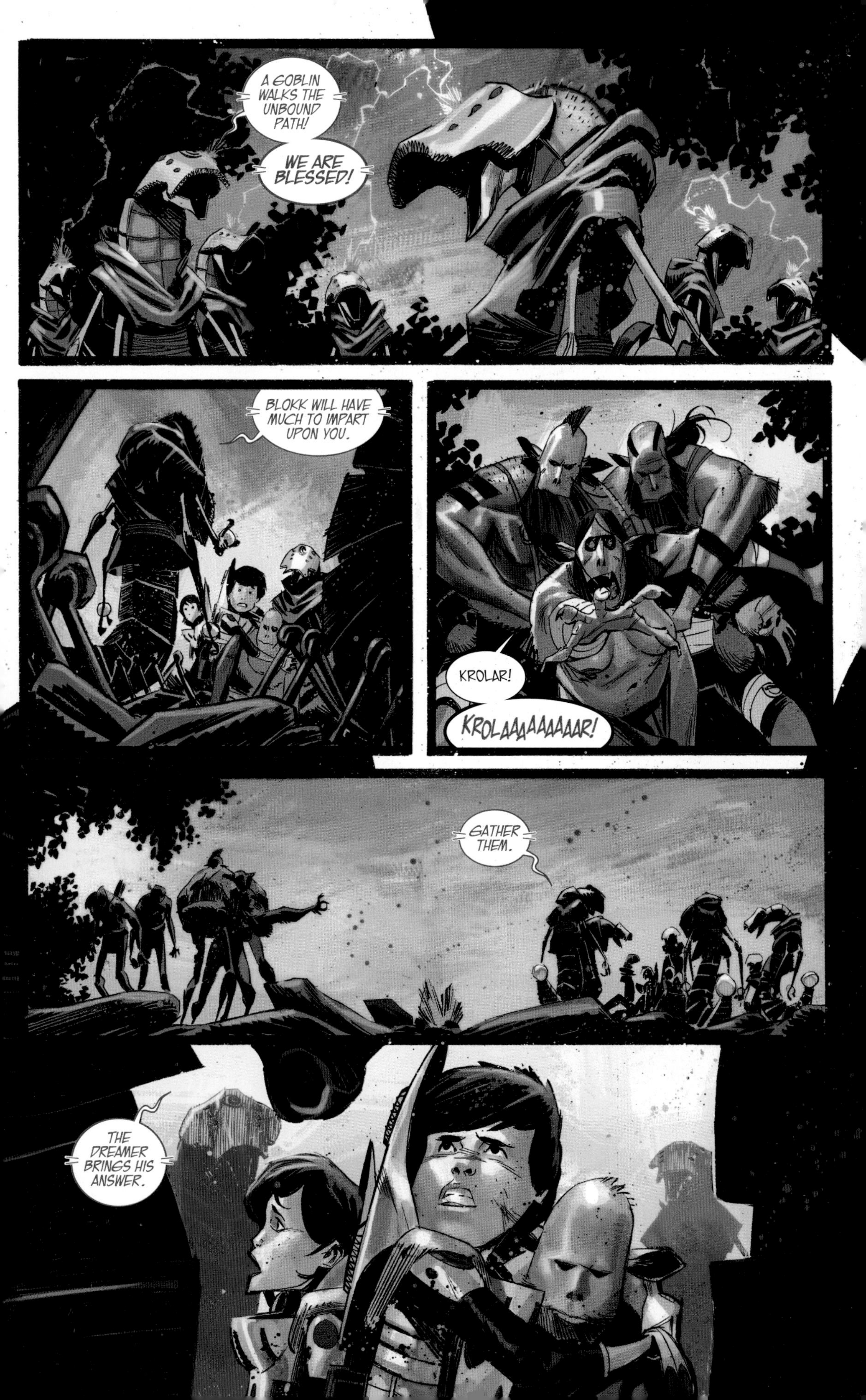
A GOBLIN WALKS THE UNBOUND PATH!
WE ARE BLESSED!
BLOKK WILL HAVE MUCH TO IMPART UPON YOU.
KROLAR!
KROLAAAAAAAAR!
GATHER THEM.
THE DREAMER BRINGS HIS ANSWER.

YOU'VE TRAVELED TO A
FOREIGN LAND AT THE
REQUEST OF AN OLD
FRIEND--

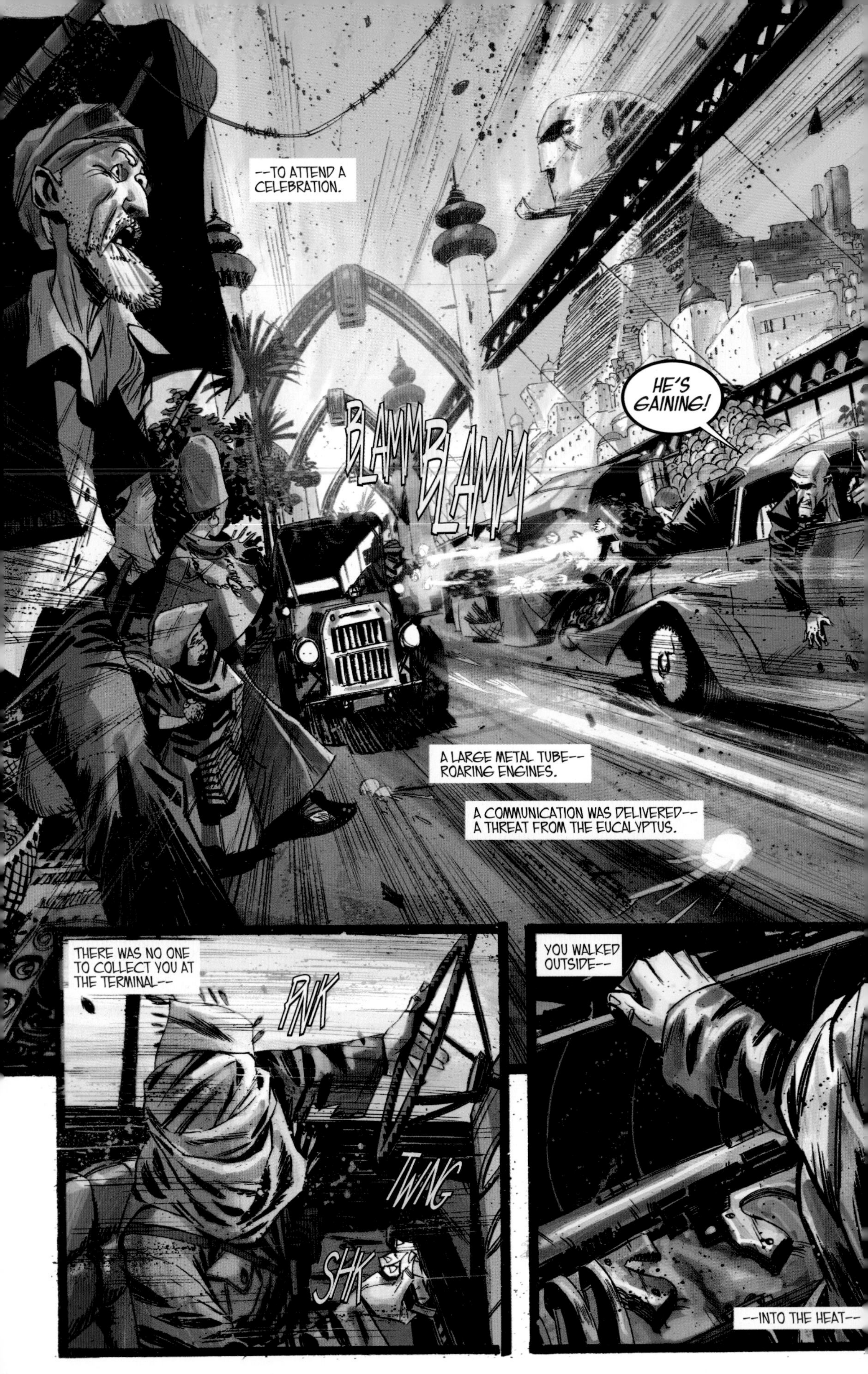
--TO ATTEND A CELEBRATION.
BLAMM BLAMM
HE'S GAINING!
A LARGE METAL TUBE-- ROARING ENGINES.
A COMMUNICATION WAS DELIVERED-- A THREAT FROM THE EUCALYPTUS.
THERE WAS NO ONE TO COLLECT YOU AT THE TERMINAL--
PNK
TWNG
SHK
YOU WALKED OUTSIDE--
--INTO THE HEAT--

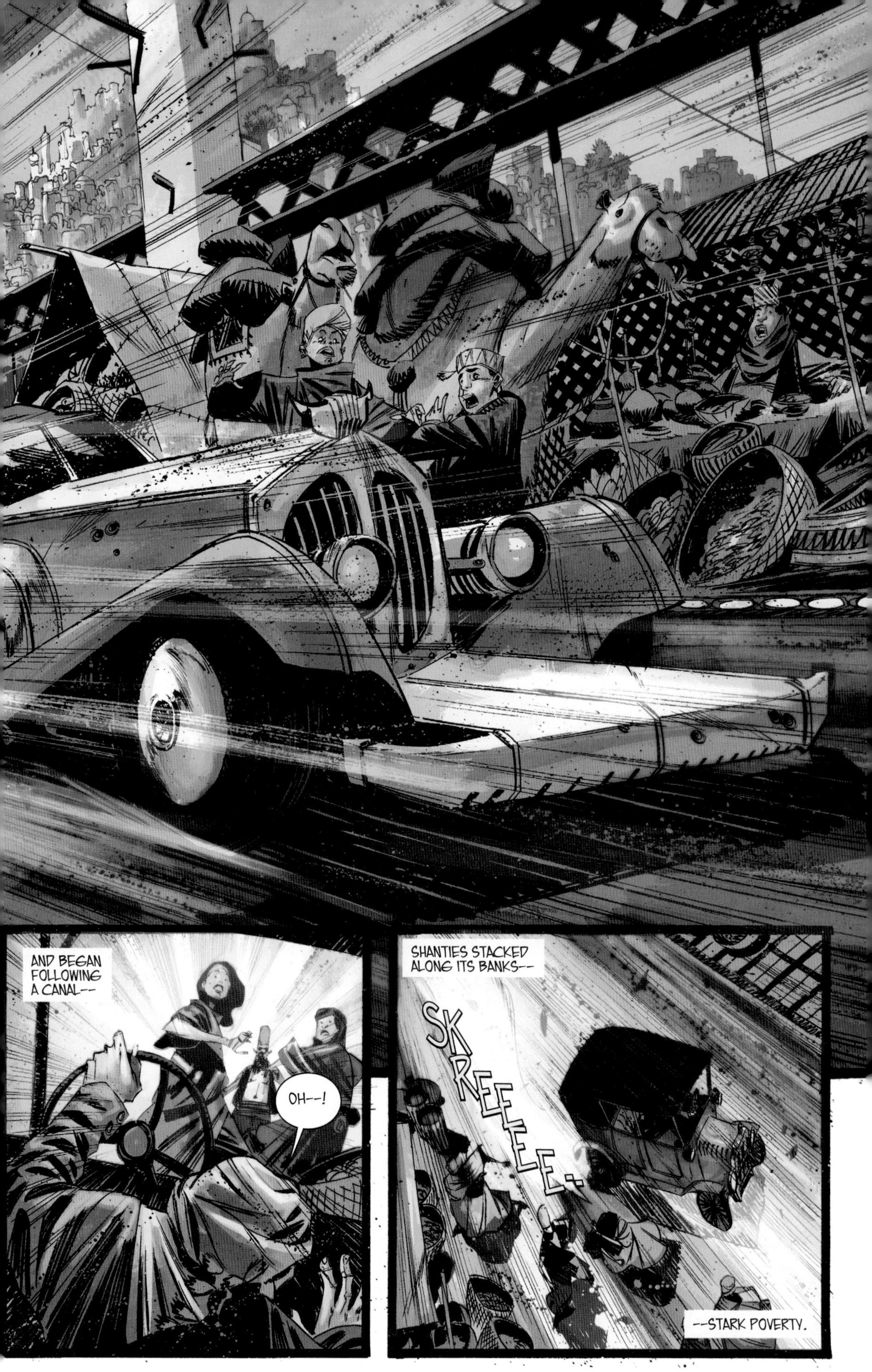
AND BEGAN FOLLOWING A CANAL--
OH--!
SHANTIES STACKED ALONG ITS BANKS--
SKREEEEEE--
--STARK POVERTY.

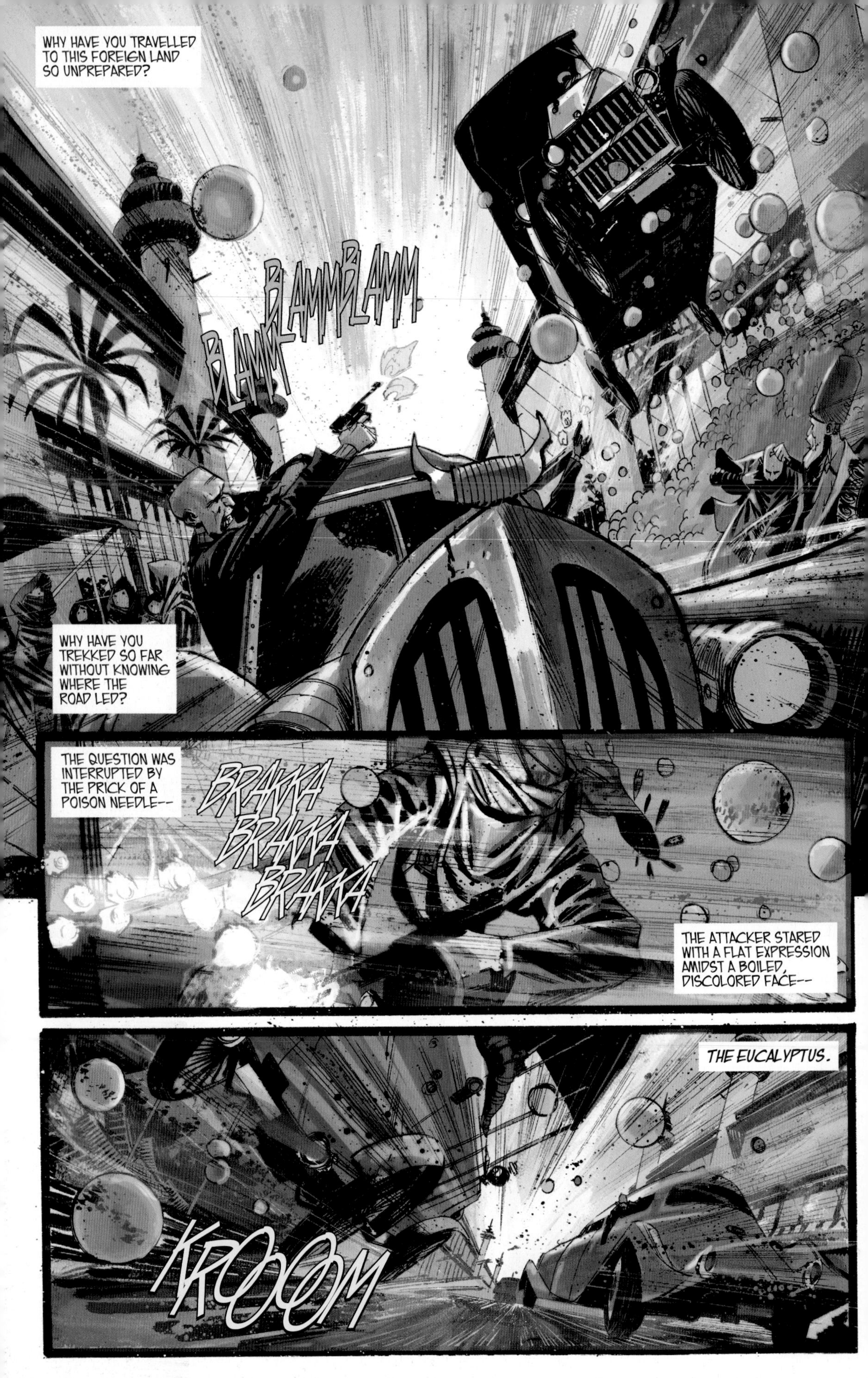
WHY HAVE YOU TRAVELLED TO THIS FOREIGN LAND SO UNPREPARED?
BLAMM BLAMM BLAMM
WHY HAVE YOU TREKKED SO FAR WITHOUT KNOWING WHERE THE ROAD LED?
THE QUESTION WAS INTERRUPTED BY THE PRICK OF A POISON NEEDLE--
BRAKKA BRAKKA BRAKKA
THE ATTACKER STARED WITH A FLAT EXPRESSION AMIDST A BOILED, DISCOLORED FACE--
THE EUCALYPTUS.
KROOOOM

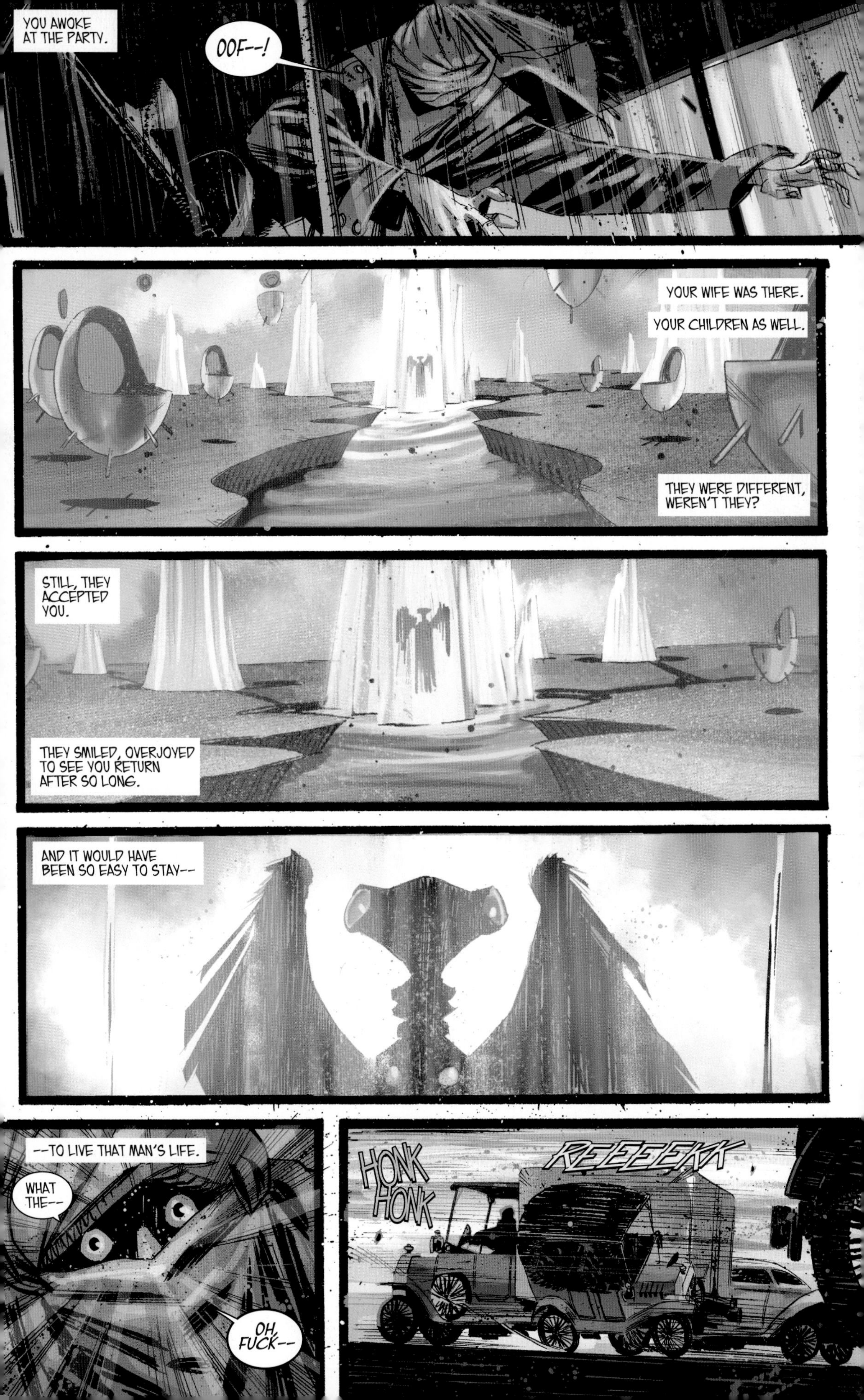
YOU AWOKE AT THE PARTY.
OOF--!
YOUR WIFE WAS THERE.
YOUR CHILDREN AS WELL.
THEY WERE DIFFERENT, WEREN'T THEY?
STILL, THEY ACCEPTED YOU.
THEY SMILED, OVERJOYED TO SEE YOU RETURN AFTER SO LONG.
AND IT WOULD HAVE BEEN SO EASY TO STAY--
--TO LIVE THAT MAN'S LIFE.
WHAT THE--
OH, FUCK--
HONK HONK
REEEEKK

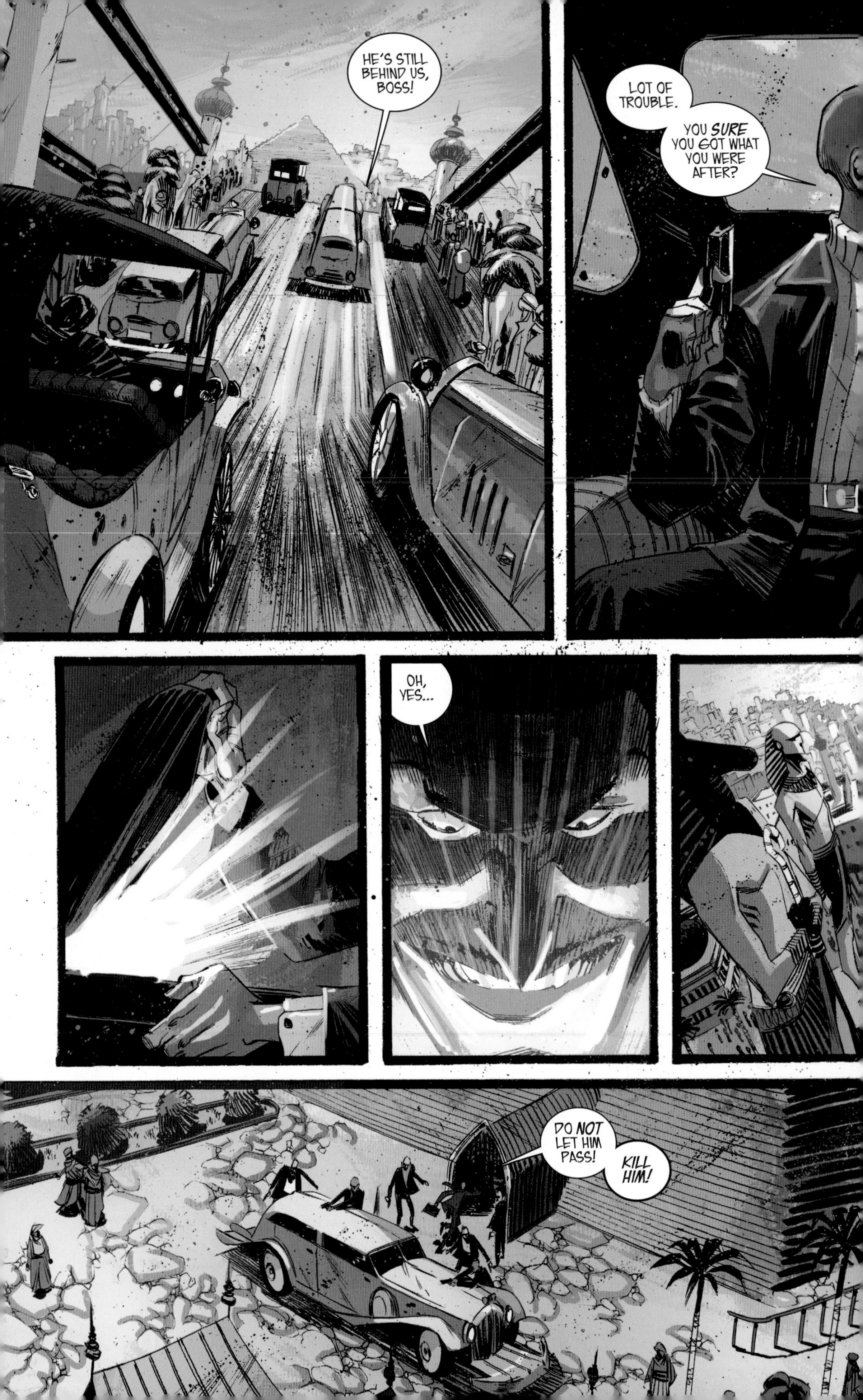
HE'S STILL BEHIND US, BOSS!
LOT OF TROUBLE.
YOU SURE YOU GOT WHAT YOU WERE AFTER?
OH, YES...
DO NOT LET HIM PASS!
KILL HIM!

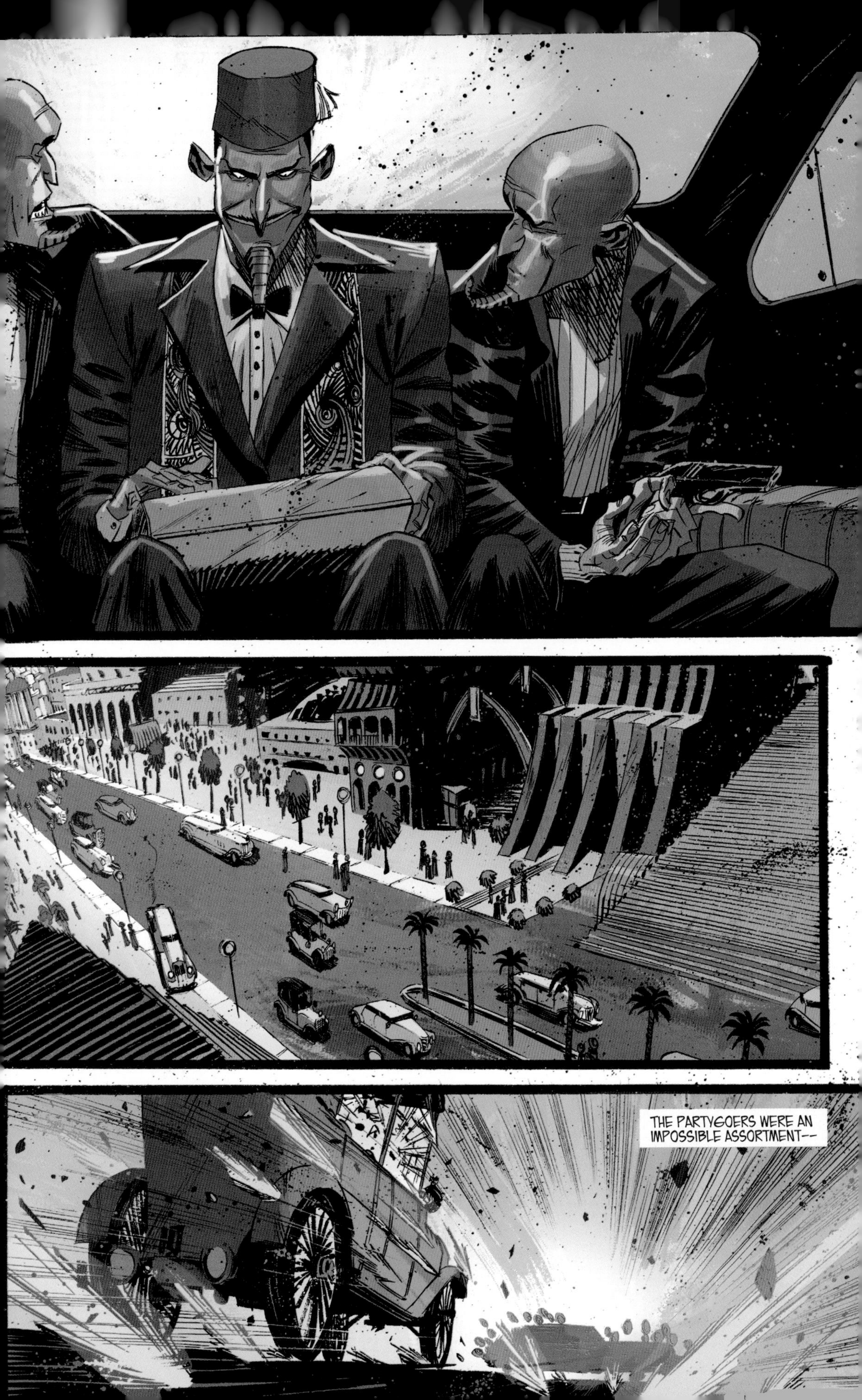
THE PARTYGOERS WERE AN IMPOSSIBLE ASSORTMENT--

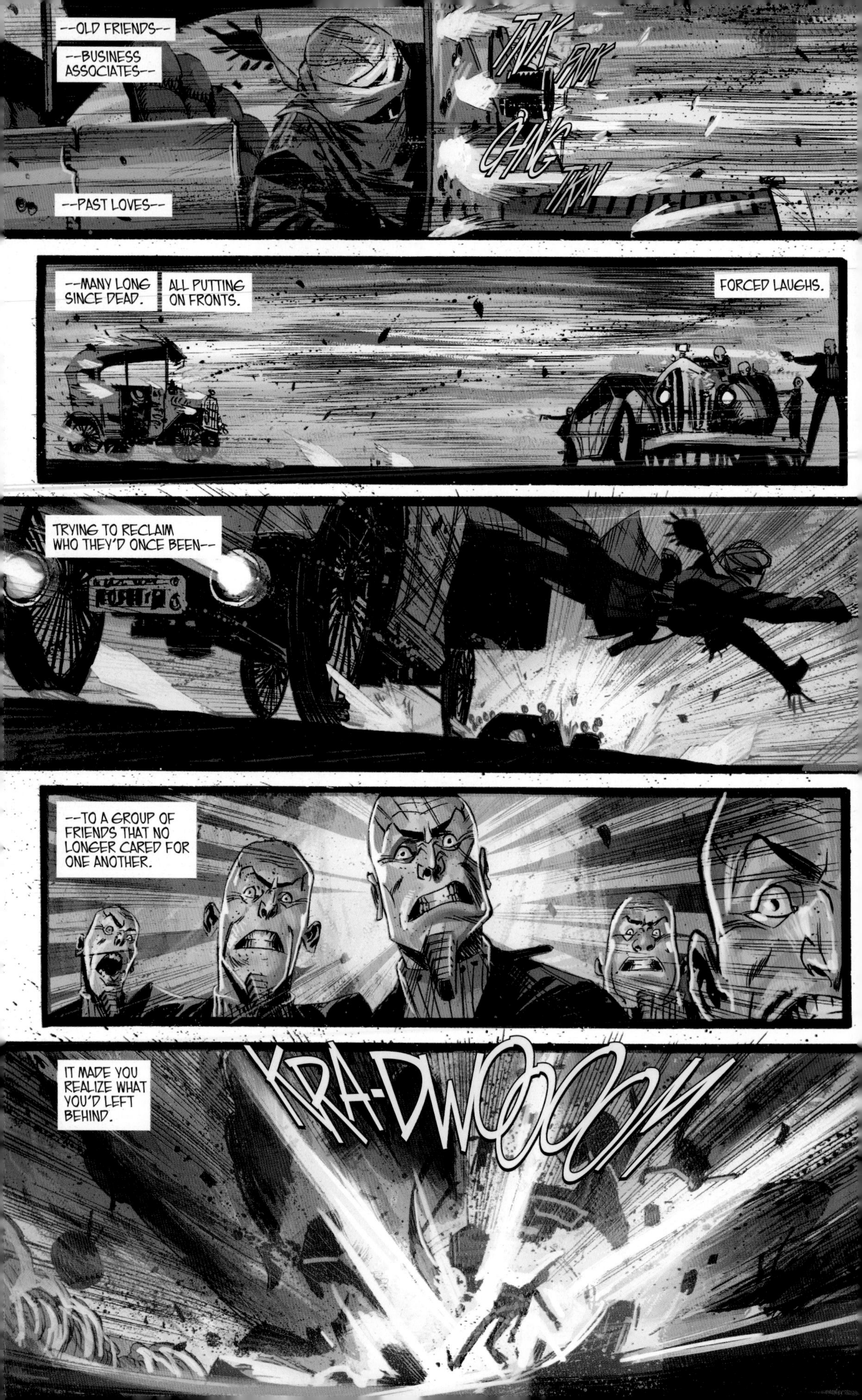
--OLD FRIENDS--
--BUSINESS ASSOCIATES--
--PAST LOVES--
TNK PNK
CHNG TKN
--MANY LONG SINCE DEAD.
ALL PUTTING ON FRONTS.
FORCED LAUGHS.
TRYING TO RECLAIM WHO THEY'D ONCE BEEN--
--TO A GROUP OF FRIENDS THAT NO LONGER CARED FOR ONE ANOTHER.
IT MADE YOU REALIZE WHAT YOU'D LEFT BEHIND.
KRA-DWOOOOM

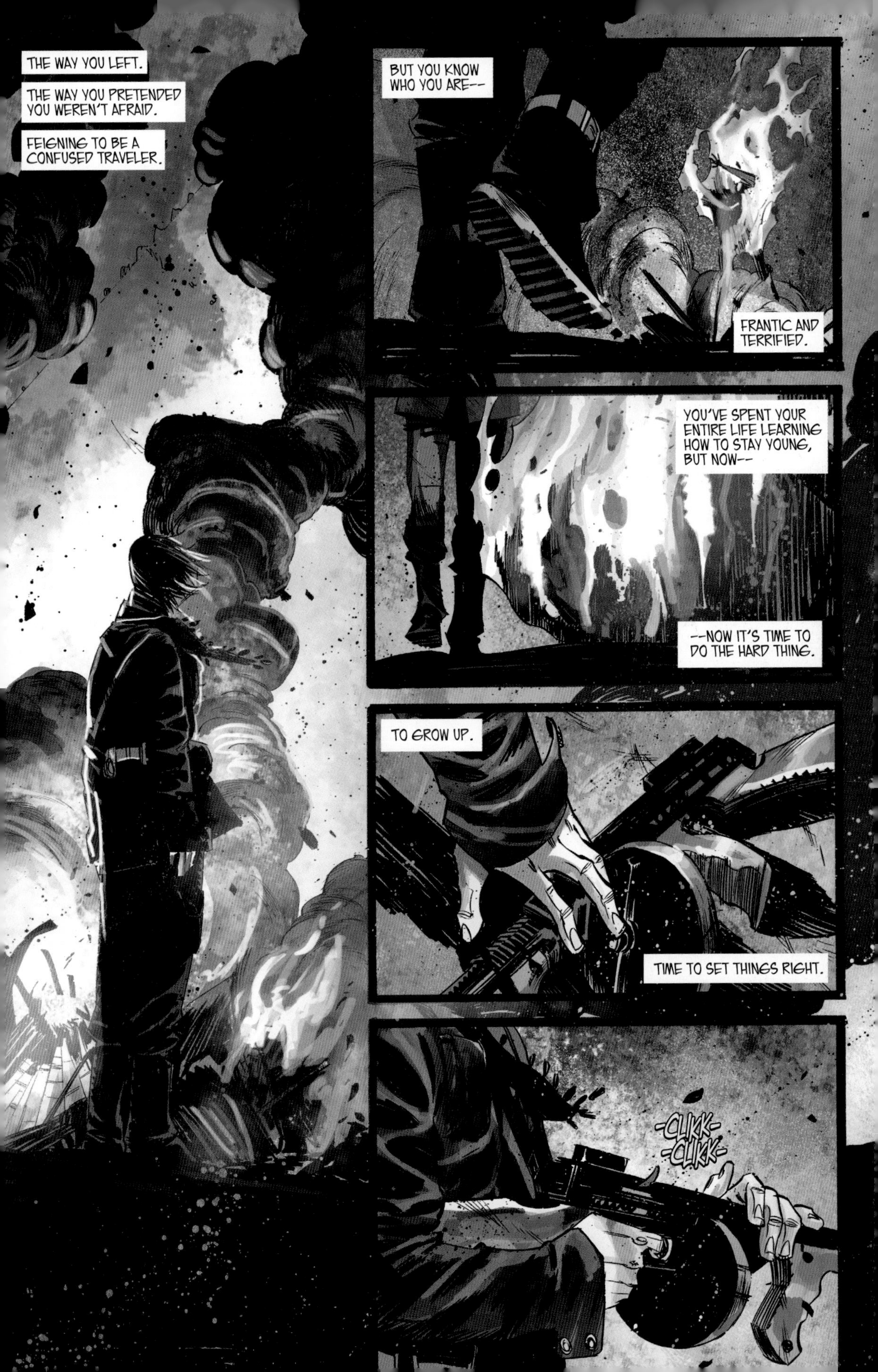
THE WAY YOU LEFT.
THE WAY YOU PRETENDED YOU WEREN'T AFRAID.
FEIGNING TO BE A CONFUSED TRAVELER.
BUT YOU KNOW WHO YOU ARE--
FRANTIC AND TERRIFIED.
YOU'VE SPENT YOUR ENTIRE LIFE LEARNING HOW TO STAY YOUNG, BUT NOW--
--NOW IT'S TIME TO DO THE HARD THING.
TO GROW UP.
TIME TO SET THINGS RIGHT.
-CLIKK-
-CLIKK-

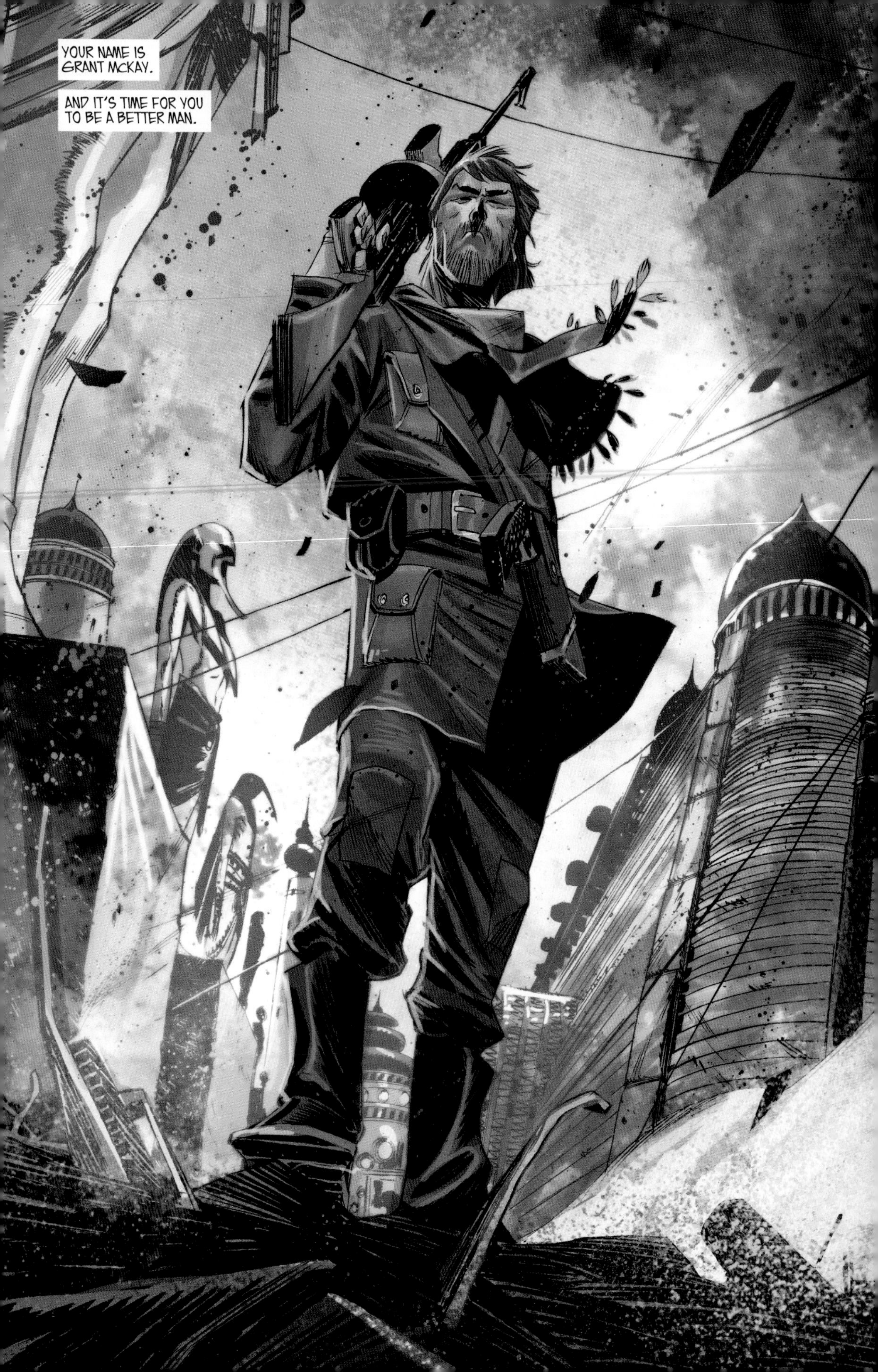
YOUR NAME IS GRANT MCKAY.
AND IT'S TIME FOR YOU TO BE A BETTER MAN.

10

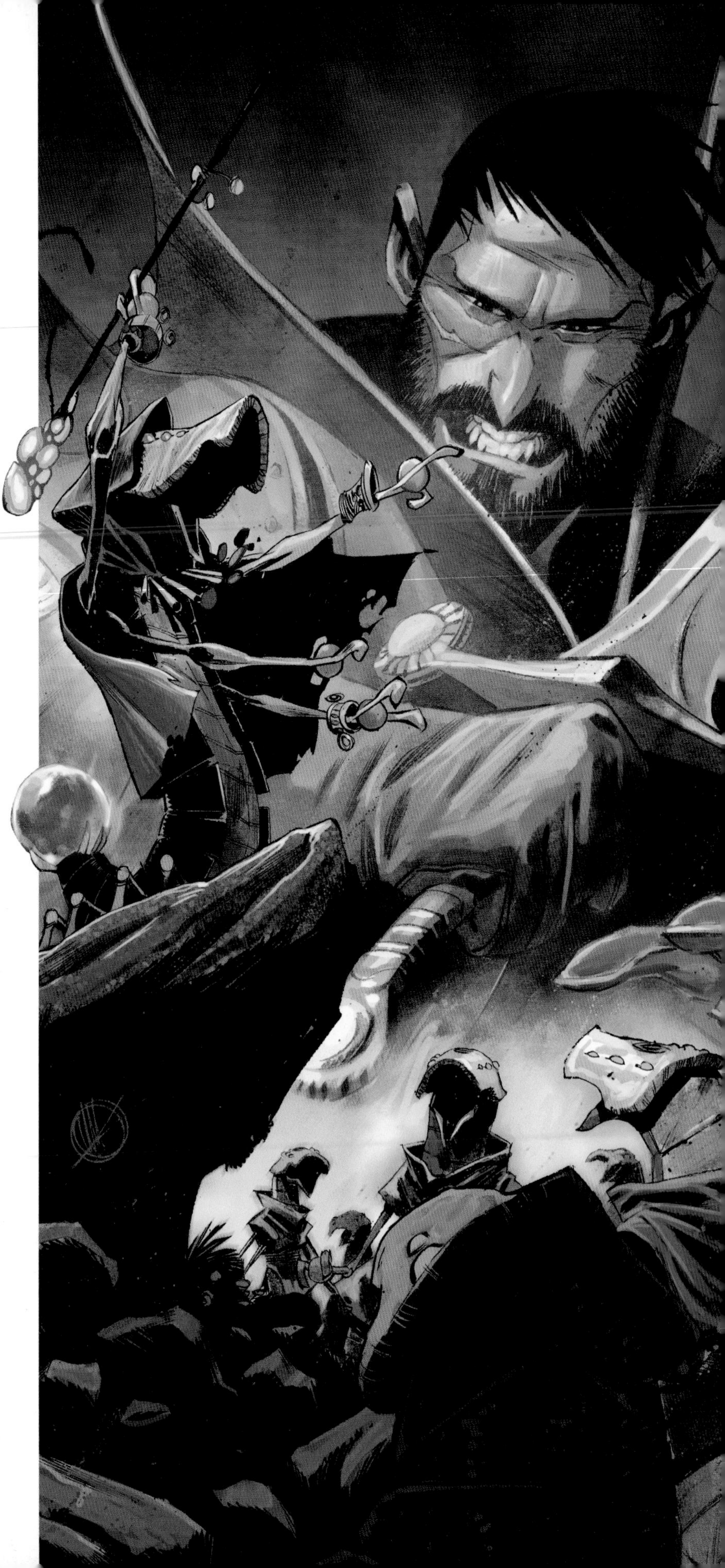

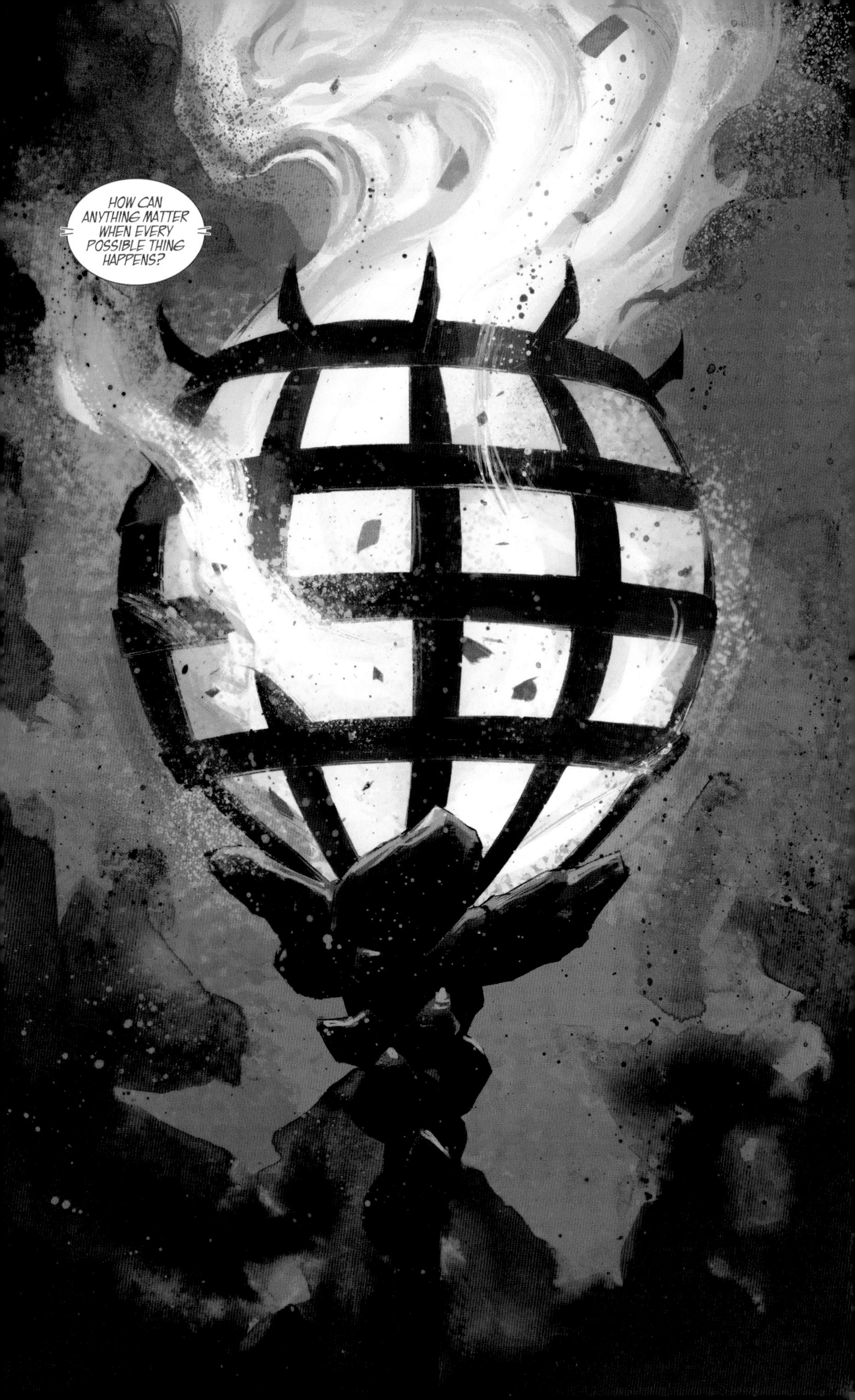
HOW CAN ANYTHING MATTER WHEN EVERY POSSIBLE THING HAPPENS?

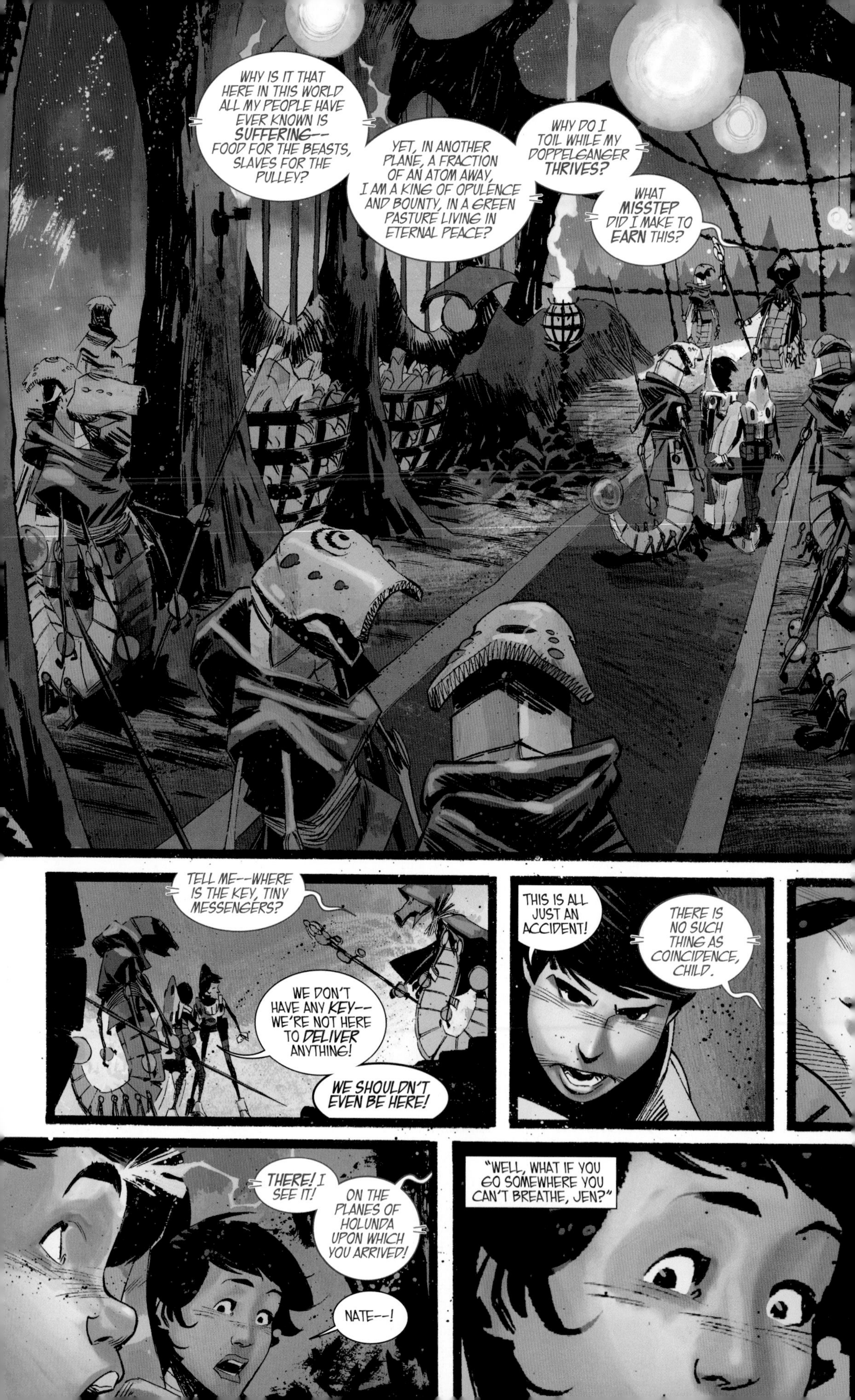
WHY IS IT THAT HERE IN THIS WORLD ALL MY PEOPLE HAVE EVER KNOWN IS SUFFERING-- FOOD FOR THE BEASTS, SLAVES FOR THE PULLEY?
YET, IN ANOTHER PLANE, A FRACTION OF AN ATOM AWAY, I AM A KING OF OPULENCE AND BOUNTY, IN A GREEN PASTURE LIVING IN ETERNAL PEACE?
WHY DO I TOIL WHILE MY DOPPELGANGER THRIVES?
WHAT MISSTEP DID I MAKE TO EARN THIS?
TELL ME--WHERE IS THE KEY, TINY MESSENGERS?
WE DON'T HAVE ANY KEY-- WE'RE NOT HERE TO DELIVER ANYTHING!
WE SHOULDN'T EVEN BE HERE!
THIS IS ALL JUST AN ACCIDENT!
THERE IS NO SUCH THING AS COINCIDENCE, CHILD.
THERE! I SEE IT!
ON THE PLANES OF HOLUNDA UPON WHICH YOU ARRIVED!
NATE--!
"WELL, WHAT IF YOU GO SOMEWHERE YOU CAN'T BREATHE, JEN?"

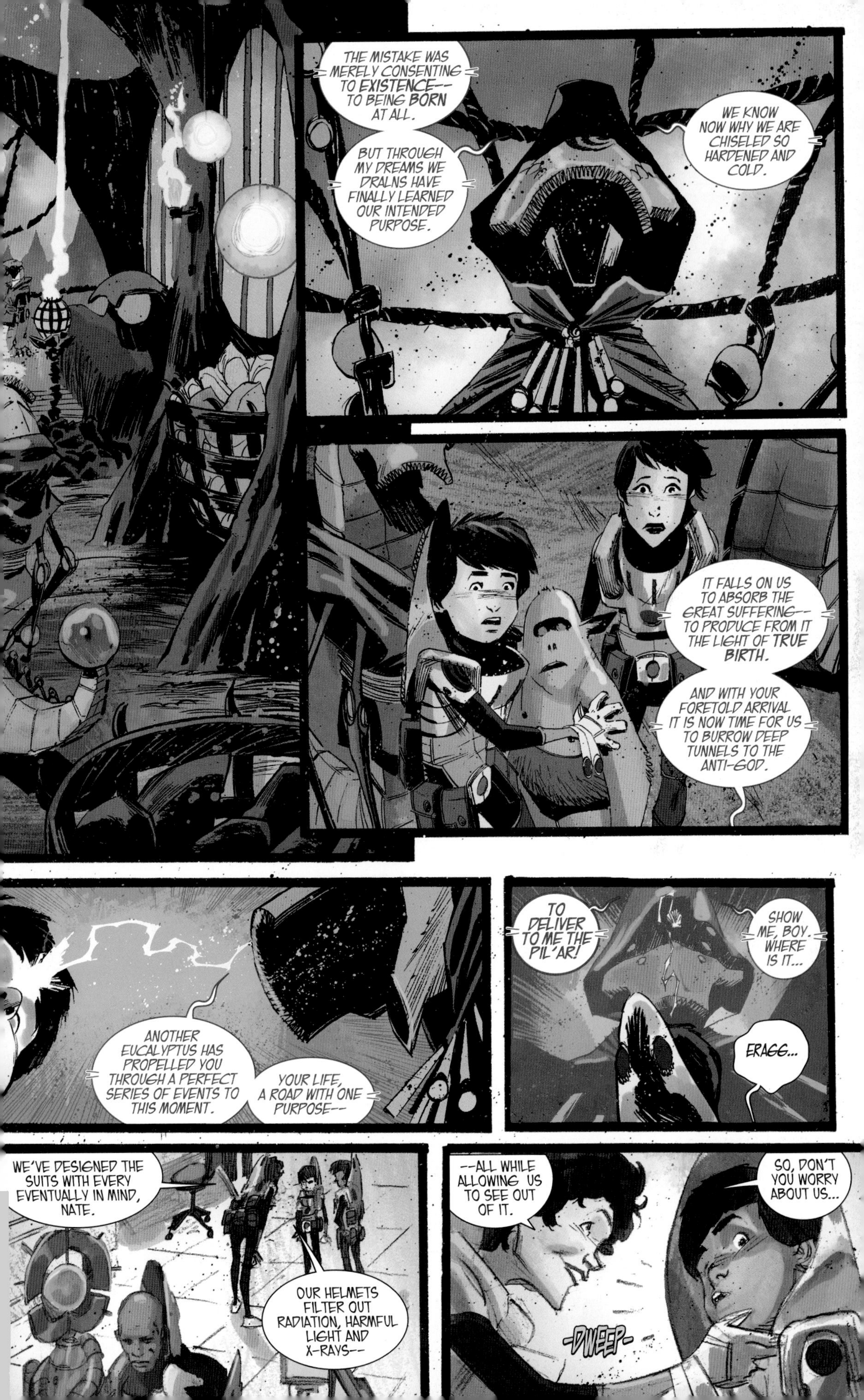
THE MISTAKE WAS MERELY CONSENTING TO EXISTENCE-- TO BEING BORN AT ALL.
BUT THROUGH MY DREAMS WE DRALNS HAVE FINALLY LEARNED OUR INTENDED PURPOSE.
WE KNOW NOW WHY WE ARE CHISELED SO HARDENED AND COLD.
IT FALLS ON US TO ABSORB THE GREAT SUFFERING-- TO PRODUCE FROM IT THE LIGHT OF TRUE BIRTH.
AND WITH YOUR FORETOLD ARRIVAL IT IS NOW TIME FOR US TO BURROW DEEP TUNNELS TO THE ANTI-GOD.
ANOTHER EUCALYPTUS HAS PROPELLED YOU THROUGH A PERFECT SERIES OF EVENTS TO THIS MOMENT.
YOUR LIFE, A ROAD WITH ONE PURPOSE--
TO DELIVER TO ME THE PIL'AR!
SHOW ME, BOY. WHERE IS IT...
ERAGG...
WE'VE DESIGNED THE SUITS WITH EVERY EVENTUALLY IN MIND, NATE.
OUR HELMETS FILTER OUT RADIATION, HARMFUL LIGHT AND X-RAYS--
--ALL WHILE ALLOWING US TO SEE OUT OF IT.
SO, DON'T YOU WORRY ABOUT US...
-DWEEP-

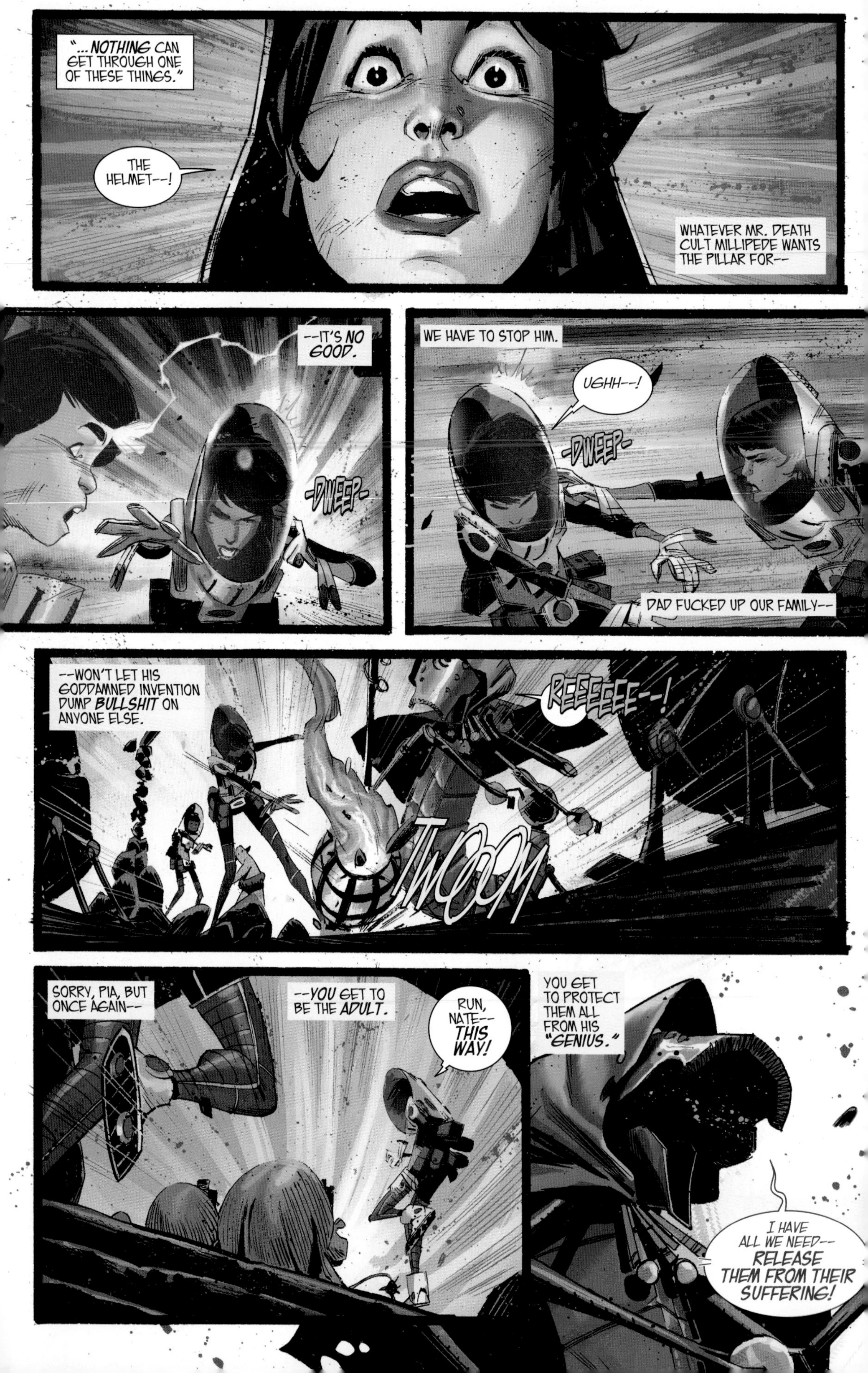

"...NOTHING CAN GET THROUGH ONE OF THESE THINGS."
THE HELMET--!
WHATEVER MR. DEATH CULT MILLIPEDE WANTS THE PILLAR FOR--
--IT'S NO GOOD.
-DWEEP-
WE HAVE TO STOP HIM.
UGHH--!
-DWEEP-
DAD FUCKED UP OUR FAMILY--
--WON'T LET HIS GODDAMNED INVENTION DUMP BULLSHIT ON ANYONE ELSE.
REEEEEE--!
TWOOM
SORRY, PIA, BUT ONCE AGAIN--
--YOU GET TO BE THE ADULT.
RUN, NATE-- THIS WAY!
YOU GET TO PROTECT THEM ALL FROM HIS "GENIUS."
I HAVE ALL WE NEED-- RELEASE THEM FROM THEIR SUFFERING!

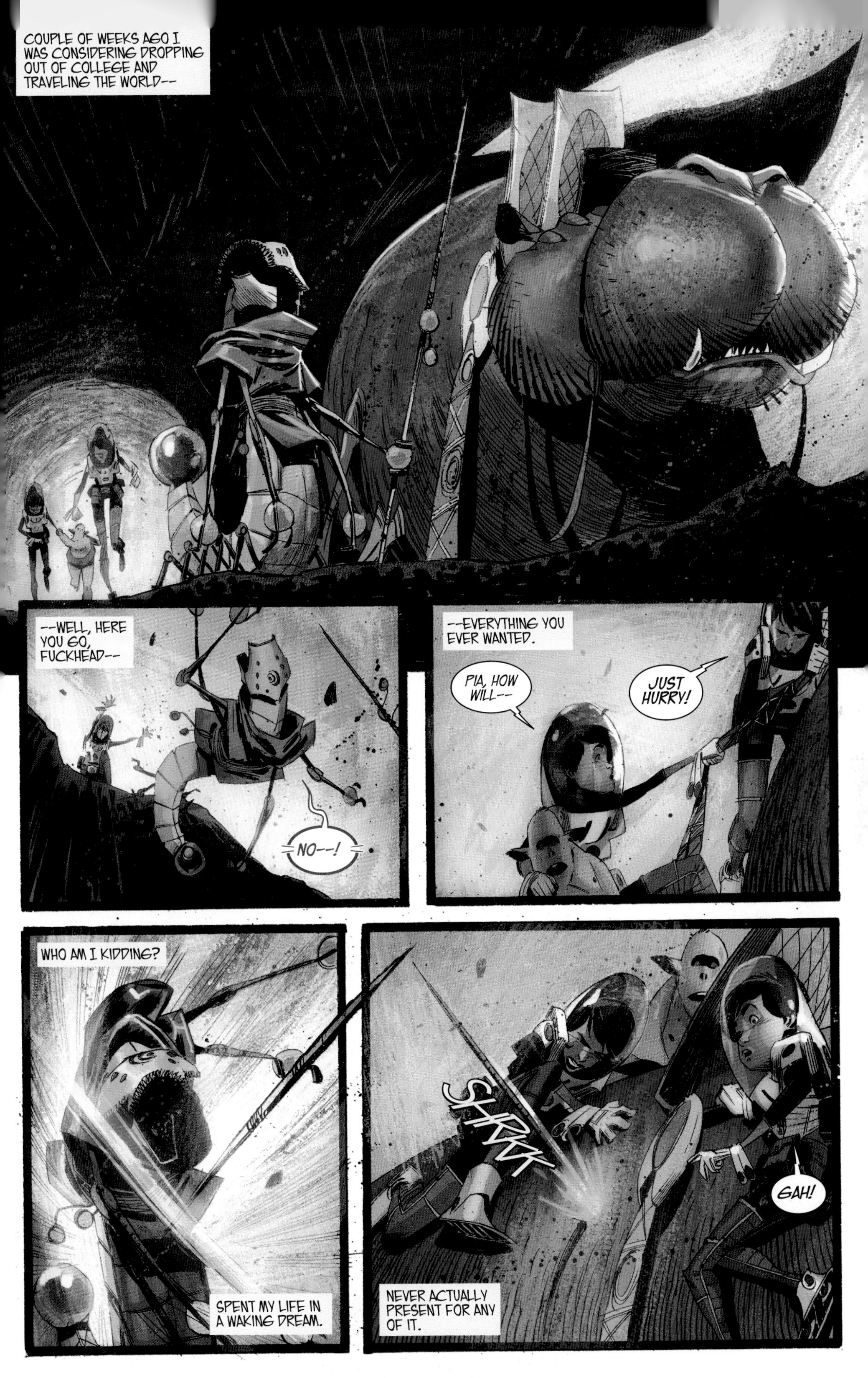

COUPLE OF WEEKS AGO I WAS CONSIDERING DROPPING OUT OF COLLEGE AND TRAVELING THE WORLD--
--WELL, HERE YOU GO, FUCKHEAD--
NO--!
--EVERYTHING YOU EVER WANTED.
PIA, HOW WILL--
JUST HURRY!
WHO AM I KIDDING?
SPENT MY LIFE IN A WAKING DREAM.
SHRKK
GAH!
NEVER ACTUALLY PRESENT FOR ANY OF IT.

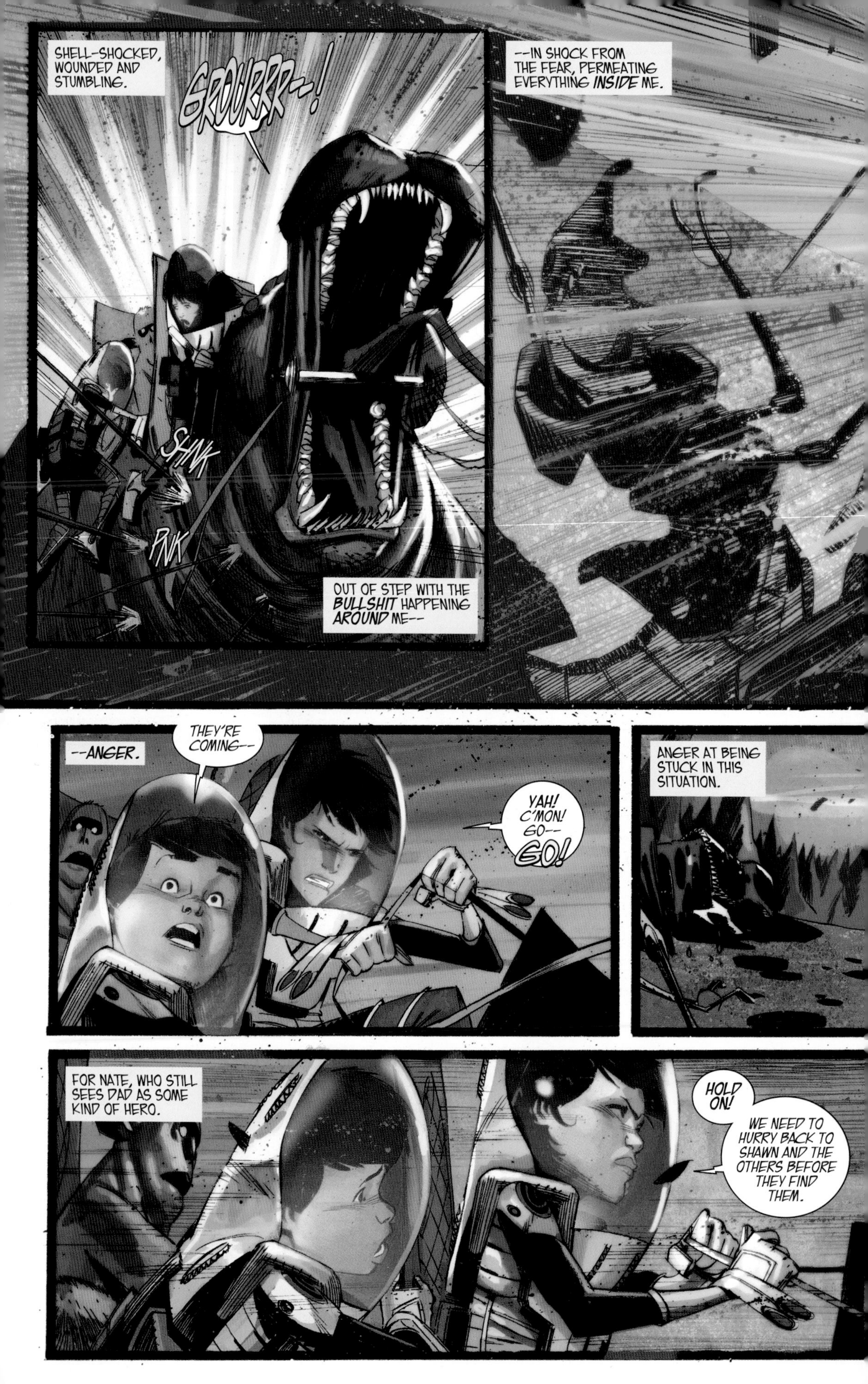
SHELL-SHOCKED, WOUNDED AND STUMBLING.
GROURRR--!
--IN SHOCK FROM THE FEAR, PERMEATING EVERYTHING INSIDE ME.
SHNK
PNK
OUT OF STEP WITH THE BULLSHIT HAPPENING AROUND ME--
--ANGER.
THEY'RE COMING--
YAH! C'MON! GO-- GO!
ANGER AT BEING STUCK IN THIS SITUATION.
FOR NATE, WHO STILL SEES DAD AS SOME KIND OF HERO.
HOLD ON!
WE NEED TO HURRY BACK TO SHAWN AND THE OTHERS BEFORE THEY FIND THEM.

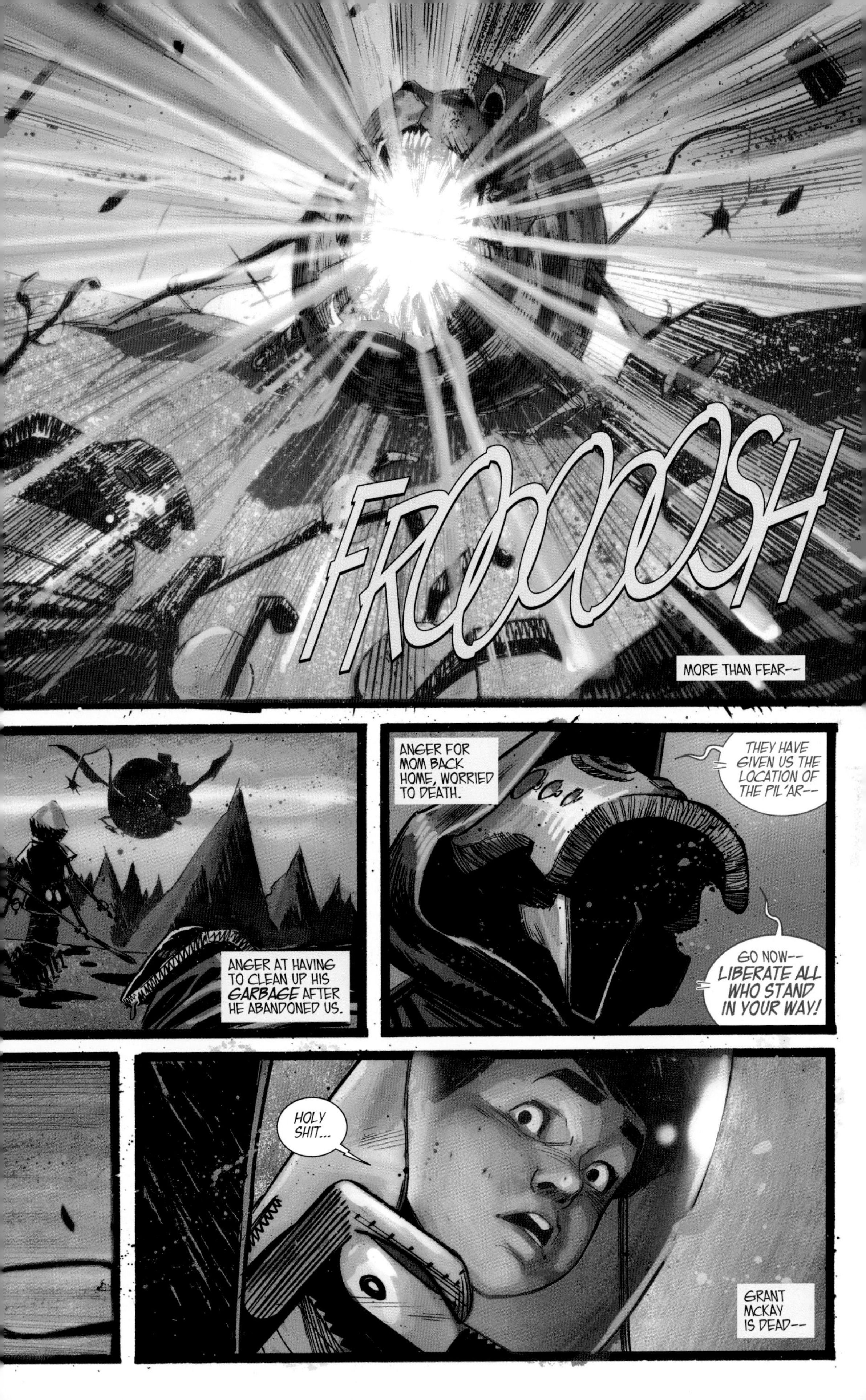
FROOOOOSH
MORE THAN FEAR--
ANGER AT HAVING TO CLEAN UP HIS GARBAGE AFTER HE ABANDONED US.
ANGER FOR MOM BACK HOME, WORRIED TO DEATH.
THEY HAVE GIVEN US THE LOCATION OF THE PIL'AR--
GO NOW-- LIBERATE ALL WHO STAND IN YOUR WAY!
HOLY SHIT...
GRANT MCKAY IS DEAD--

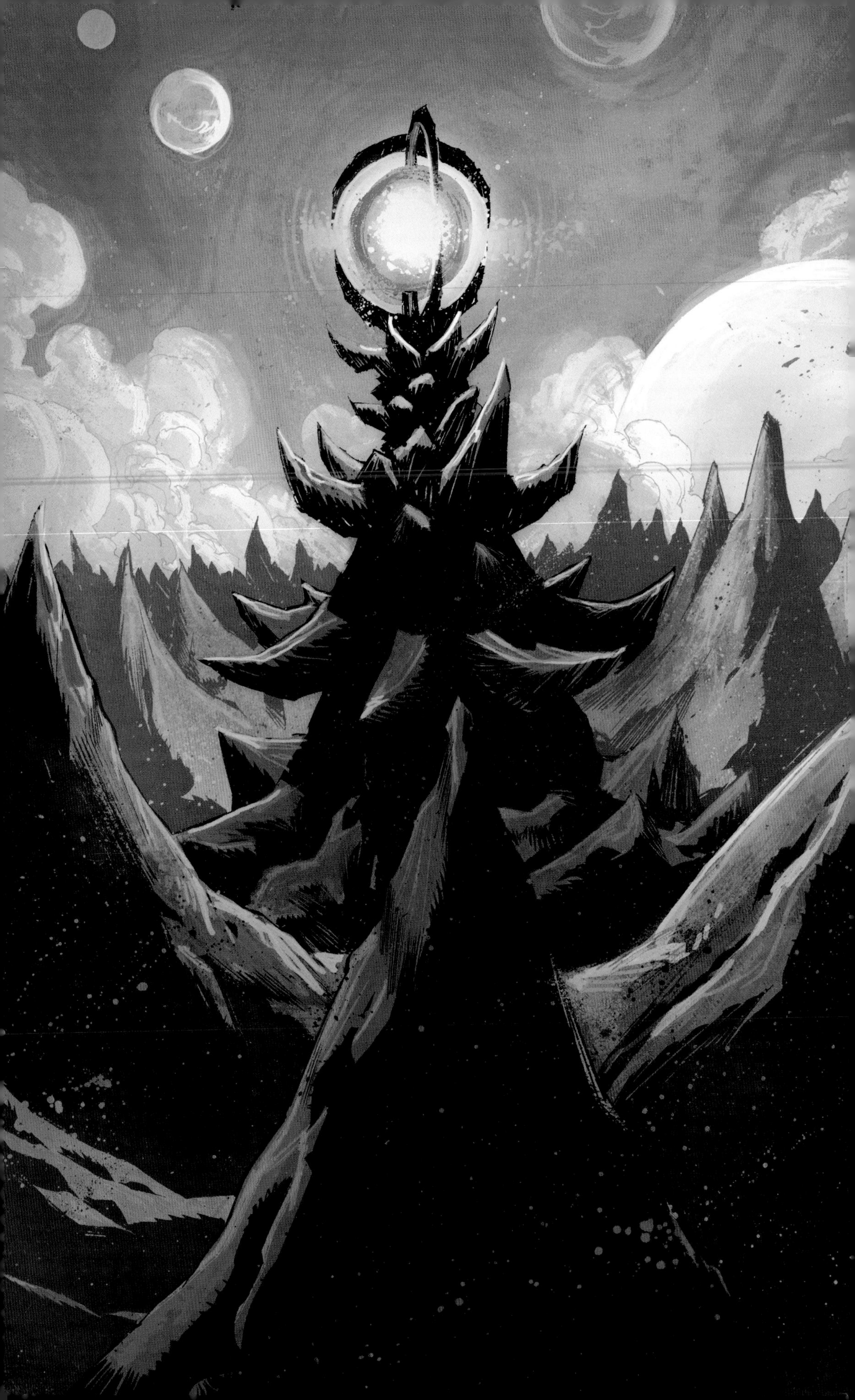

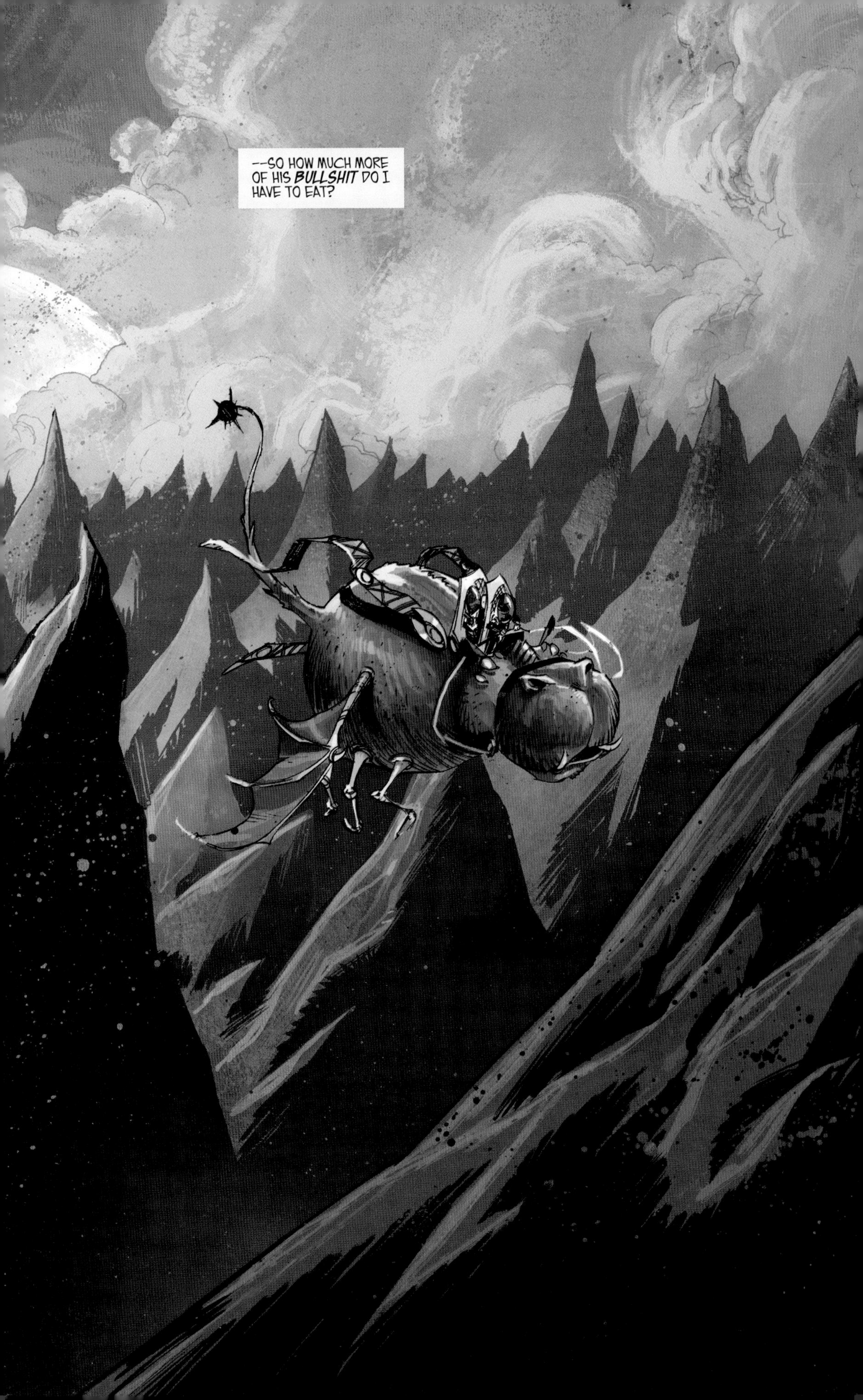
--SO HOW MUCH MORE OF HIS *BULLSHIT* DO I HAVE TO EAT?

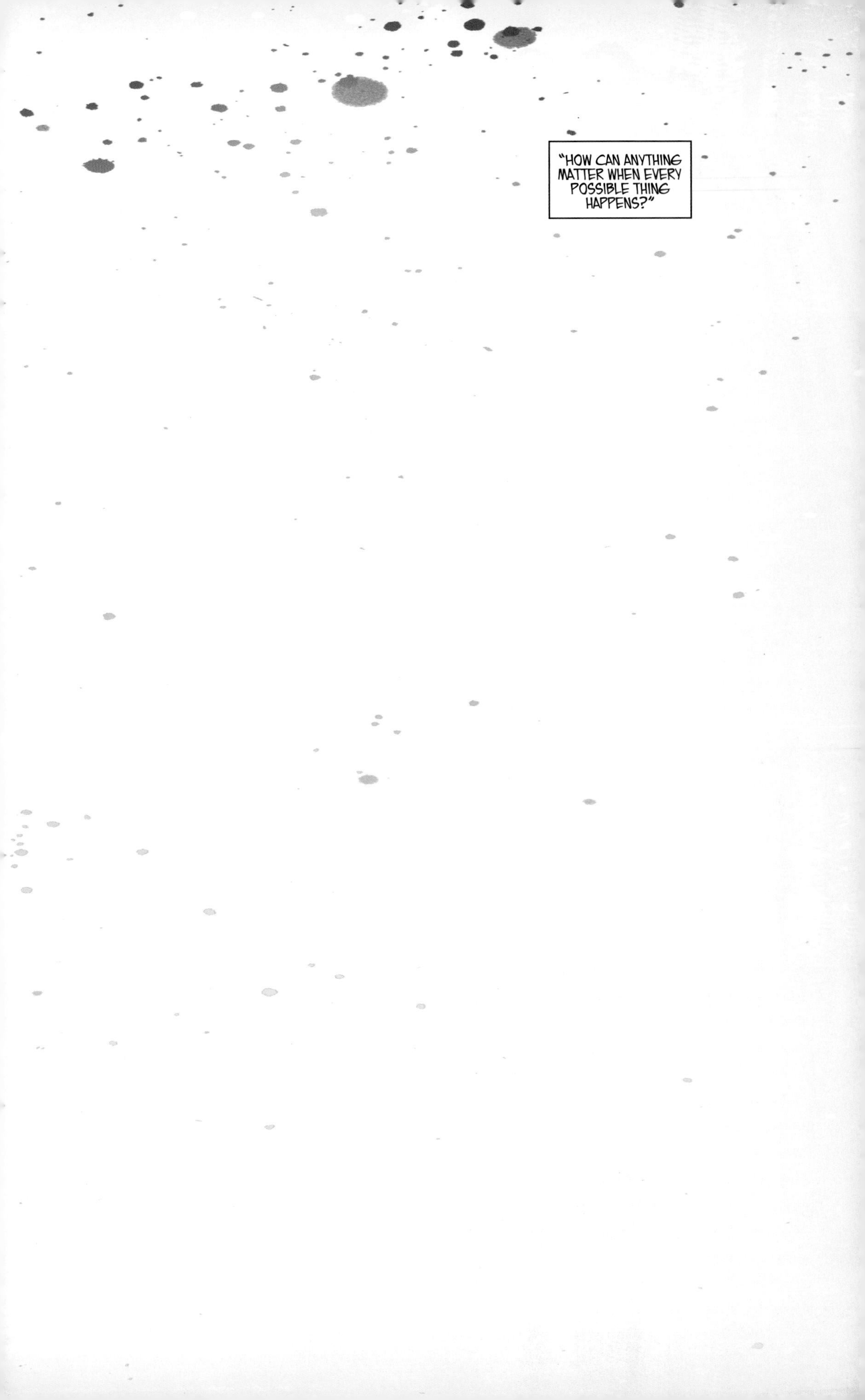
"HOW CAN ANYTHING MATTER WHEN EVERY POSSIBLE THING HAPPENS?"

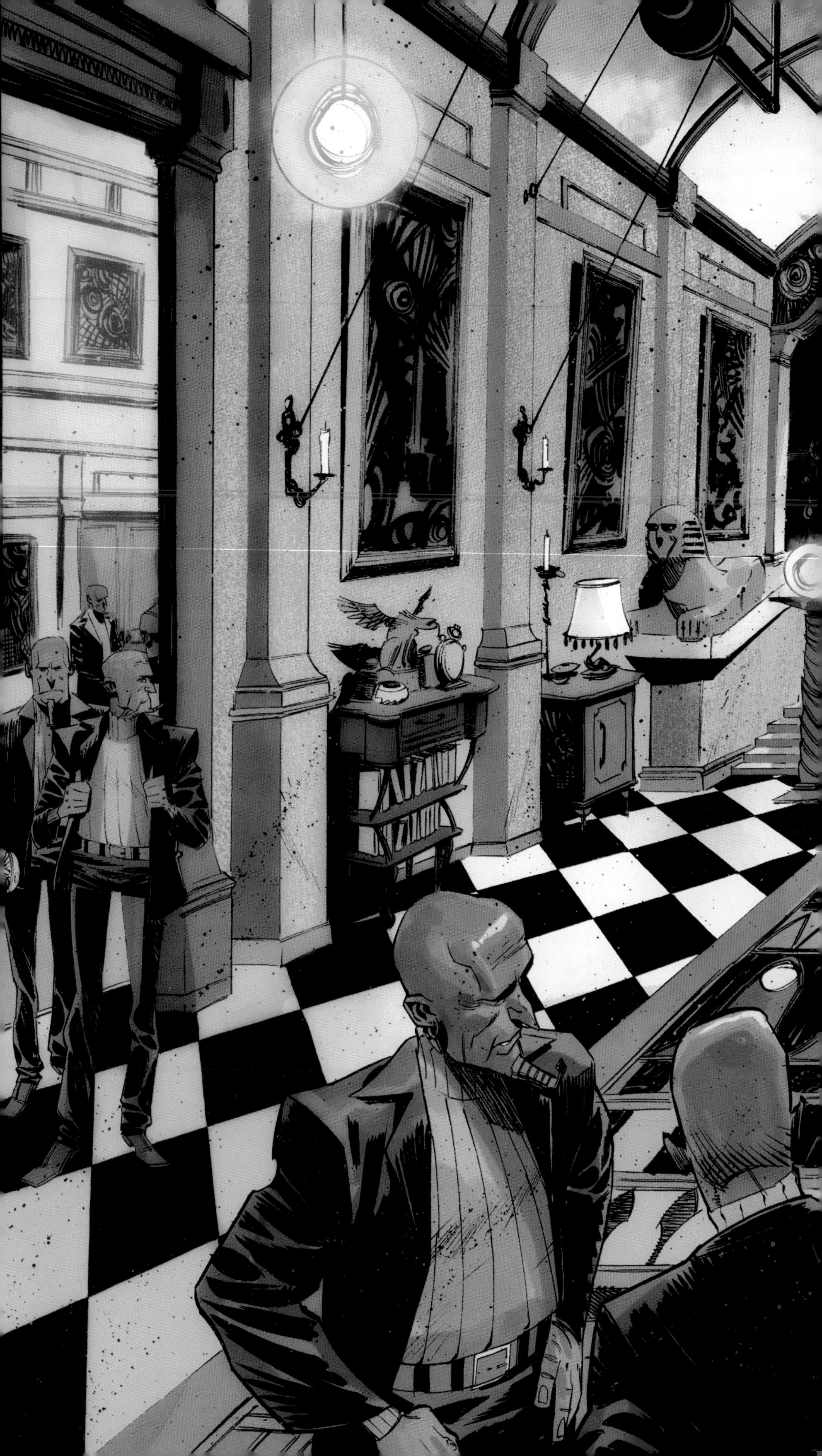

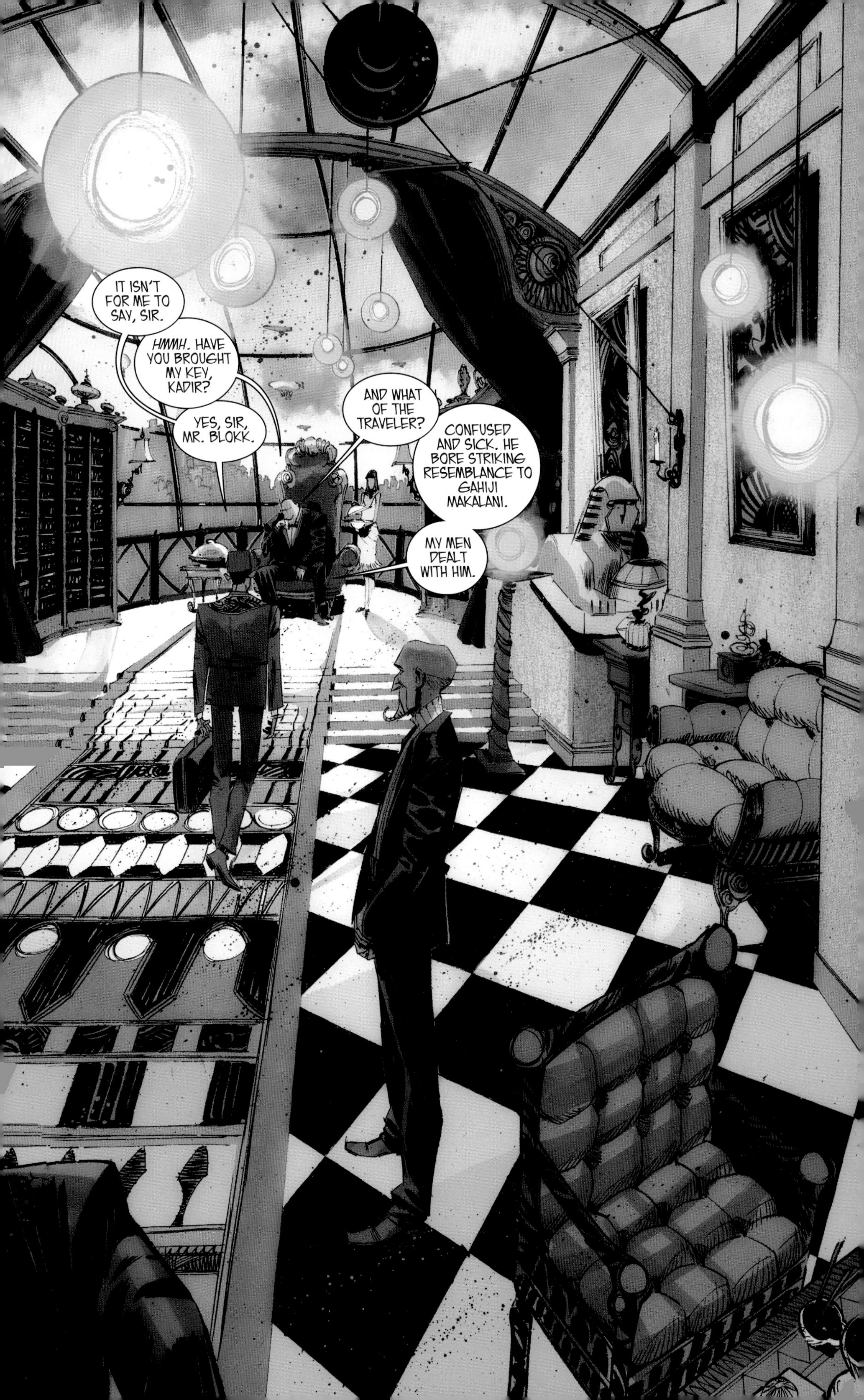
IT ISN'T FOR ME TO SAY, SIR.
HMMH. HAVE YOU BROUGHT MY KEY, KADIR?
YES, SIR, MR. BLOKK.
AND WHAT OF THE TRAVELER?
CONFUSED AND SICK. HE BORE STRIKING RESEMBLANCE TO GAHIJI MAKALANI.
MY MEN DEALT WITH HIM.

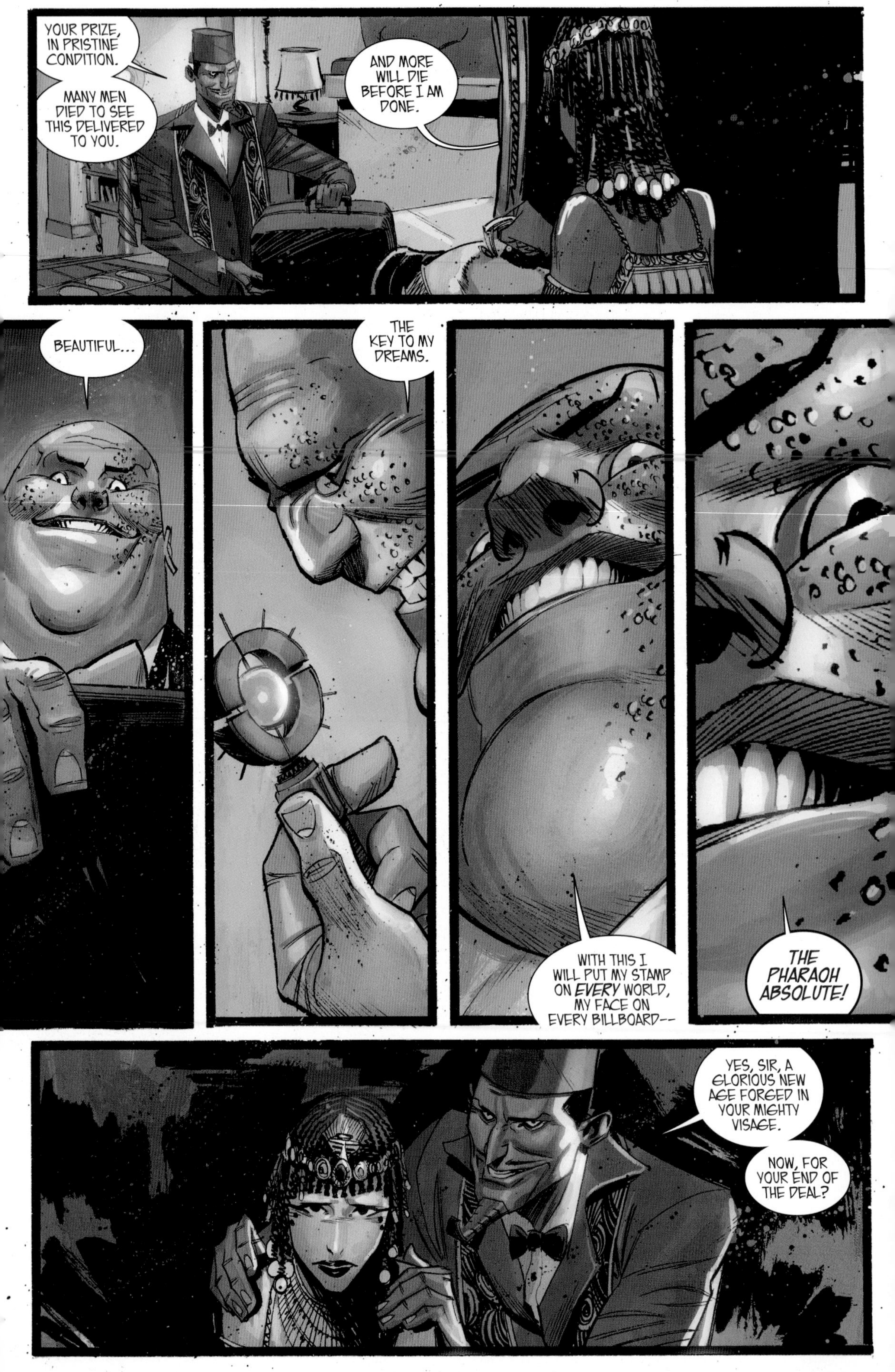
YOUR PRIZE, IN PRISTINE CONDITION.
MANY MEN DIED TO SEE THIS DELIVERED TO YOU.
AND MORE WILL DIE BEFORE I AM DONE.
BEAUTIFUL...
THE KEY TO MY DREAMS.
WITH THIS I WILL PUT MY STAMP ON *EVERY* WORLD, MY FACE ON EVERY BILLBOARD--
THE PHARAOH ABSOLUTE!
YES, SIR, A GLORIOUS NEW AGE FORGED IN YOUR MIGHTY VISAGE.
NOW, FOR YOUR END OF THE DEAL?

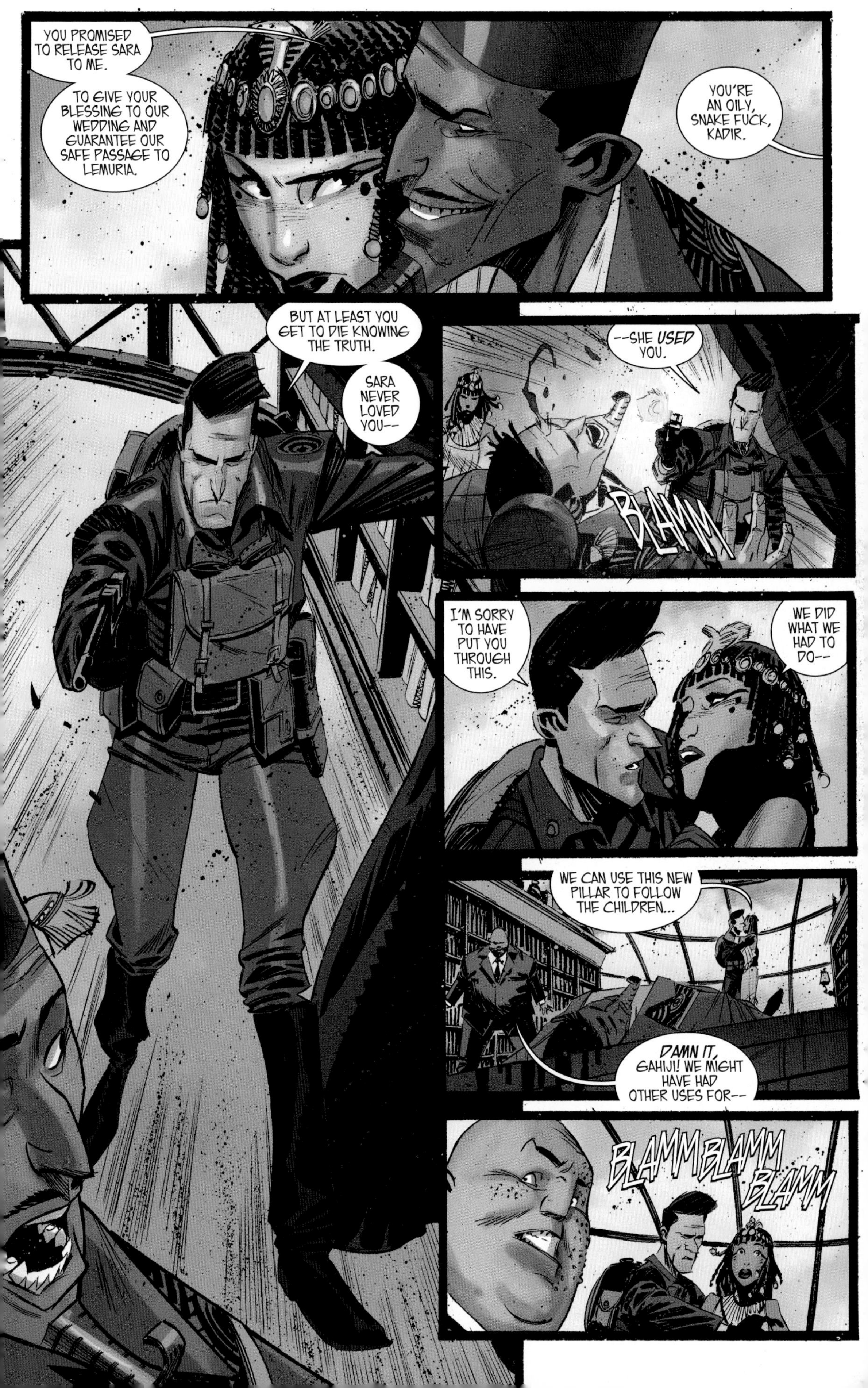
YOU PROMISED TO RELEASE SARA TO ME.
TO GIVE YOUR BLESSING TO OUR WEDDING AND GUARANTEE OUR SAFE PASSAGE TO LEMURIA.
YOU'RE AN OILY, SNAKE FUCK, KADIR.
BUT AT LEAST YOU GET TO DIE KNOWING THE TRUTH.
SARA NEVER LOVED YOU--
--SHE USED YOU.
BLAMM
I'M SORRY TO HAVE PUT YOU THROUGH THIS.
WE DID WHAT WE HAD TO DO--
WE CAN USE THIS NEW PILLAR TO FOLLOW THE CHILDREN...
DAMN IT, GAHIJI! WE MIGHT HAVE HAD OTHER USES FOR--
BLAMM BLAMM BLAMM

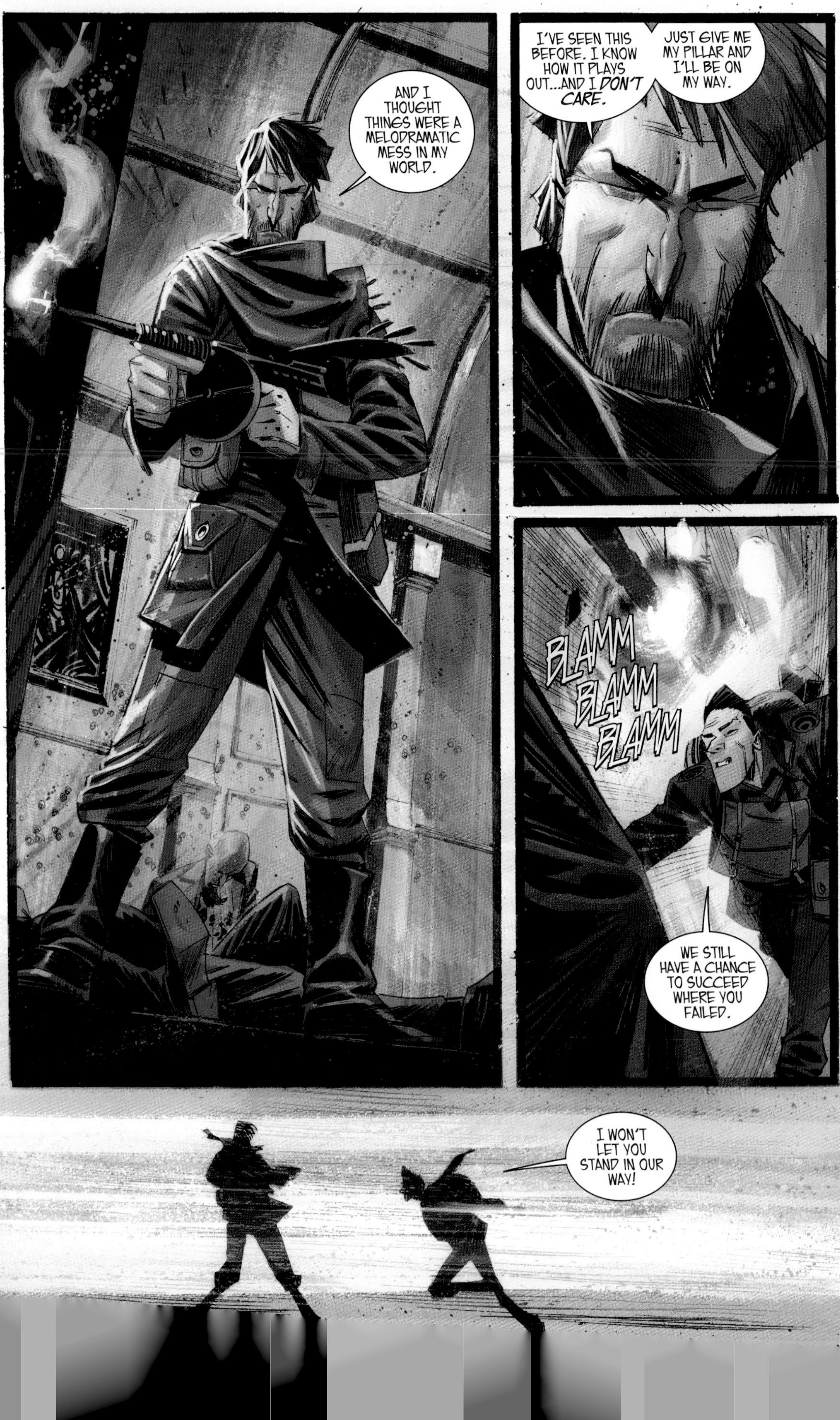
AND I THOUGHT THINGS WERE A MELODRAMATIC MESS IN MY WORLD.
I'VE SEEN THIS BEFORE. I KNOW HOW IT PLAYS OUT...AND I DON'T CARE.
JUST GIVE ME MY PILLAR AND I'LL BE ON MY WAY.
BLAMM BLAMM BLAMM
WE STILL HAVE A CHANCE TO SUCCEED WHERE YOU FAILED.
I WON'T LET YOU STAND IN OUR WAY!

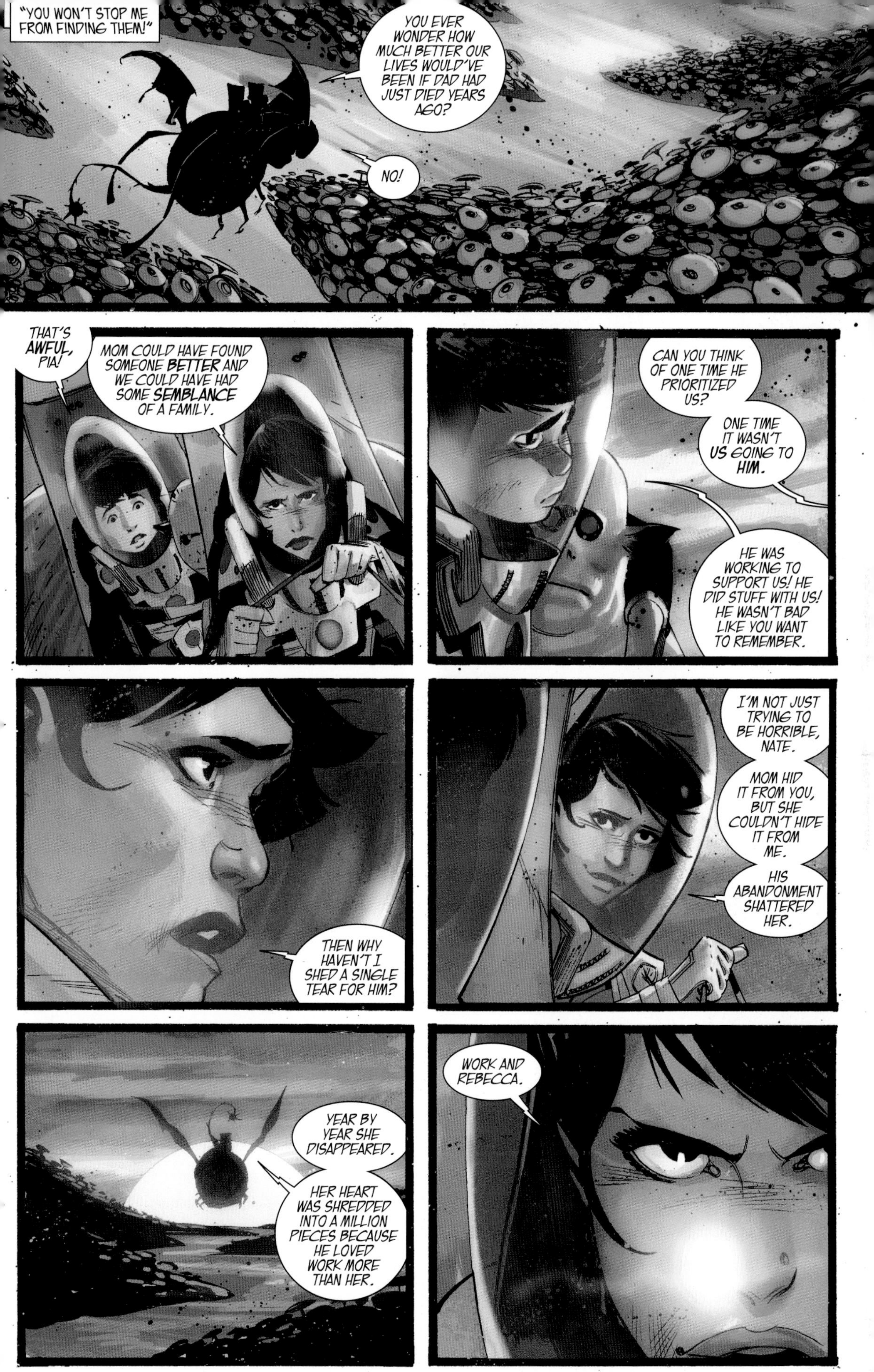
"YOU WON'T STOP ME FROM FINDING THEM!"
YOU EVER WONDER HOW MUCH BETTER OUR LIVES WOULD'VE BEEN IF DAD HAD JUST DIED YEARS AGO?
NO!
THAT'S AWFUL, PIA!
MOM COULD HAVE FOUND SOMEONE BETTER AND WE COULD HAVE HAD SOME SEMBLANCE OF A FAMILY.
CAN YOU THINK OF ONE TIME HE PRIORITIZED US?
ONE TIME IT WASN'T US GOING TO HIM.
HE WAS WORKING TO SUPPORT US! HE DID STUFF WITH US! HE WASN'T BAD LIKE YOU WANT TO REMEMBER.
THEN WHY HAVEN'T I SHED A SINGLE TEAR FOR HIM?
I'M NOT JUST TRYING TO BE HORRIBLE, NATE.
MOM HID IT FROM YOU, BUT SHE COULDN'T HIDE IT FROM ME.
HIS ABANDONMENT SHATTERED HER.
YEAR BY YEAR SHE DISAPPEARED.
HER HEART WAS SHREDDED INTO A MILLION PIECES BECAUSE HE LOVED WORK MORE THAN HER.
WORK AND REBECCA.

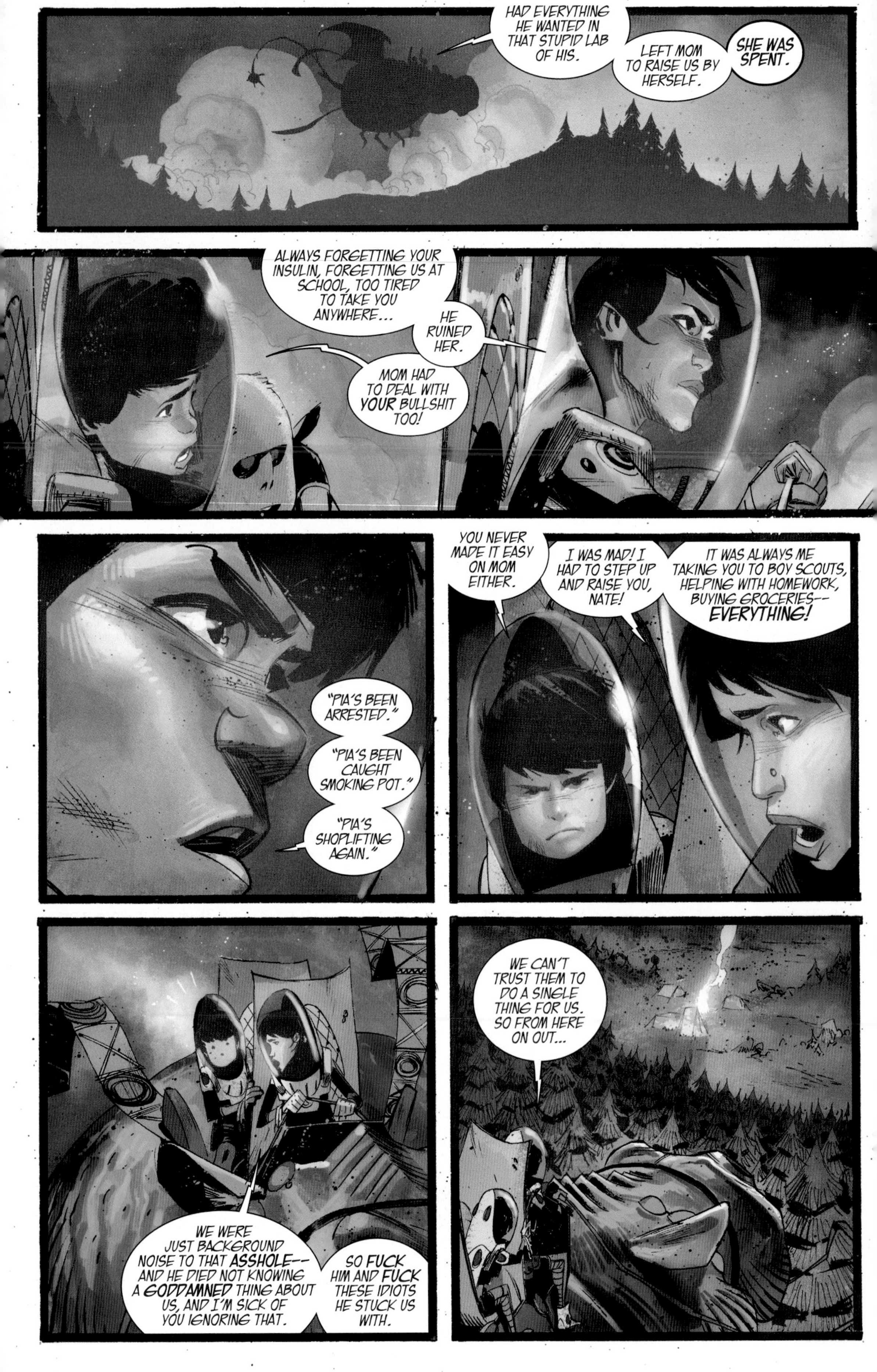
HAD EVERYTHING HE WANTED IN THAT STUPID LAB OF HIS.
LEFT MOM TO RAISE US BY HERSELF.
SHE WAS SPENT.
ALWAYS FORGETTING YOUR INSULIN, FORGETTING US AT SCHOOL, TOO TIRED TO TAKE YOU ANYWHERE...
HE RUINED HER.
MOM HAD TO DEAL WITH YOUR BULLSHIT TOO!
"PIA'S BEEN ARRESTED."
"PIA'S BEEN CAUGHT SMOKING POT."
"PIA'S SHOPLIFTING AGAIN."
YOU NEVER MADE IT EASY ON MOM EITHER.
I WAS MAD! I HAD TO STEP UP AND RAISE YOU, NATE!
IT WAS ALWAYS ME TAKING YOU TO BOY SCOUTS, HELPING WITH HOMEWORK, BUYING GROCERIES-- EVERYTHING!
WE WERE JUST BACKGROUND NOISE TO THAT ASSHOLE-- AND HE DIED NOT KNOWING A GODDAMNED THING ABOUT US, AND I'M SICK OF YOU IGNORING THAT.
SO FUCK HIM AND FUCK THESE IDIOTS HE STUCK US WITH.
WE CAN'T TRUST THEM TO DO A SINGLE THING FOR US. SO FROM HERE ON OUT...

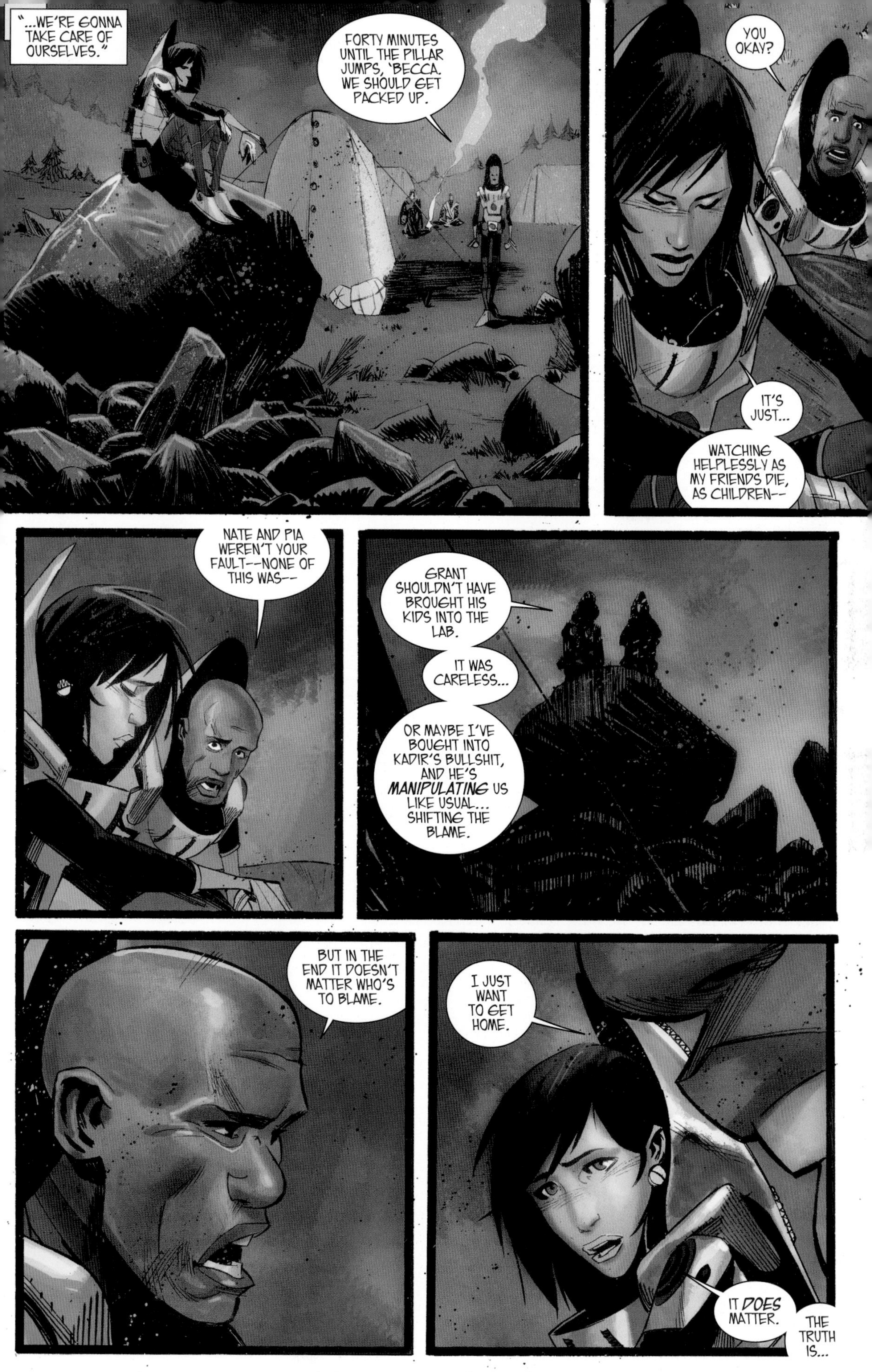
"...WE'RE GONNA TAKE CARE OF OURSELVES."
FORTY MINUTES UNTIL THE PILLAR JUMPS, 'BECCA. WE SHOULD GET PACKED UP.
YOU OKAY?
IT'S JUST...
WATCHING HELPLESSLY AS MY FRIENDS DIE, AS CHILDREN--
NATE AND PIA WEREN'T YOUR FAULT--NONE OF THIS WAS--
GRANT SHOULDN'T HAVE BROUGHT HIS KIDS INTO THE LAB.
IT WAS CARELESS...
OR MAYBE I'VE BOUGHT INTO KADIR'S BULLSHIT, AND HE'S *MANIPULATING* US LIKE USUAL... SHIFTING THE BLAME.
BUT IN THE END IT DOESN'T MATTER WHO'S TO BLAME.
I JUST WANT TO GET HOME.
IT *DOES* MATTER.
THE TRUTH IS...

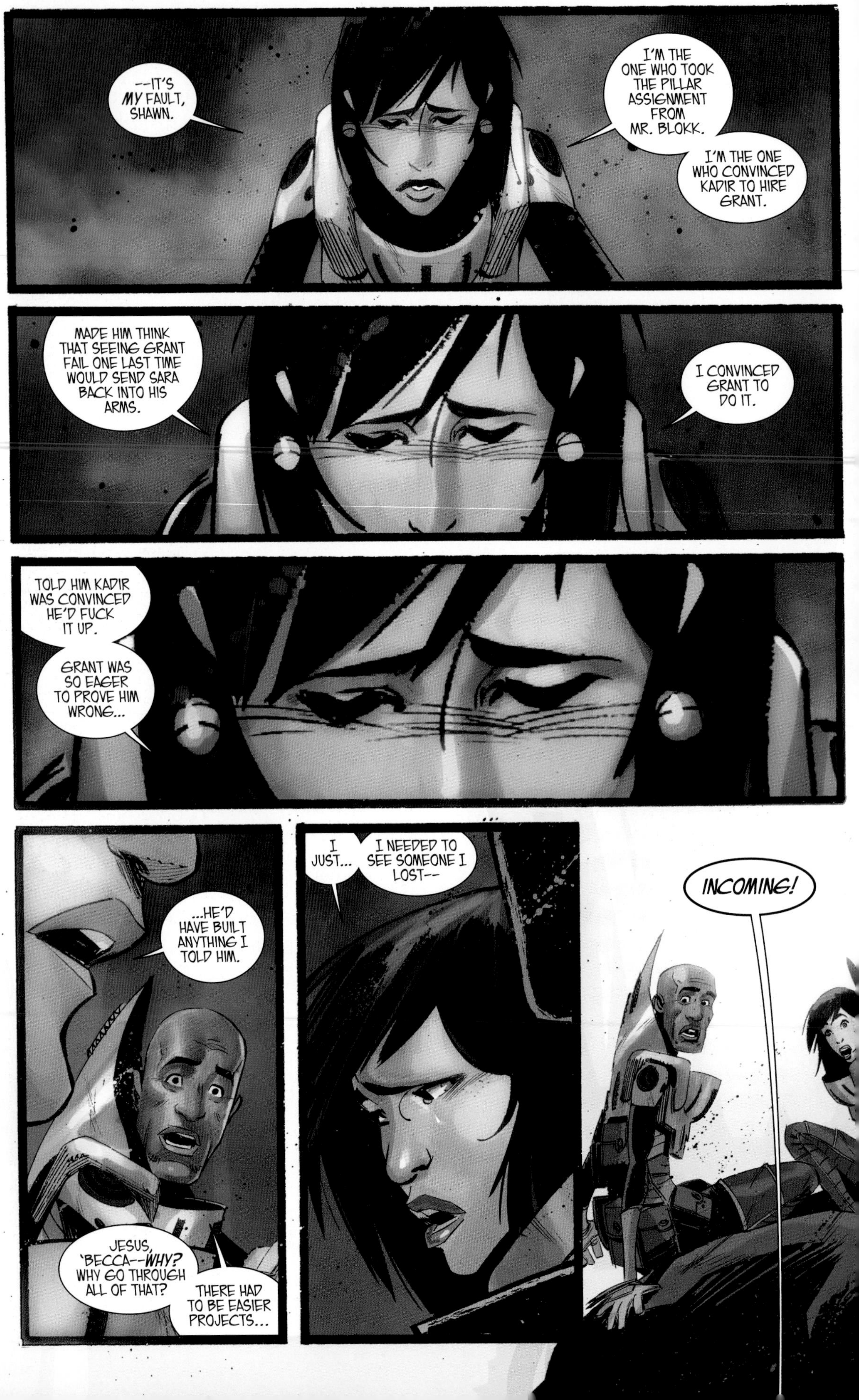
--IT'S MY FAULT, SHAWN.
I'M THE ONE WHO TOOK THE PILLAR ASSIGNMENT FROM MR. BLOKK.
I'M THE ONE WHO CONVINCED KADIR TO HIRE GRANT.
MADE HIM THINK THAT SEEING GRANT FAIL ONE LAST TIME WOULD SEND SARA BACK INTO HIS ARMS.
I CONVINCED GRANT TO DO IT.
TOLD HIM KADIR WAS CONVINCED HE'D FUCK IT UP.
GRANT WAS SO EAGER TO PROVE HIM WRONG...
...HE'D HAVE BUILT ANYTHING I TOLD HIM.
JESUS, 'BECCA--WHY? WHY GO THROUGH ALL OF THAT?
THERE HAD TO BE EASIER PROJECTS...
I JUST...
I NEEDED TO SEE SOMEONE I LOST--
INCOMING!

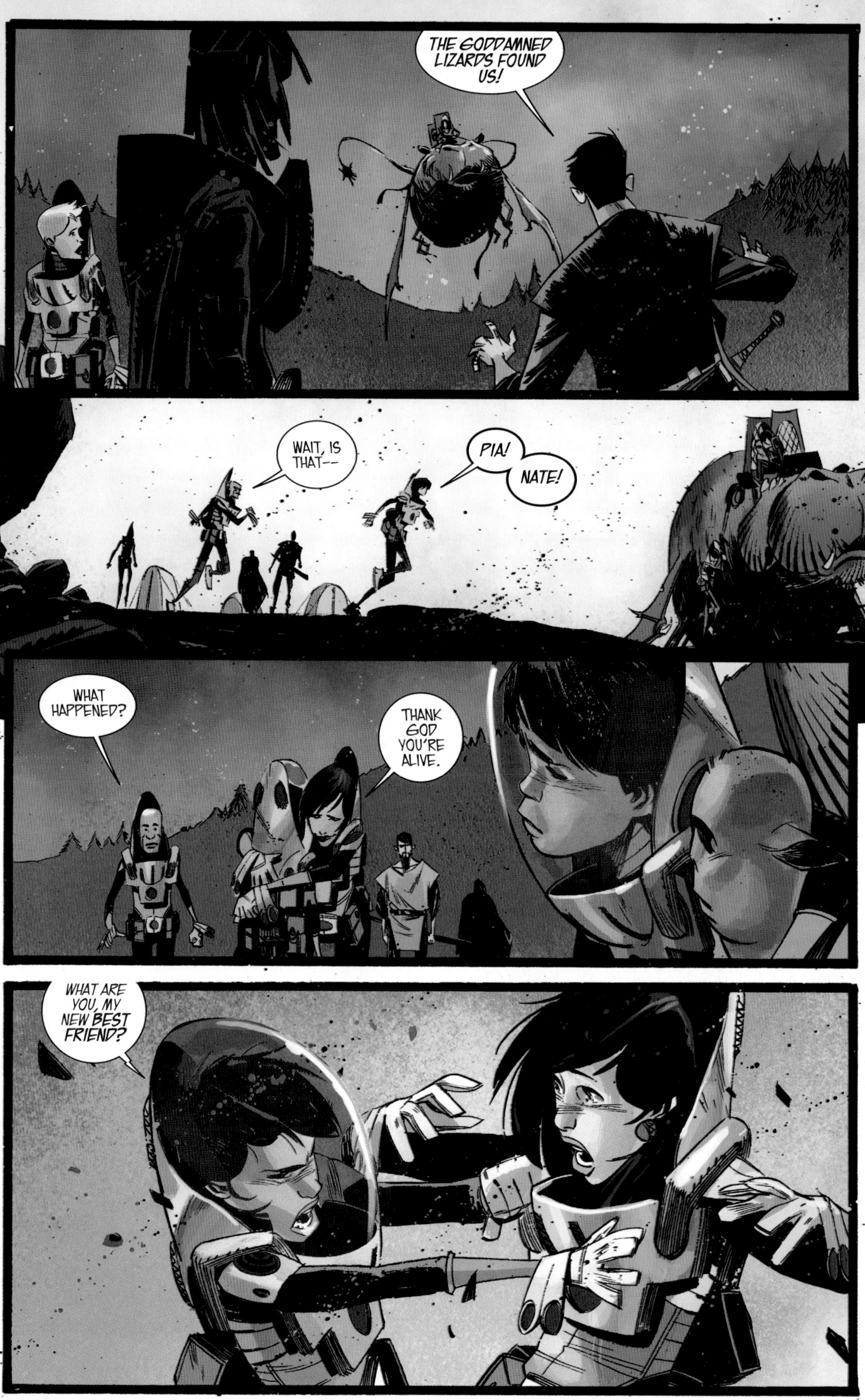
THE GODDAMNED LIZARDS FOUND US!
WAIT, IS THAT--
PIA!
NATE!
WHAT HAPPENED?
THANK GOD YOU'RE ALIVE.
WHAT ARE YOU, MY NEW BEST FRIEND?

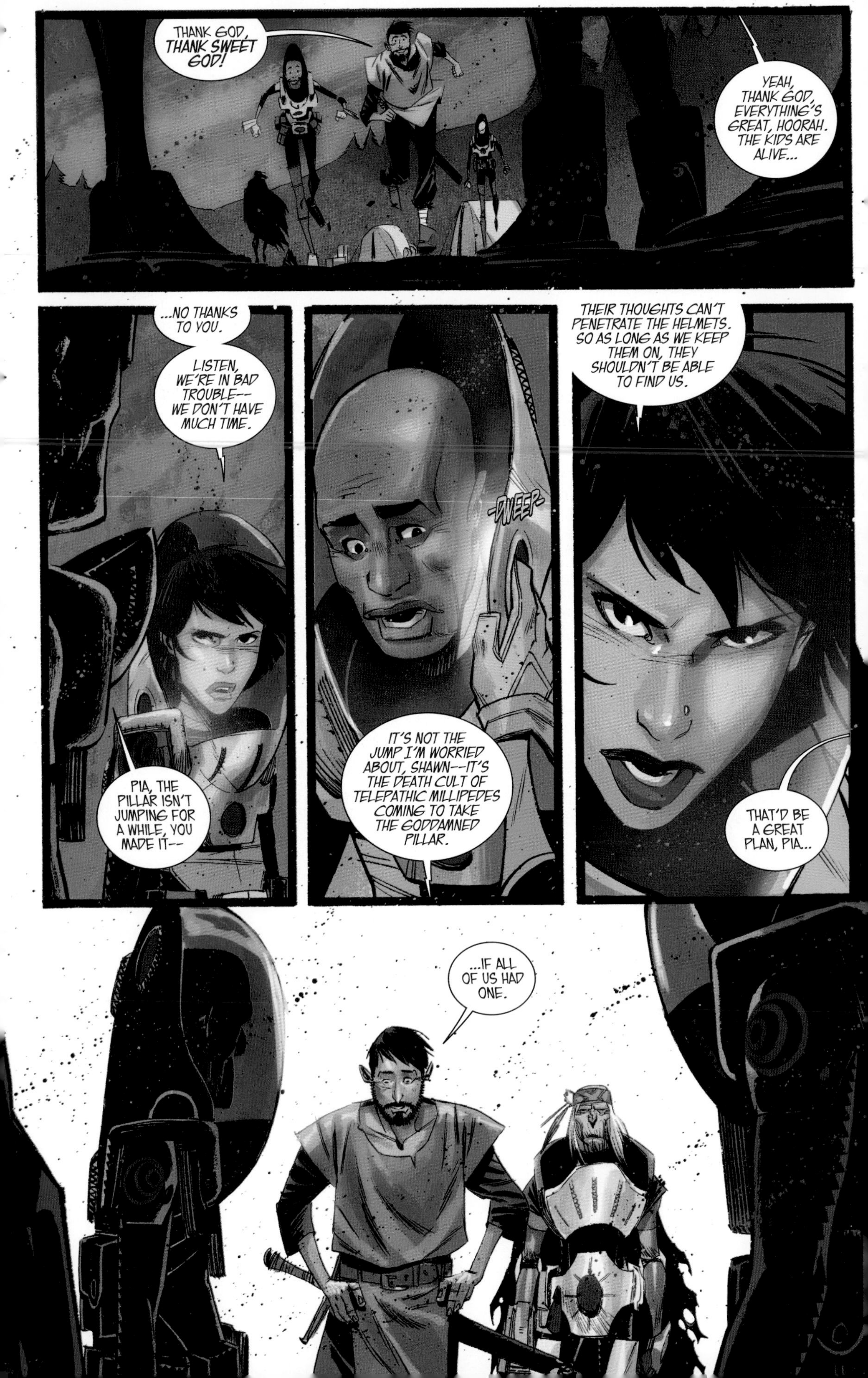
THANK GOD, THANK SWEET GOD!
YEAH, THANK GOD, EVERYTHING'S GREAT, HOORAH. THE KIDS ARE ALIVE...
...NO THANKS TO YOU.
LISTEN, WE'RE IN BAD TROUBLE-- WE DON'T HAVE MUCH TIME.
PIA, THE PILLAR ISN'T JUMPING FOR A WHILE, YOU MADE IT--
-DWEEP-
IT'S NOT THE JUMP I'M WORRIED ABOUT, SHAWN--IT'S THE DEATH CULT OF TELEPATHIC MILLIPEDES COMING TO TAKE THE GODDAMNED PILLAR.
THEIR THOUGHTS CAN'T PENETRATE THE HELMETS. SO AS LONG AS WE KEEP THEM ON, THEY SHOULDN'T BE ABLE TO FIND US.
THAT'D BE A GREAT PLAN, PIA...
...IF ALL OF US HAD ONE.

11

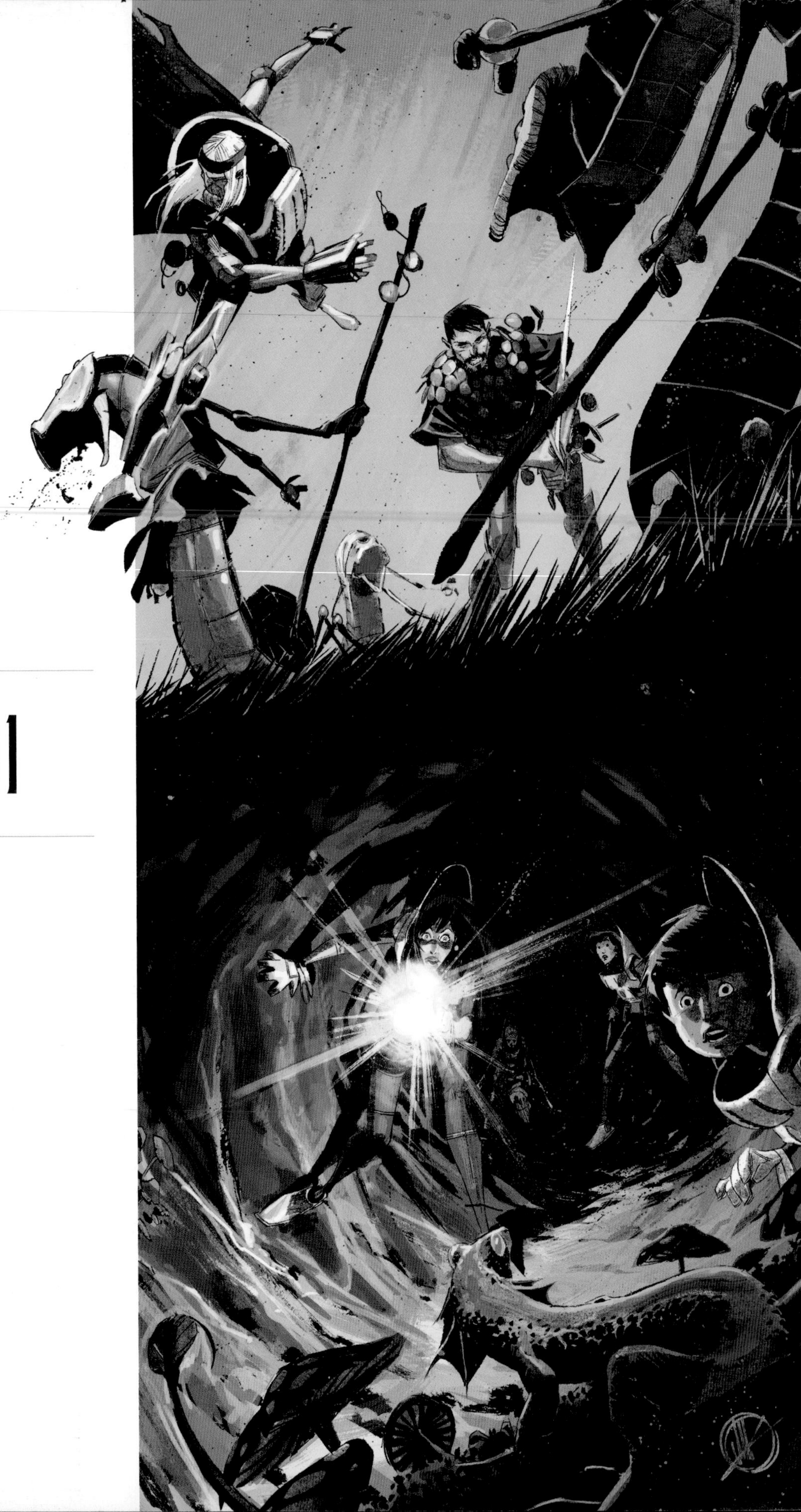

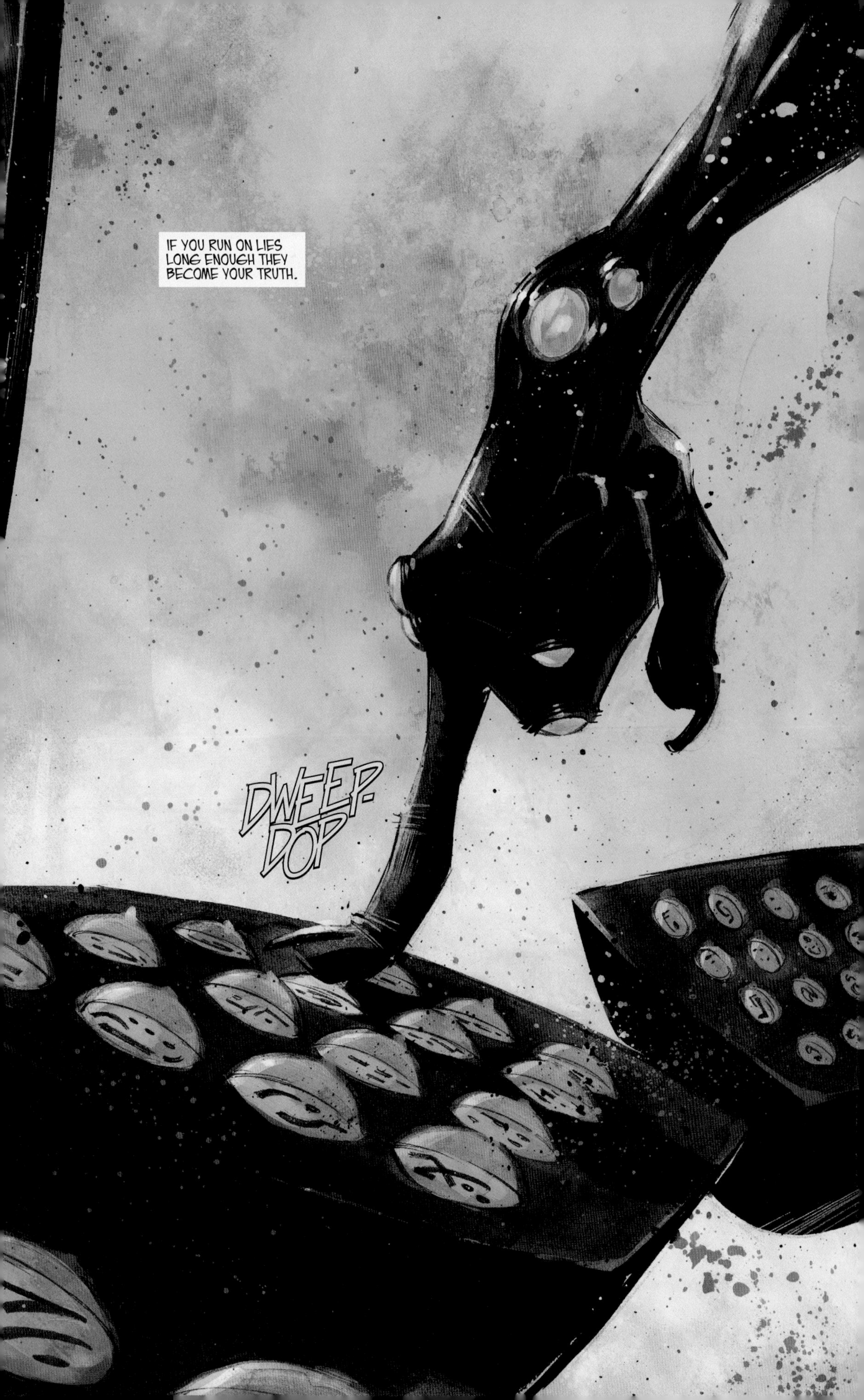
IF YOU RUN ON LIES LONG ENOUGH THEY BECOME YOUR TRUTH.
DWEEP DOP

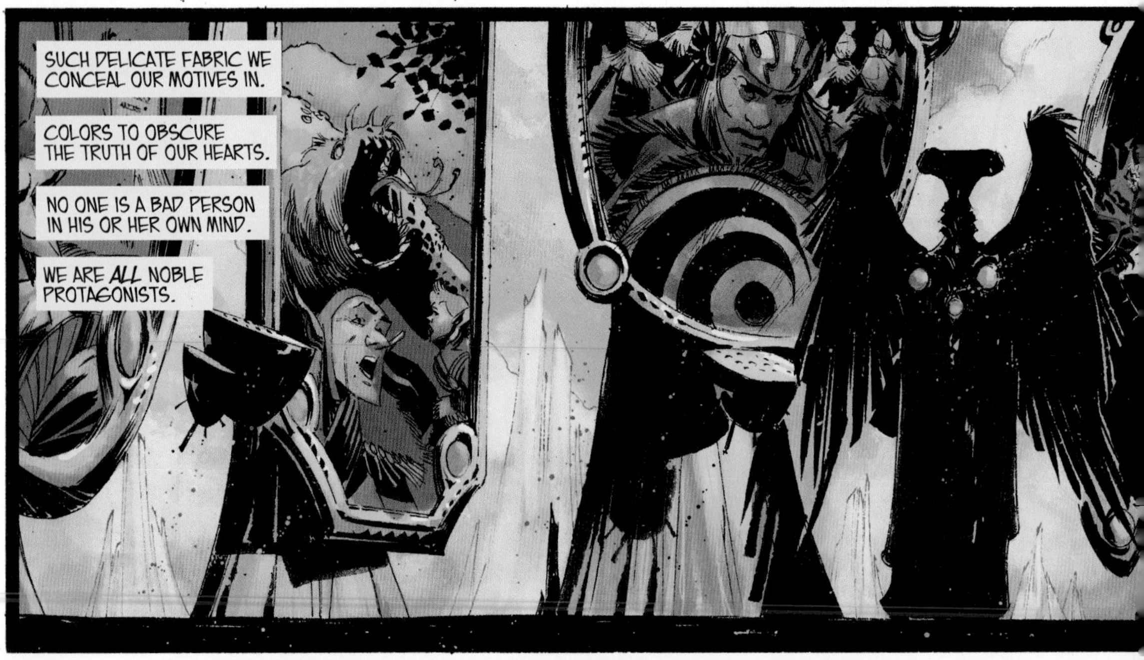
SUCH DELICATE FABRIC WE CONCEAL OUR MOTIVES IN.
COLORS TO OBSCURE THE TRUTH OF OUR HEARTS.
NO ONE IS A BAD PERSON IN HIS OR HER OWN MIND.
WE ARE ALL NOBLE PROTAGONISTS.

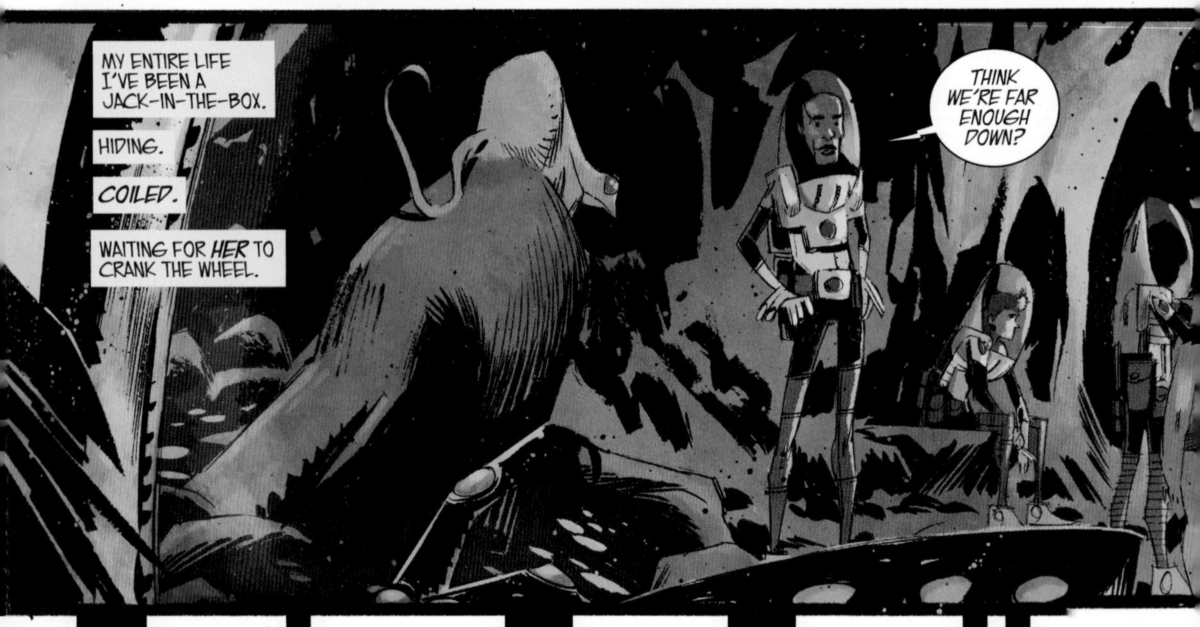
MY ENTIRE LIFE I'VE BEEN A JACK-IN-THE-BOX.
HIDING.
COILED.
WAITING FOR HER TO CRANK THE WHEEL.
THINK WE'RE FAR ENOUGH DOWN?

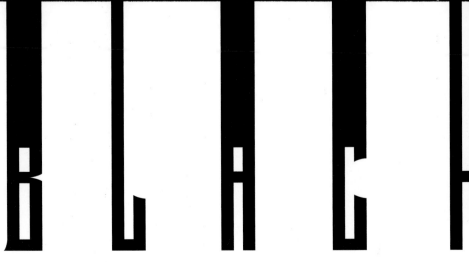

BLACK

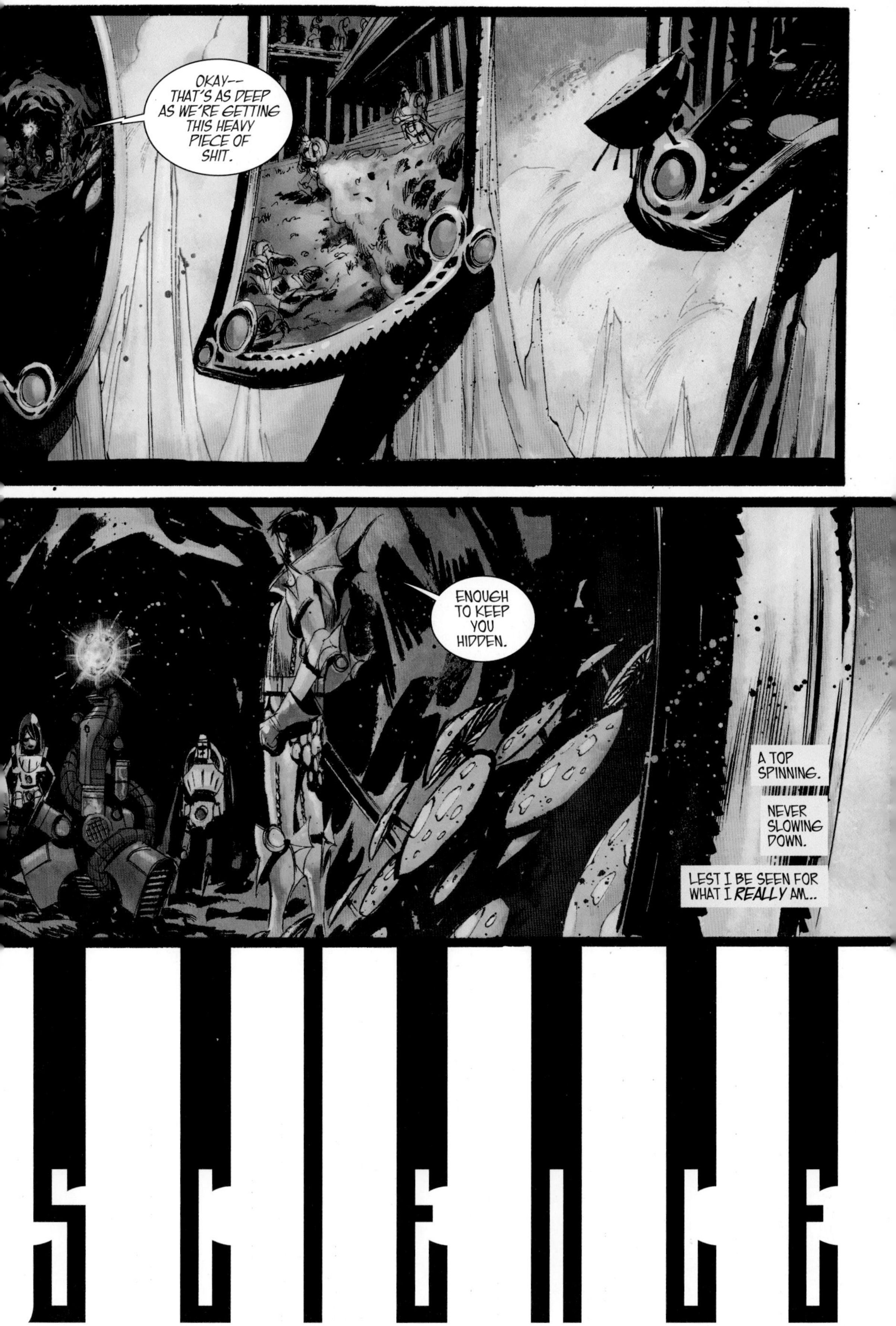
OKAY-- THAT'S AS DEEP AS WE'RE GETTING THIS HEAVY PIECE OF SHIT.
ENOUGH TO KEEP YOU HIDDEN.
A TOP SPINNING.
NEVER SLOWING DOWN.
LEST I BE SEEN FOR WHAT I *REALLY* AM...
SCIENCE

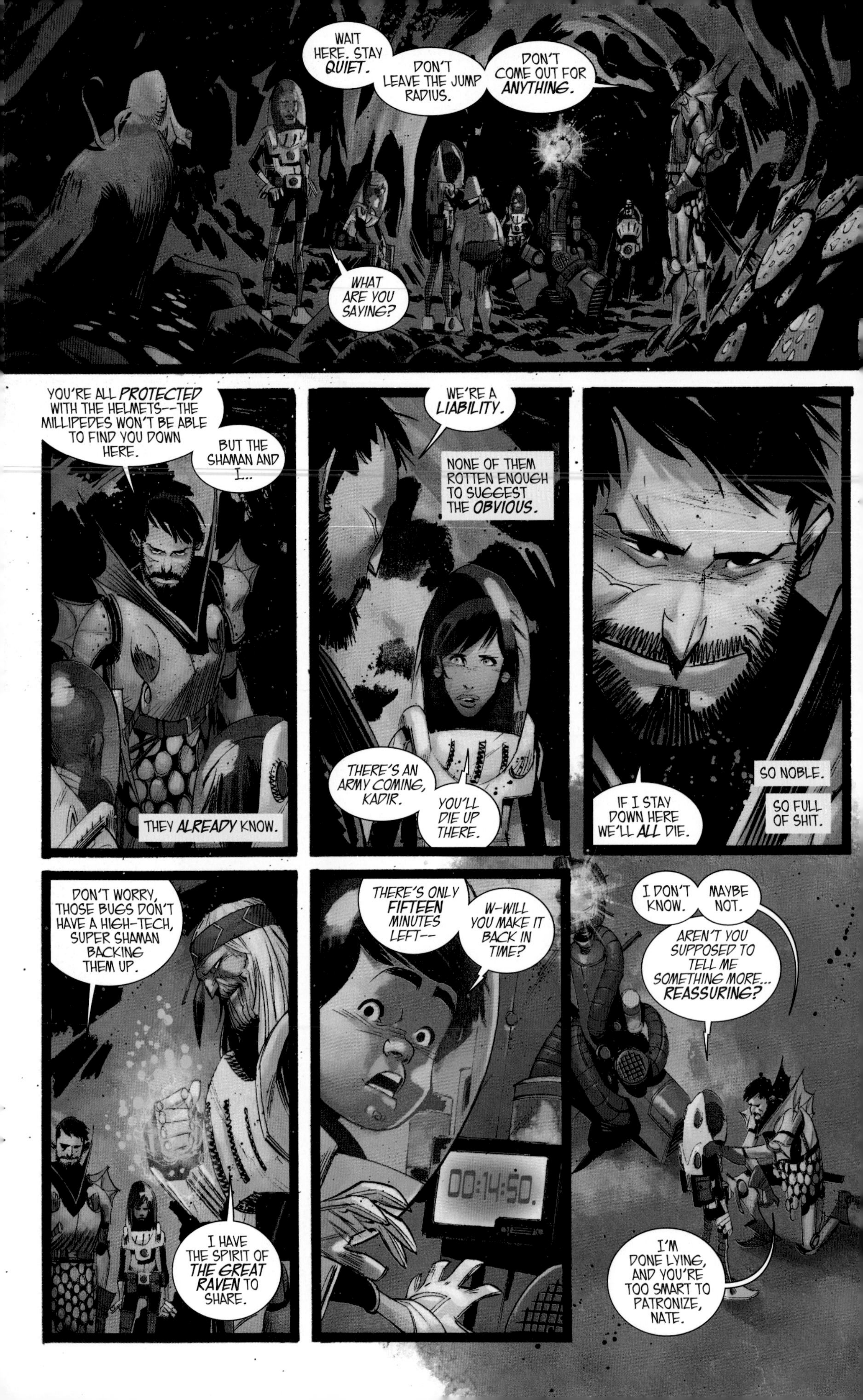

WAIT HERE. STAY QUIET.
DON'T LEAVE THE JUMP RADIUS.
DON'T COME OUT FOR ANYTHING.
WHAT ARE YOU SAYING?
YOU'RE ALL PROTECTED WITH THE HELMETS--THE MILLIPEDES WON'T BE ABLE TO FIND YOU DOWN HERE.
BUT THE SHAMAN AND I...
THEY ALREADY KNOW.
WE'RE A LIABILITY.
NONE OF THEM ROTTEN ENOUGH TO SUGGEST THE OBVIOUS.
THERE'S AN ARMY COMING, KADIR.
YOU'LL DIE UP THERE.
IF I STAY DOWN HERE WE'LL ALL DIE.
SO NOBLE.
SO FULL OF SHIT.
DON'T WORRY, THOSE BUGS DON'T HAVE A HIGH-TECH, SUPER SHAMAN BACKING THEM UP.
I HAVE THE SPIRIT OF THE GREAT RAVEN TO SHARE.
THERE'S ONLY FIFTEEN MINUTES LEFT--
W-WILL YOU MAKE IT BACK IN TIME?
00:14:50.
I DON'T KNOW.
MAYBE NOT.
AREN'T YOU SUPPOSED TO TELL ME SOMETHING MORE... REASSURING?
I'M DONE LYING, AND YOU'RE TOO SMART TO PATRONIZE, NATE.

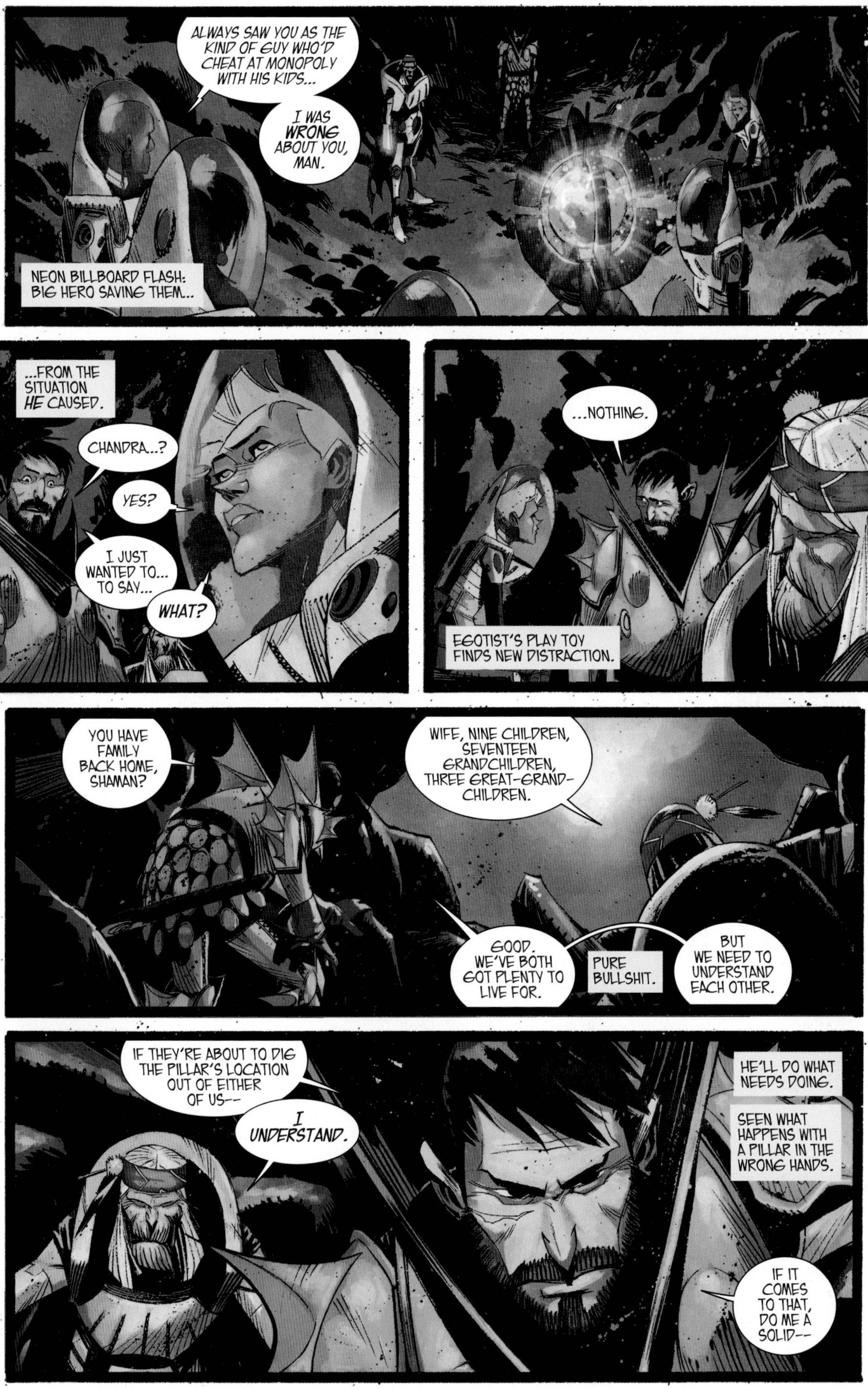
ALWAYS SAW YOU AS THE KIND OF GUY WHO'D CHEAT AT MONOPOLY WITH HIS KIDS...
I WAS WRONG ABOUT YOU, MAN.
NEON BILLBOARD FLASH: BIG HERO SAVING THEM...
...FROM THE SITUATION HE CAUSED.
CHANDRA...?
YES?
I JUST WANTED TO... TO SAY...
WHAT?
...NOTHING.
EGOTIST'S PLAY TOY FINDS NEW DISTRACTION.
YOU HAVE FAMILY BACK HOME, SHAMAN?
WIFE, NINE CHILDREN, SEVENTEEN GRANDCHILDREN, THREE GREAT-GRAND-CHILDREN.
GOOD. WE'VE BOTH GOT PLENTY TO LIVE FOR.
PURE BULLSHIT.
BUT WE NEED TO UNDERSTAND EACH OTHER.
IF THEY'RE ABOUT TO DIG THE PILLAR'S LOCATION OUT OF EITHER OF US--
I UNDERSTAND.
HE'LL DO WHAT NEEDS DOING.
SEEN WHAT HAPPENS WITH A PILLAR IN THE WRONG HANDS.
IF IT COMES TO THAT, DO ME A SOLID--

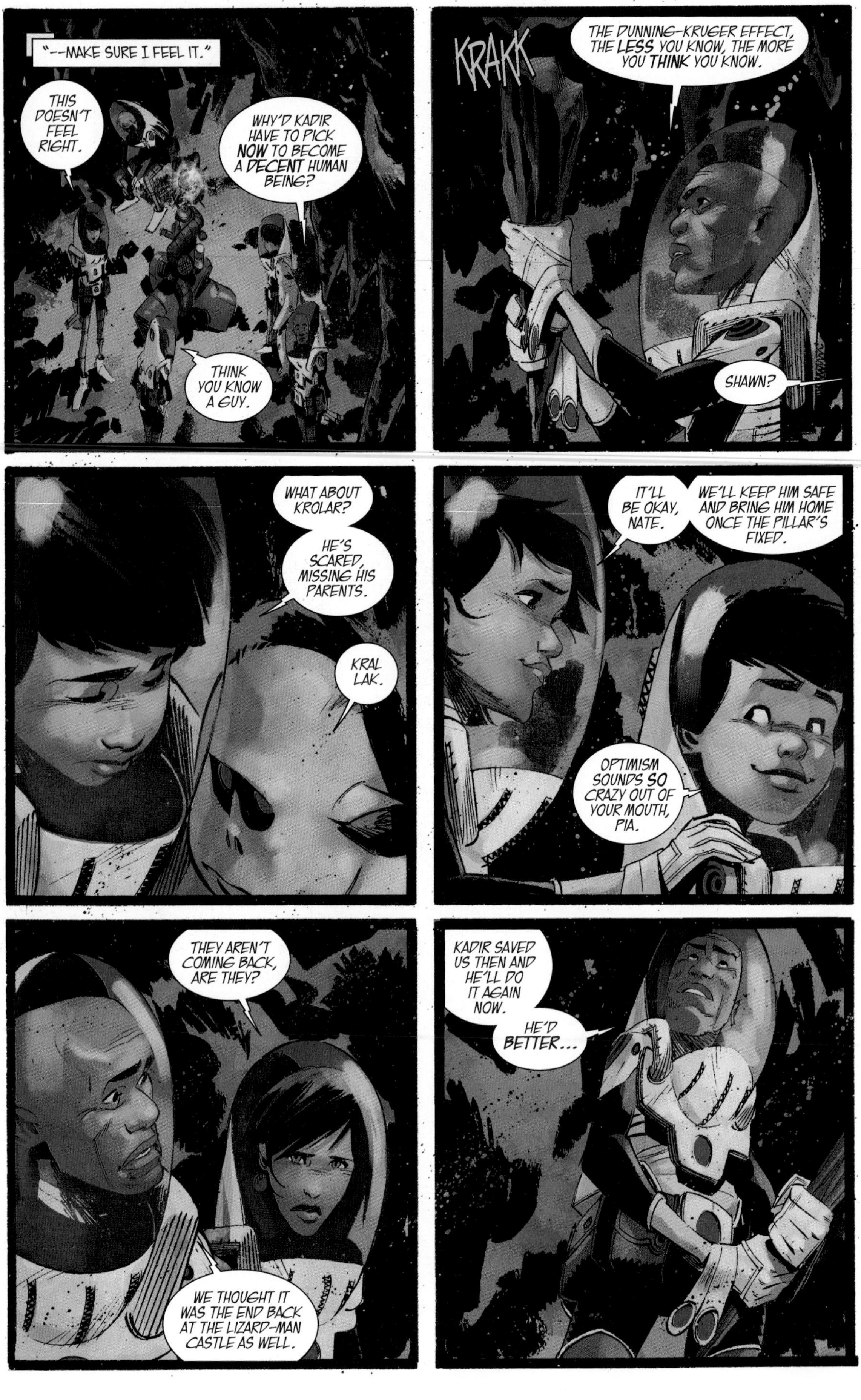
"--MAKE SURE I FEEL IT."
THIS DOESN'T FEEL RIGHT.
WHY'D KADIR HAVE TO PICK NOW TO BECOME A DECENT HUMAN BEING?
THINK YOU KNOW A GUY.
KRAKK
THE DUNNING-KRUGER EFFECT, THE LESS YOU KNOW, THE MORE YOU THINK YOU KNOW.
SHAWN?
WHAT ABOUT KROLAR?
HE'S SCARED, MISSING HIS PARENTS.
KRAL LAK.
IT'LL BE OKAY, NATE.
WE'LL KEEP HIM SAFE AND BRING HIM HOME ONCE THE PILLAR'S FIXED.
OPTIMISM SOUNDS SO CRAZY OUT OF YOUR MOUTH, PIA.
THEY AREN'T COMING BACK, ARE THEY?
WE THOUGHT IT WAS THE END BACK AT THE LIZARD-MAN CASTLE AS WELL.
KADIR SAVED US THEN AND HE'LL DO IT AGAIN NOW.
HE'D BETTER...

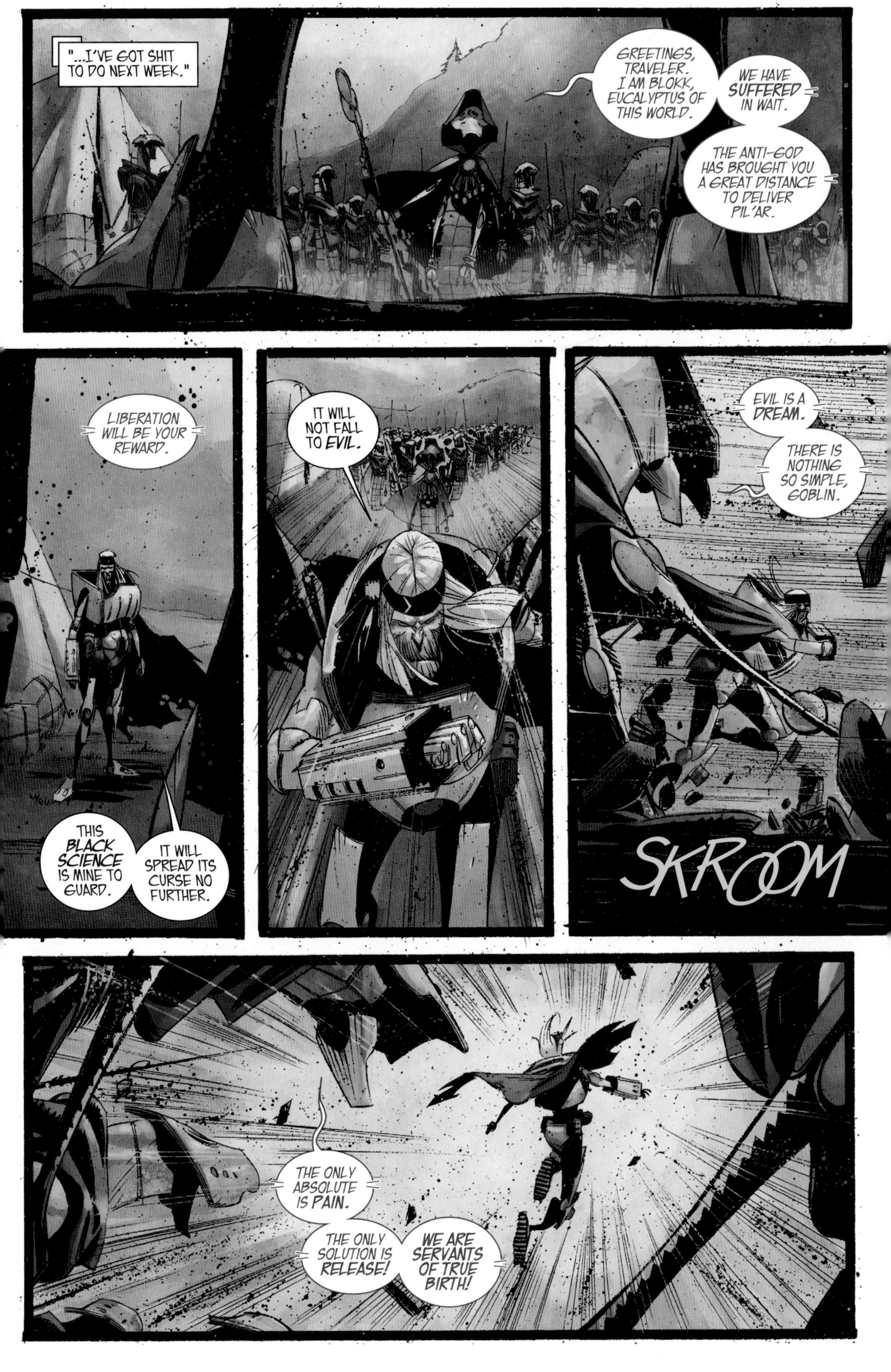
"...I'VE GOT SHIT TO DO NEXT WEEK."
GREETINGS, TRAVELER. I AM BLOKK, EUCALYPTUS OF THIS WORLD.
WE HAVE SUFFERED IN WAIT.
THE ANTI-GOD HAS BROUGHT YOU A GREAT DISTANCE TO DELIVER PIL'AR.
LIBERATION WILL BE YOUR REWARD.
THIS BLACK SCIENCE IS MINE TO GUARD.
IT WILL SPREAD ITS CURSE NO FURTHER.
IT WILL NOT FALL TO EVIL.
EVIL IS A DREAM.
THERE IS NOTHING SO SIMPLE, GOBLIN.
SKROOM
THE ONLY ABSOLUTE IS PAIN.
THE ONLY SOLUTION IS RELEASE!
WE ARE SERVANTS OF TRUE BIRTH!

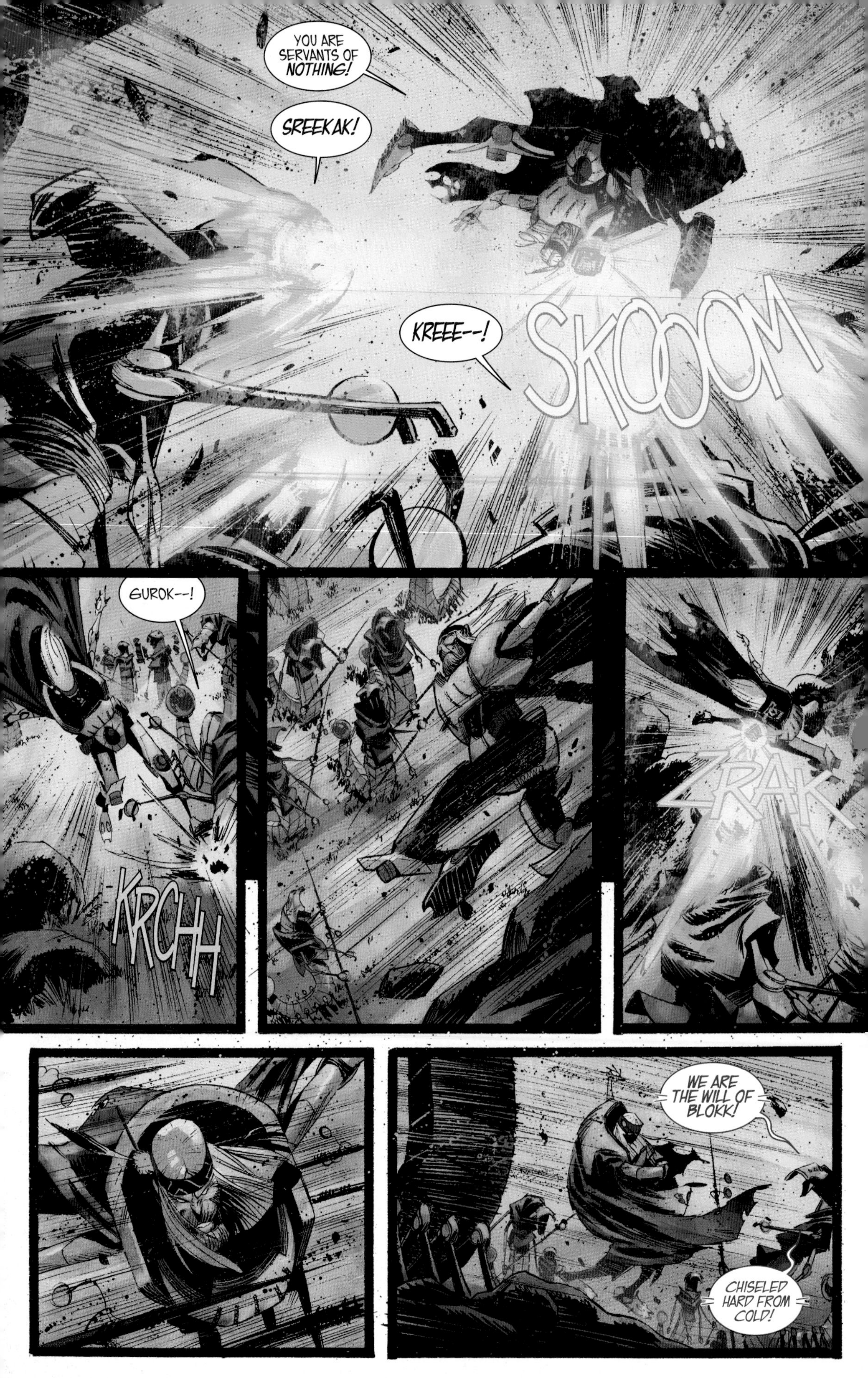
YOU ARE SERVANTS OF NOTHING!
SREEKAK!
KREEE--!
SKOOOM
GUROK--!
KRCHH
ZRAK
WE ARE THE WILL OF BLOKK!
CHISELED HARD FROM COLD!

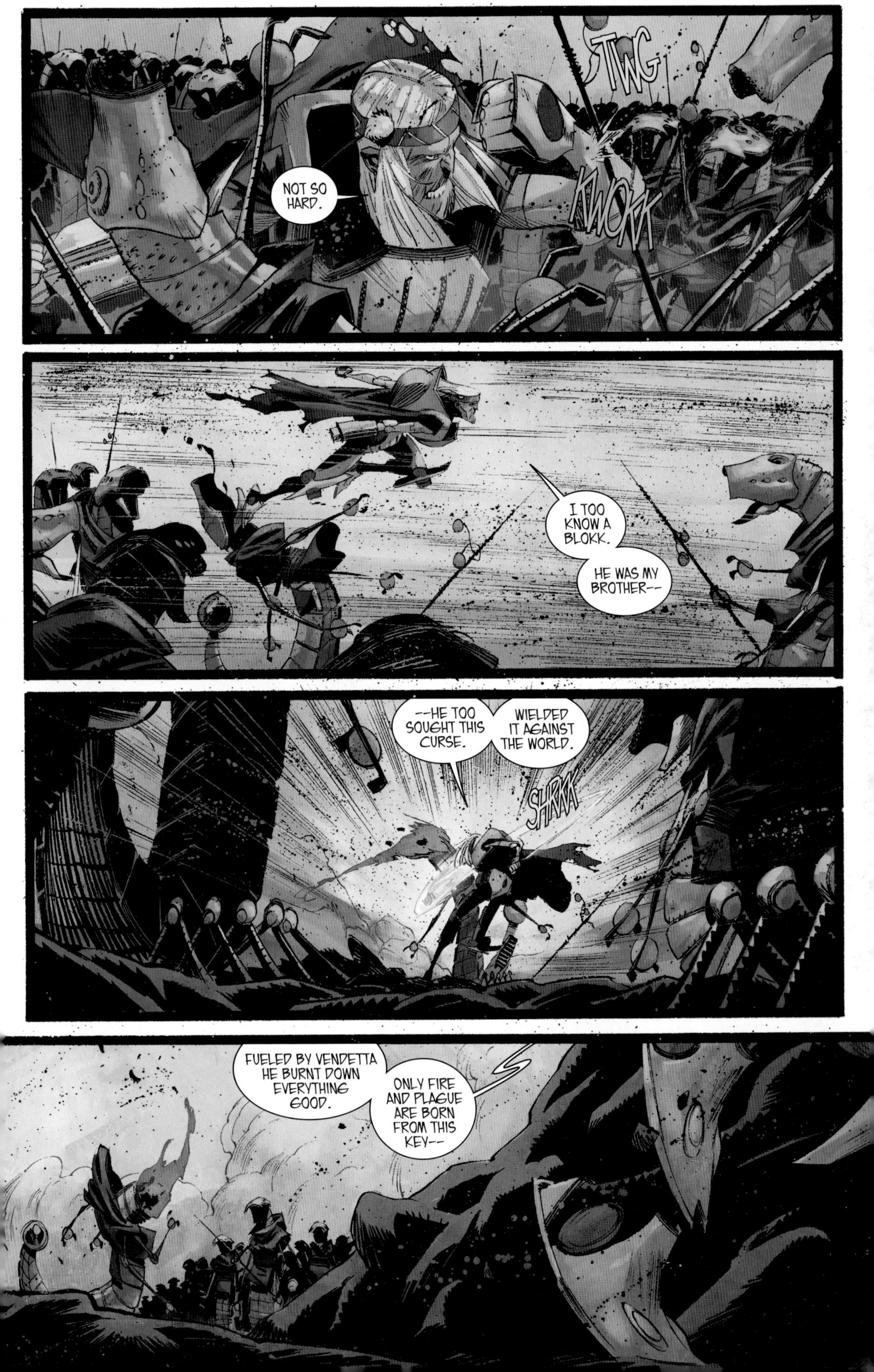
TWG
NOT SO HARD.
KWOKK
I TOO KNOW A BLOKK.
HE WAS MY BROTHER--
--HE TOO SOUGHT THIS CURSE.
WIELDED IT AGAINST THE WORLD.
SHRKK
FUELED BY VENDETTA HE BURNT DOWN EVERYTHING GOOD.
ONLY FIRE AND PLAGUE ARE BORN FROM THIS KEY--

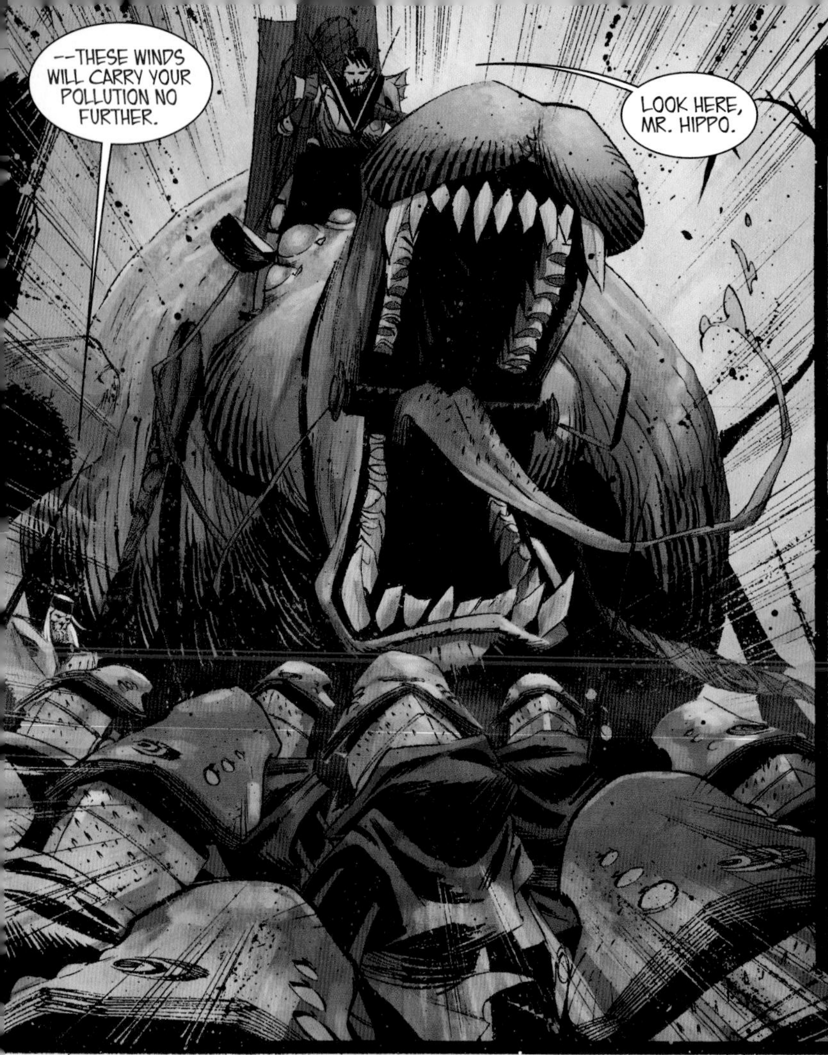
--THESE WINDS WILL CARRY YOUR POLLUTION NO FURTHER.
LOOK HERE, MR. HIPPO.

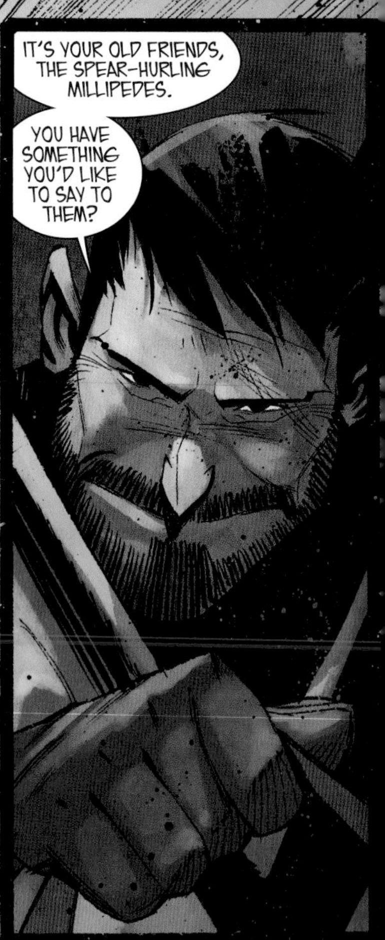
IT'S YOUR OLD FRIENDS, THE SPEAR-HURLING MILLIPEDES.
YOU HAVE SOMETHING YOU'D LIKE TO SAY TO THEM?

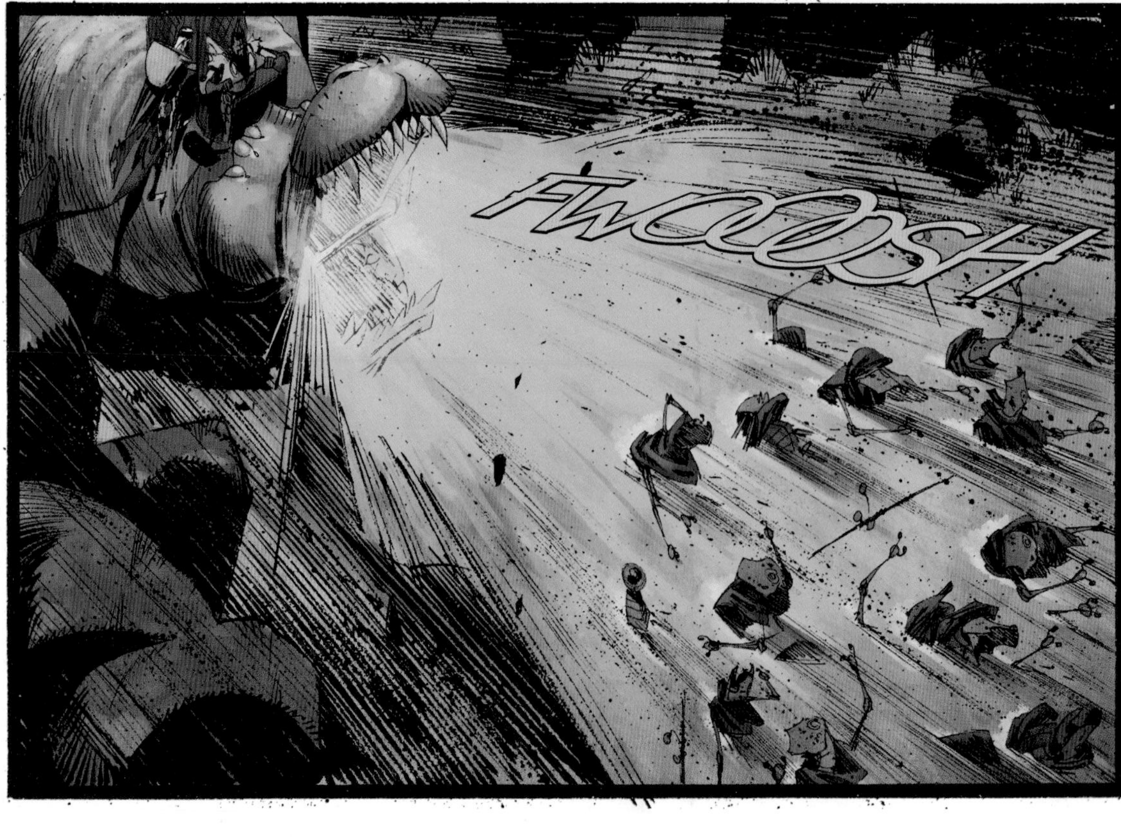
FWOOOSH

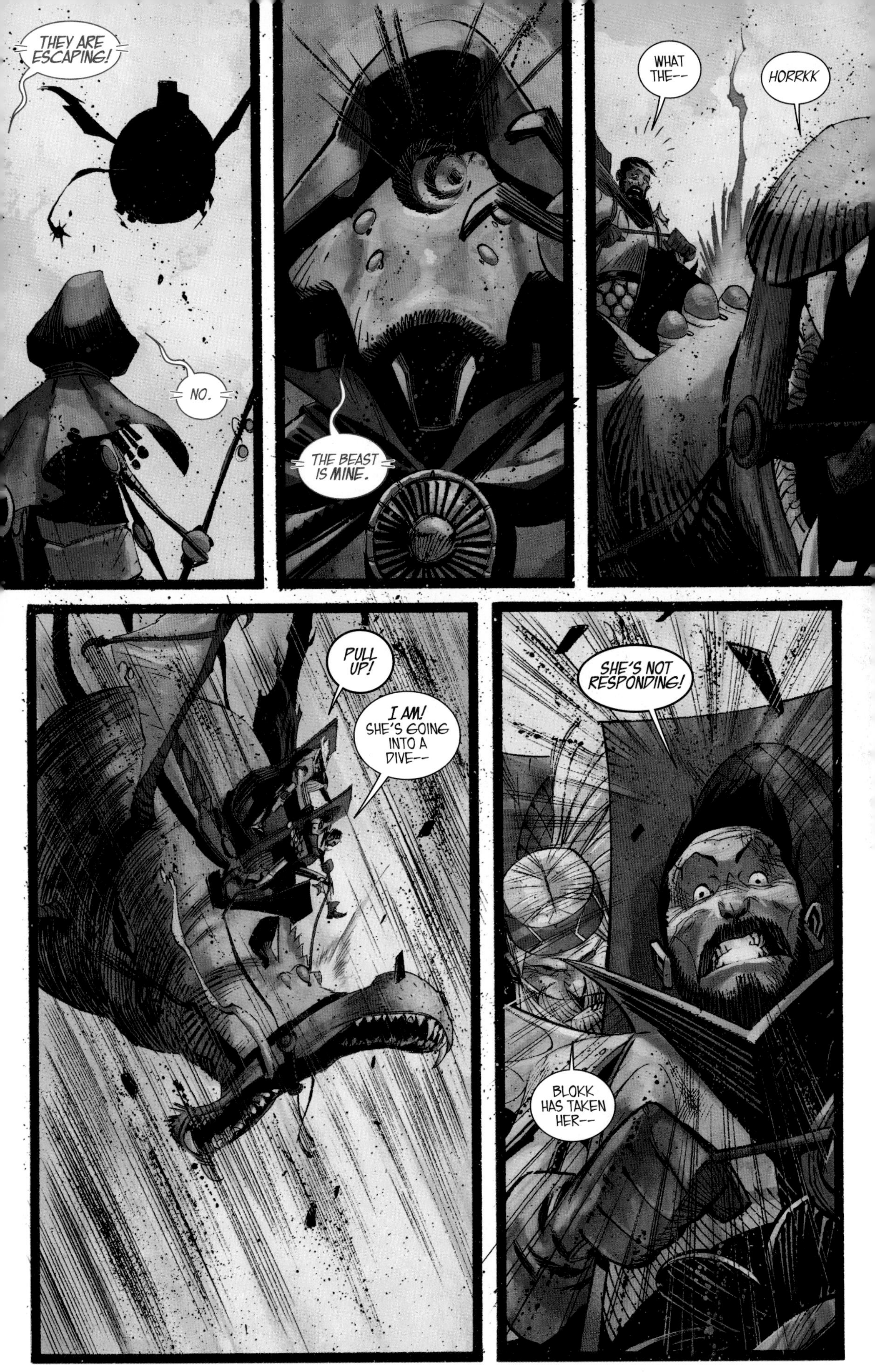
THEY ARE ESCAPING!
NO.
THE BEAST IS MINE.
WHAT THE--
HORRKK
PULL UP!
I AM! SHE'S GOING INTO A DIVE--
SHE'S NOT RESPONDING!
BLOKK HAS TAKEN HER--

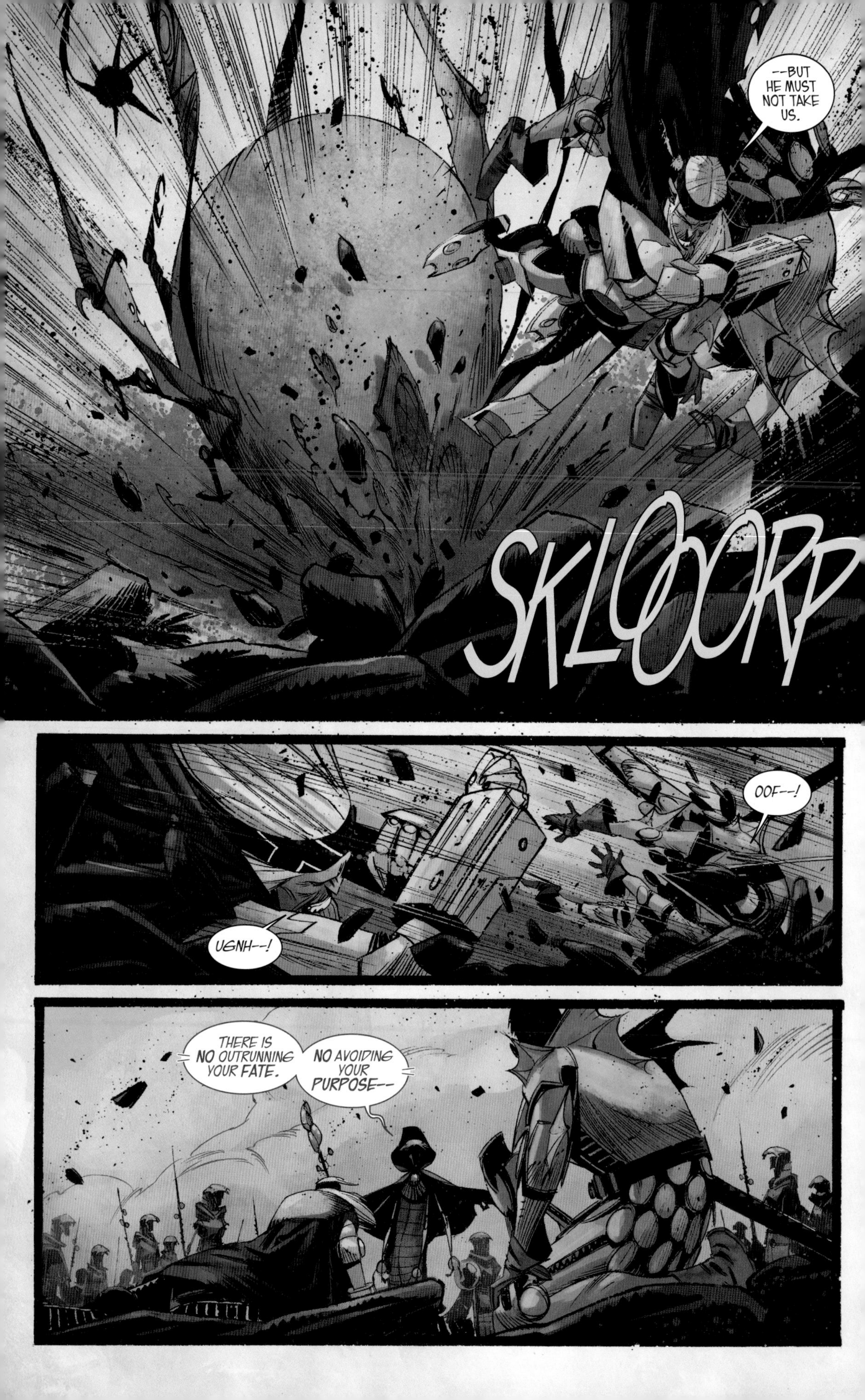
--BUT HE MUST NOT TAKE US.
SKLOOORP
OOF--!
UGNH--!
THERE IS NO OUTRUNNING YOUR FATE.
NO AVOIDING YOUR PURPOSE--

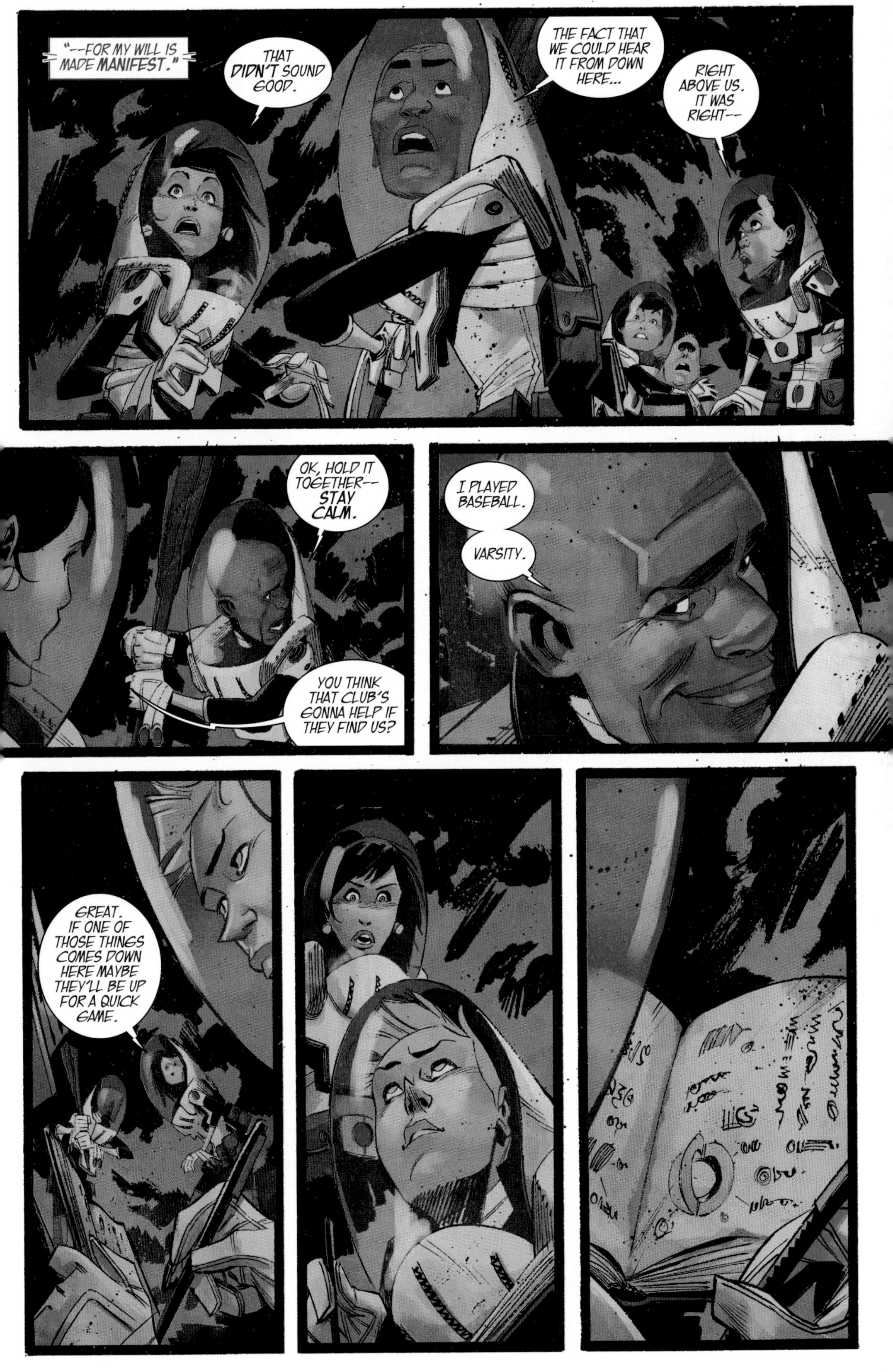
"--FOR MY WILL IS MADE MANIFEST."
THAT DIDN'T SOUND GOOD.
THE FACT THAT WE COULD HEAR IT FROM DOWN HERE...
RIGHT ABOVE US. IT WAS RIGHT--
OK, HOLD IT TOGETHER-- STAY CALM.
YOU THINK THAT CLUB'S GONNA HELP IF THEY FIND US?
I PLAYED BASEBALL.
VARSITY.
GREAT. IF ONE OF THOSE THINGS COMES DOWN HERE MAYBE THEY'LL BE UP FOR A QUICK GAME.

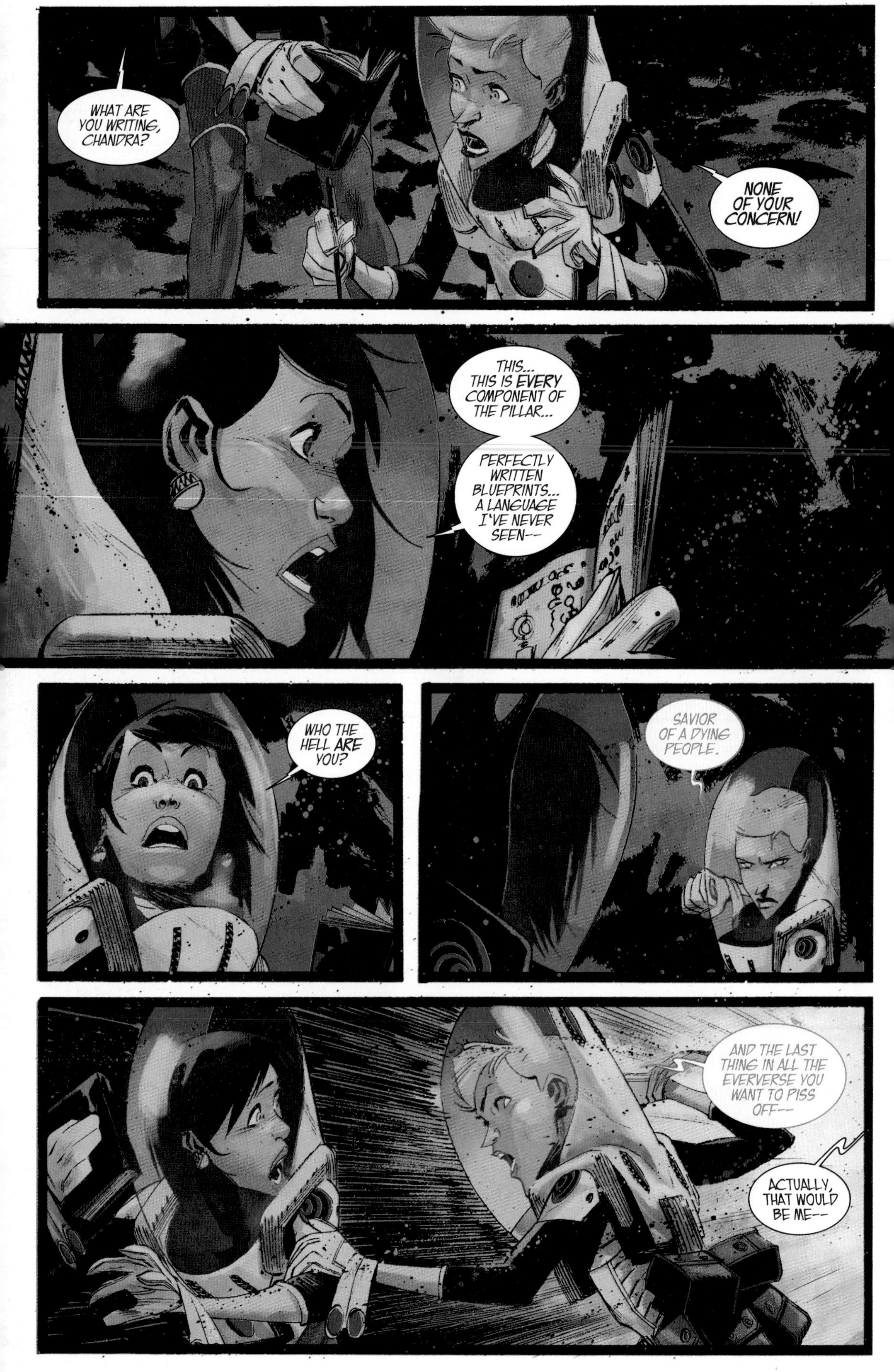
WHAT ARE YOU WRITING, CHANDRA?
NONE OF YOUR CONCERN!
THIS... THIS IS EVERY COMPONENT OF THE PILLAR...
PERFECTLY WRITTEN BLUEPRINTS... A LANGUAGE I'VE NEVER SEEN--
WHO THE HELL ARE YOU?
SAVIOR OF A DYING PEOPLE.
AND THE LAST THING IN ALL THE EVERVERSE YOU WANT TO PISS OFF--
ACTUALLY, THAT WOULD BE ME--

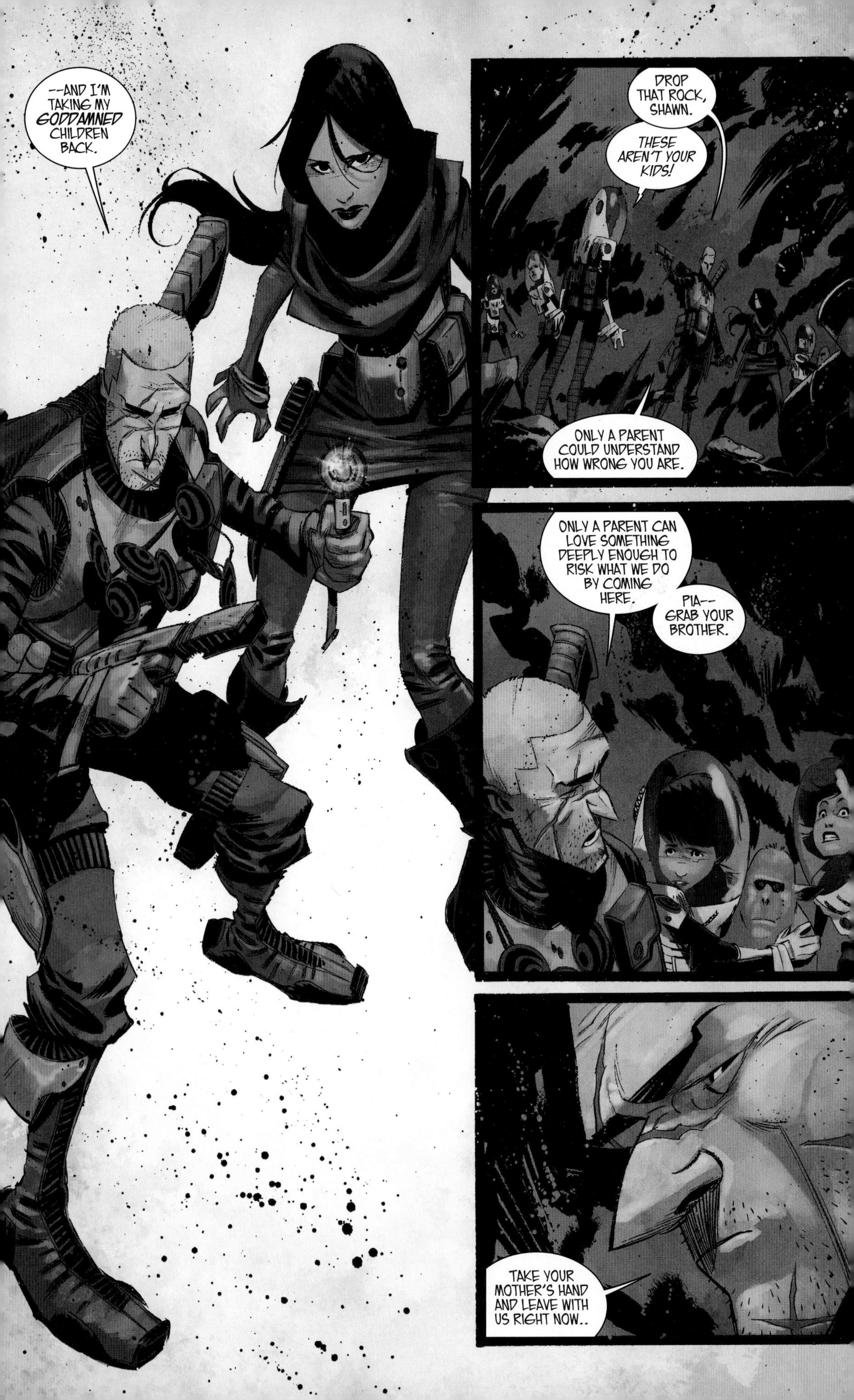
--AND I'M TAKING MY *GODDAMNED* CHILDREN BACK.
DROP THAT ROCK, SHAWN.
THESE AREN'T YOUR KIDS!
ONLY A PARENT COULD UNDERSTAND HOW WRONG YOU ARE.
ONLY A PARENT CAN LOVE SOMETHING DEEPLY ENOUGH TO RISK WHAT WE DO BY COMING HERE.
PIA-- GRAB YOUR BROTHER.
TAKE YOUR MOTHER'S HAND AND LEAVE WITH US RIGHT NOW..

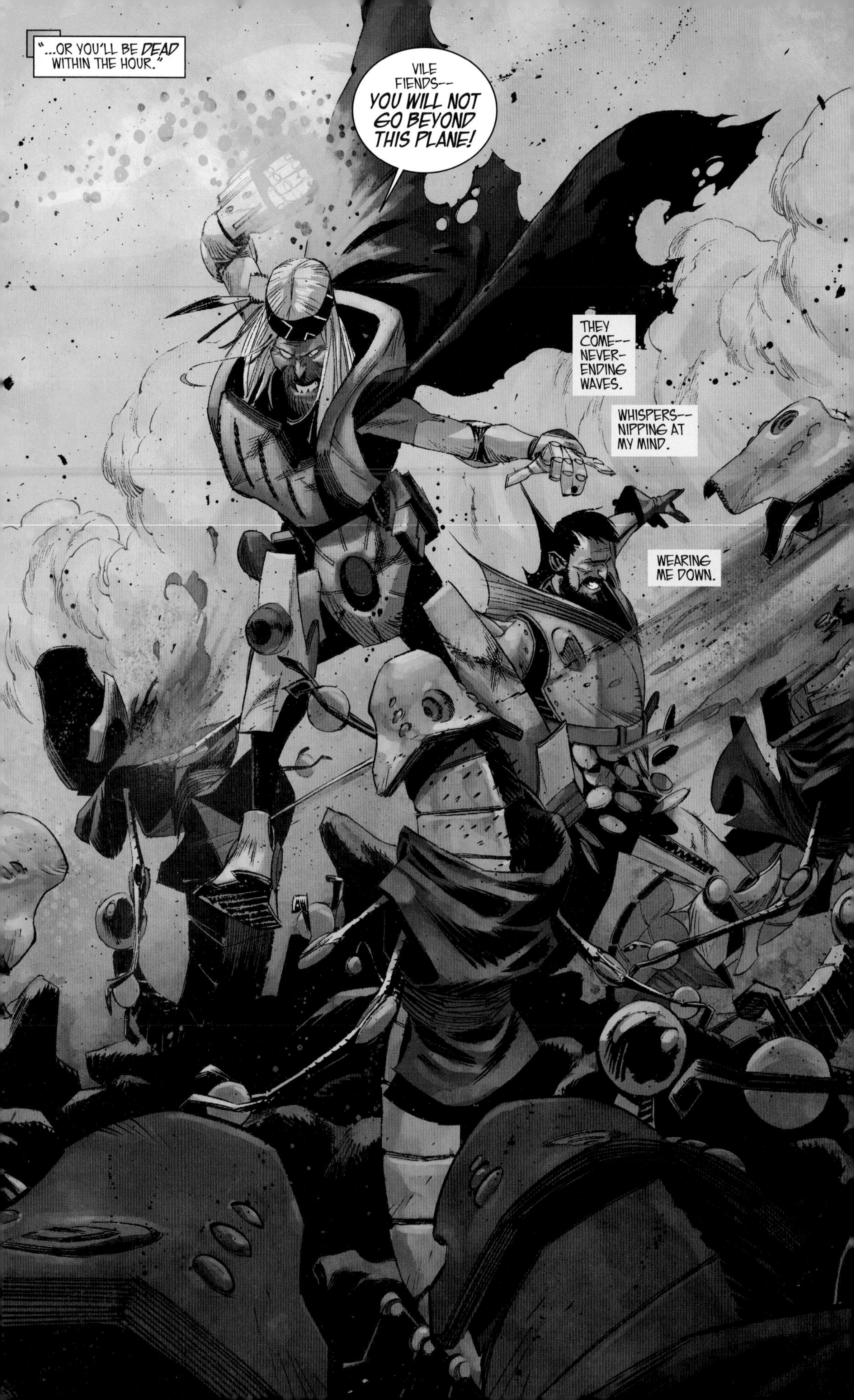
"...OR YOU'LL BE DEAD WITHIN THE HOUR."
VILE FIENDS-- YOU WILL NOT GO BEYOND THIS PLANE!
THEY COME-- NEVER-ENDING WAVES.
WHISPERS-- NIPPING AT MY MIND.
WEARING ME DOWN.

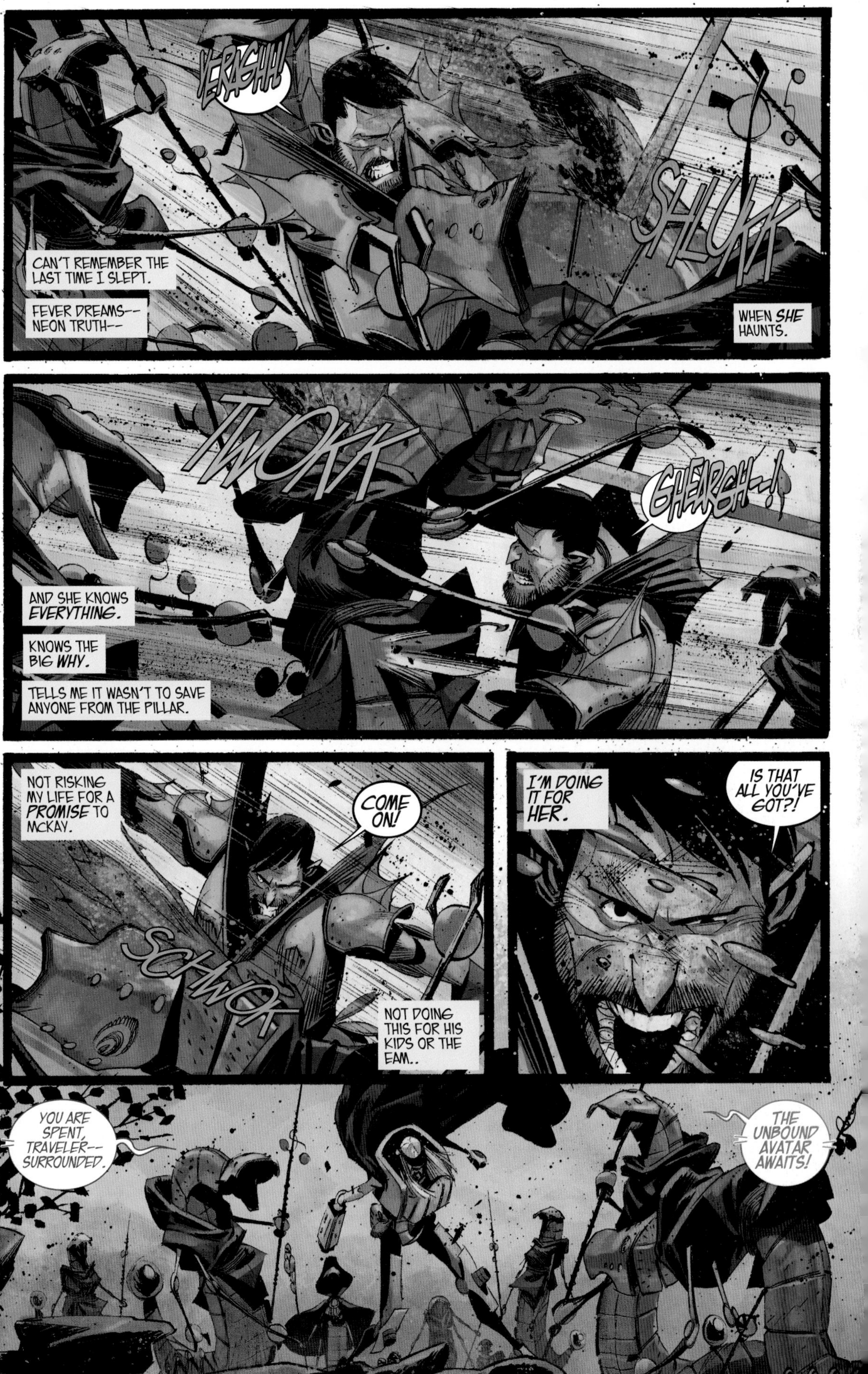
YERAGHH!
SHLUKK
CAN'T REMEMBER THE LAST TIME I SLEPT.
FEVER DREAMS-- NEON TRUTH--
WHEN SHE HAUNTS.
TWOKK
GHEARGH--!
AND SHE KNOWS EVERYTHING.
KNOWS THE BIG WHY.
TELLS ME IT WASN'T TO SAVE ANYONE FROM THE PILLAR.
NOT RISKING MY LIFE FOR A PROMISE TO MCKAY.
COME ON!
SCHWOK
NOT DOING THIS FOR HIS KIDS OR THE EAM..
I'M DOING IT FOR HER.
IS THAT ALL YOU'VE GOT?!
YOU ARE SPENT, TRAVELER-- SURROUNDED.
THE UNBOUND AVATAR AWAITS!

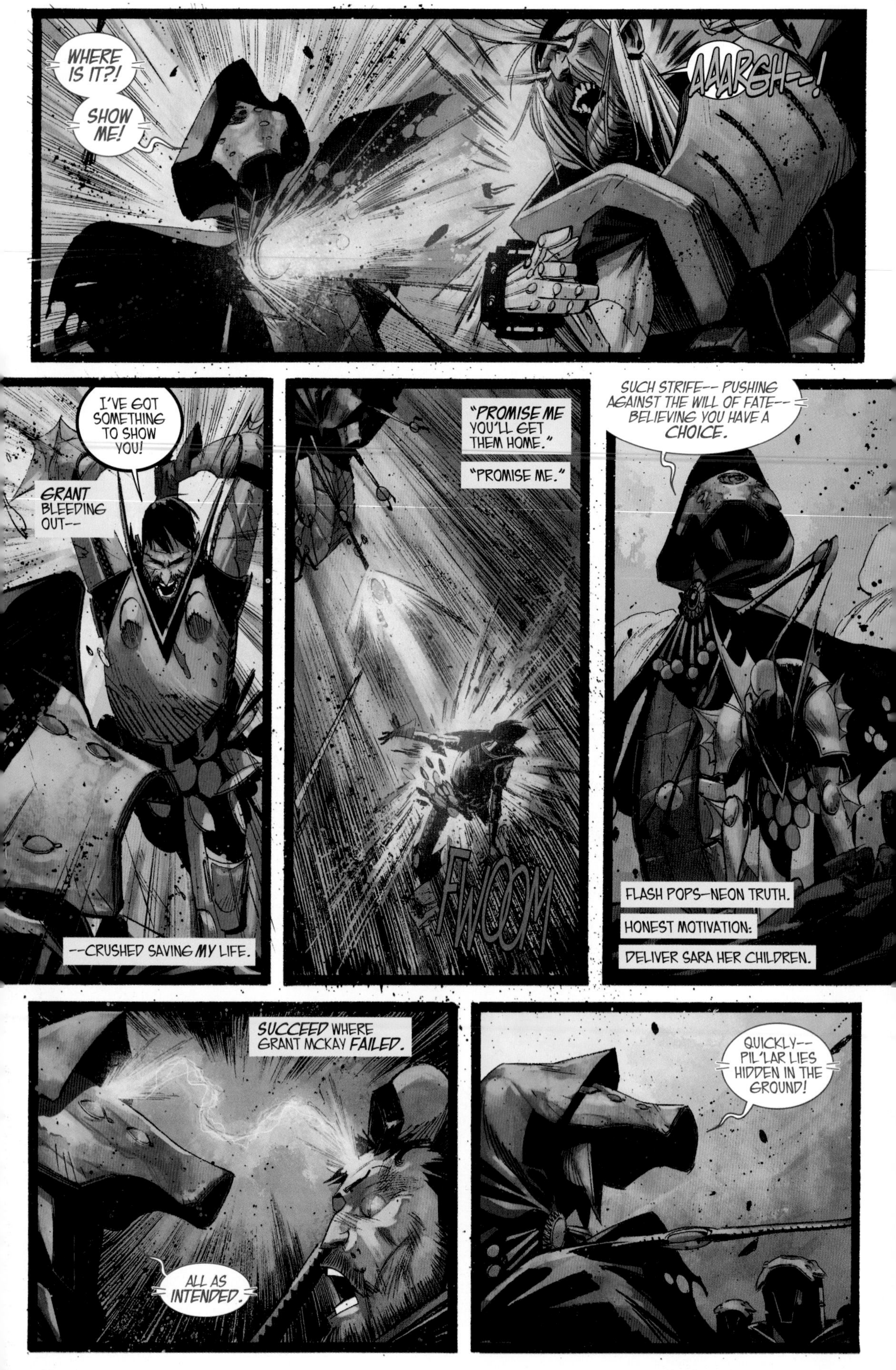
WHERE IS IT?!
SHOW ME!
AAARGH--!
I'VE GOT SOMETHING TO SHOW YOU!
GRANT BLEEDING OUT--
--CRUSHED SAVING MY LIFE.
"PROMISE ME YOU'LL GET THEM HOME."
"PROMISE ME."
FWOOM
SUCH STRIFE-- PUSHING AGAINST THE WILL OF FATE-- BELIEVING YOU HAVE A CHOICE.
FLASH POPS—NEON TRUTH.
HONEST MOTIVATION:
DELIVER SARA HER CHILDREN.
SUCCEED WHERE GRANT MCKAY FAILED.
ALL AS INTENDED.
QUICKLY-- PIL'LAR LIES HIDDEN IN THE GROUND!

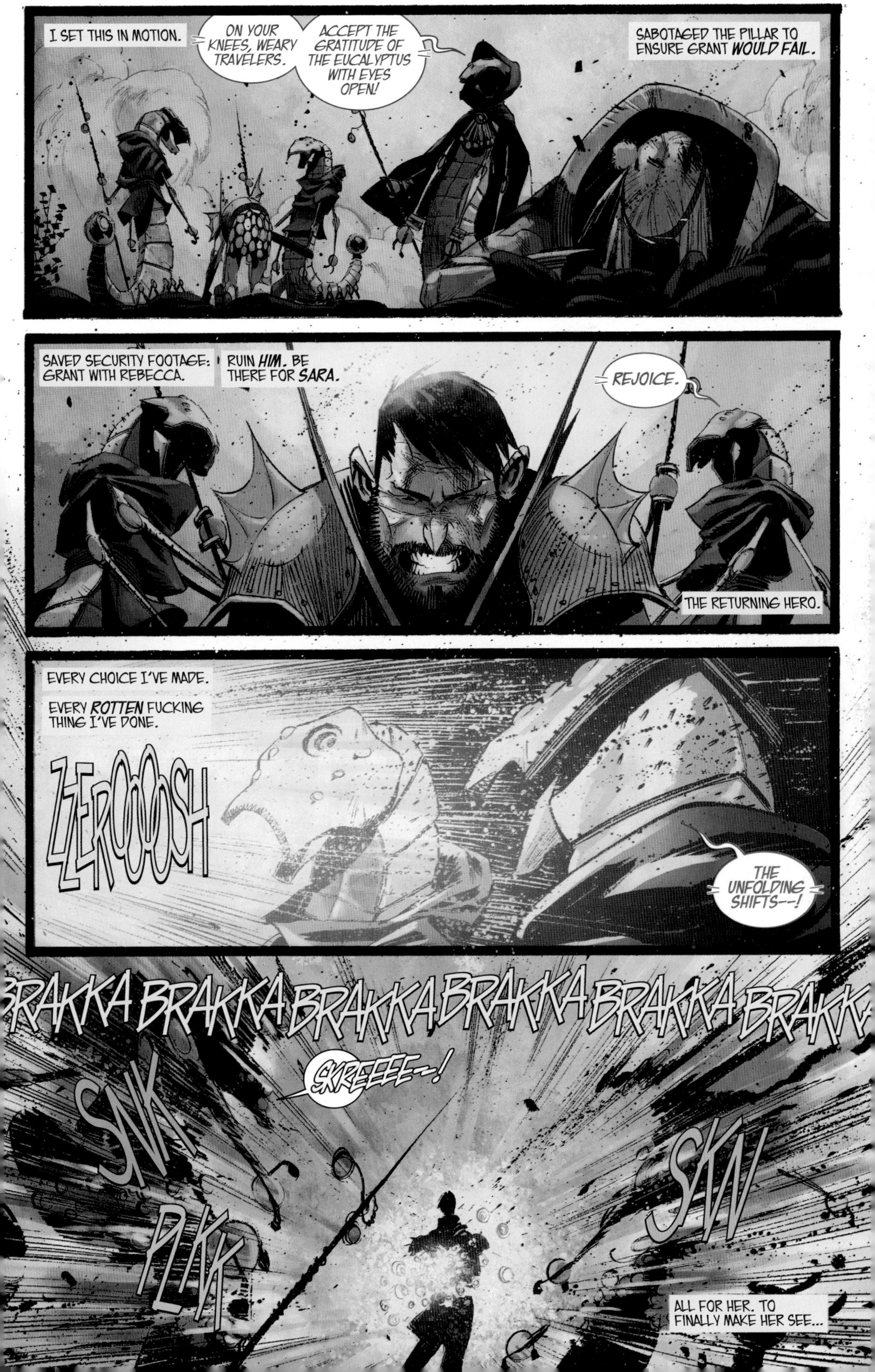
I SET THIS IN MOTION.
ON YOUR KNEES, WEARY TRAVELERS.
ACCEPT THE GRATITUDE OF THE EUCALYPTUS WITH EYES OPEN!
SABOTAGED THE PILLAR TO ENSURE GRANT WOULD FAIL.
SAVED SECURITY FOOTAGE: GRANT WITH REBECCA.
RUIN HIM. BE THERE FOR SARA.
REJOICE.
THE RETURNING HERO.
EVERY CHOICE I'VE MADE.
EVERY ROTTEN FUCKING THING I'VE DONE.
ZZEROOOOOSH
THE UNFOLDING SHIFTS--!
BRAKKA BRAKKA BRAKKA BRAKKA BRAKKA BRAKKA
SKREEEEE--!
SNK
SKW
PLKK
ALL FOR HER. TO FINALLY MAKE HER SEE...

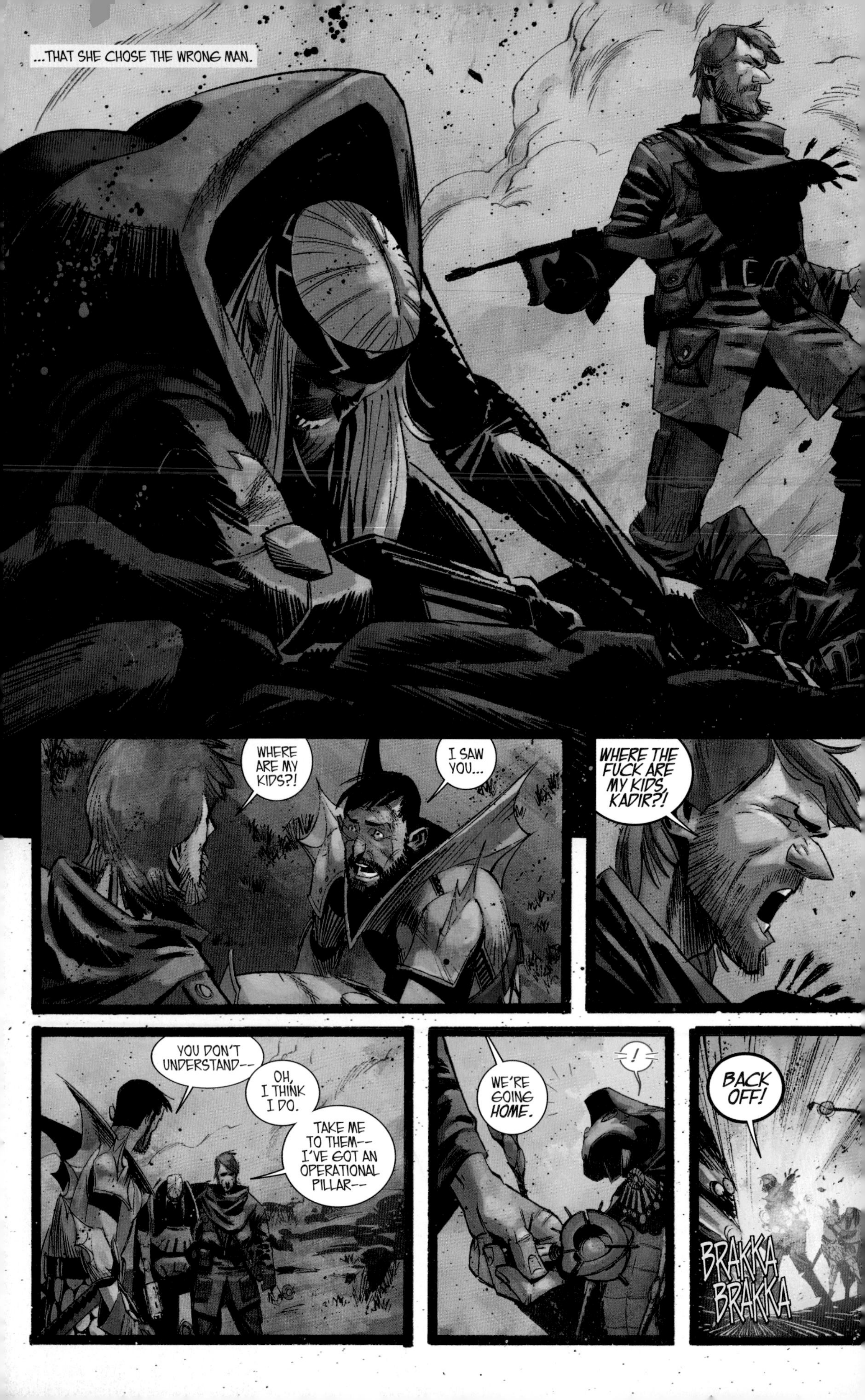
...THAT SHE CHOSE THE WRONG MAN.
WHERE ARE MY KIDS?!
I SAW YOU...
WHERE THE FUCK ARE MY KIDS, KADIR?!
YOU DON'T UNDERSTAND--
OH, I THINK I DO.
TAKE ME TO THEM-- I'VE GOT AN OPERATIONAL PILLAR--
WE'RE GOING HOME.
!
BACK OFF!
BRAKKA BRAKKA

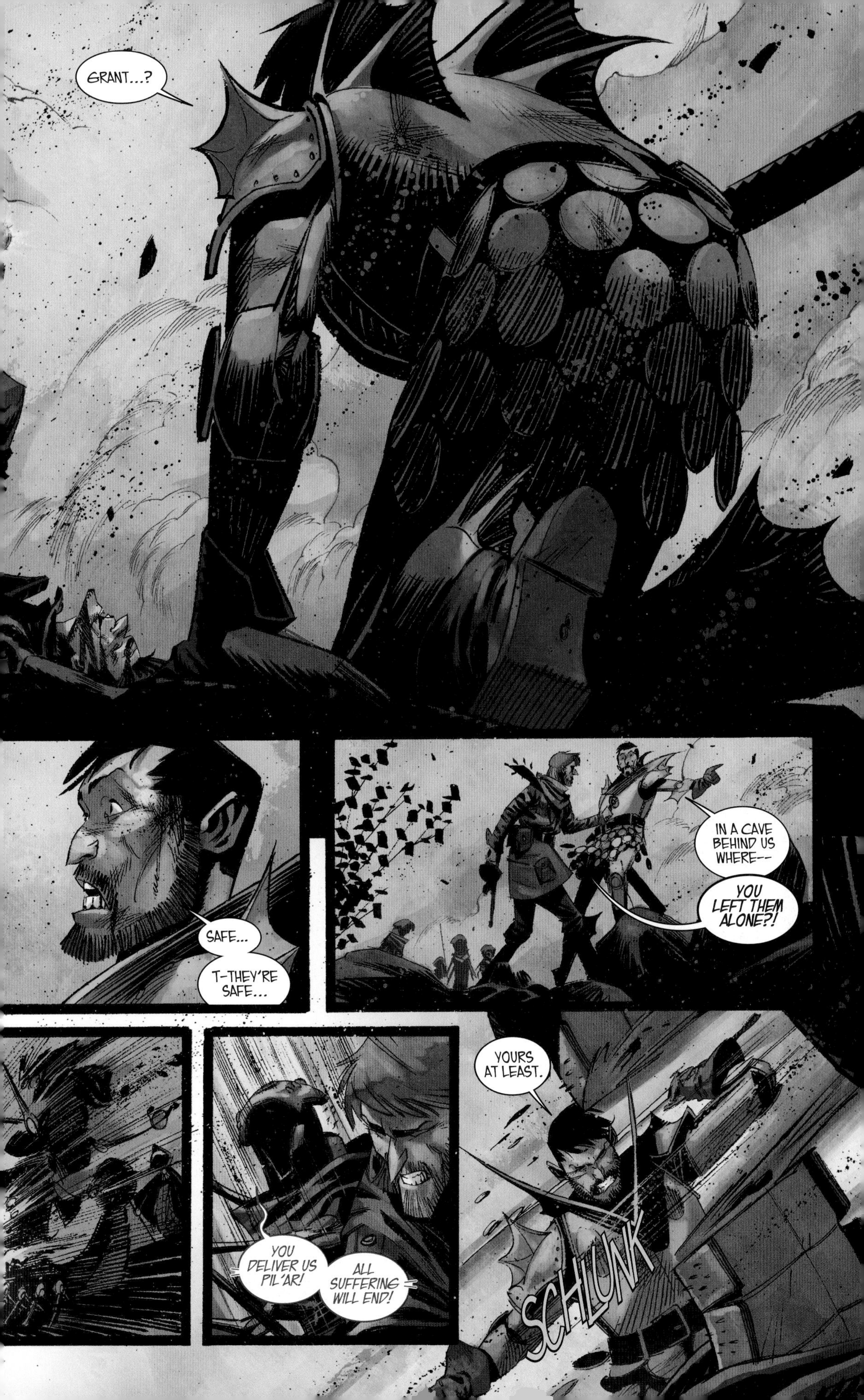
GRANT...?
SAFE...
T-THEY'RE SAFE...
IN A CAVE BEHIND US WHERE--
YOU LEFT THEM ALONE?!
YOU DELIVER US PIL'AR!
ALL SUFFERING WILL END!
YOURS AT LEAST.
SCHLUNK

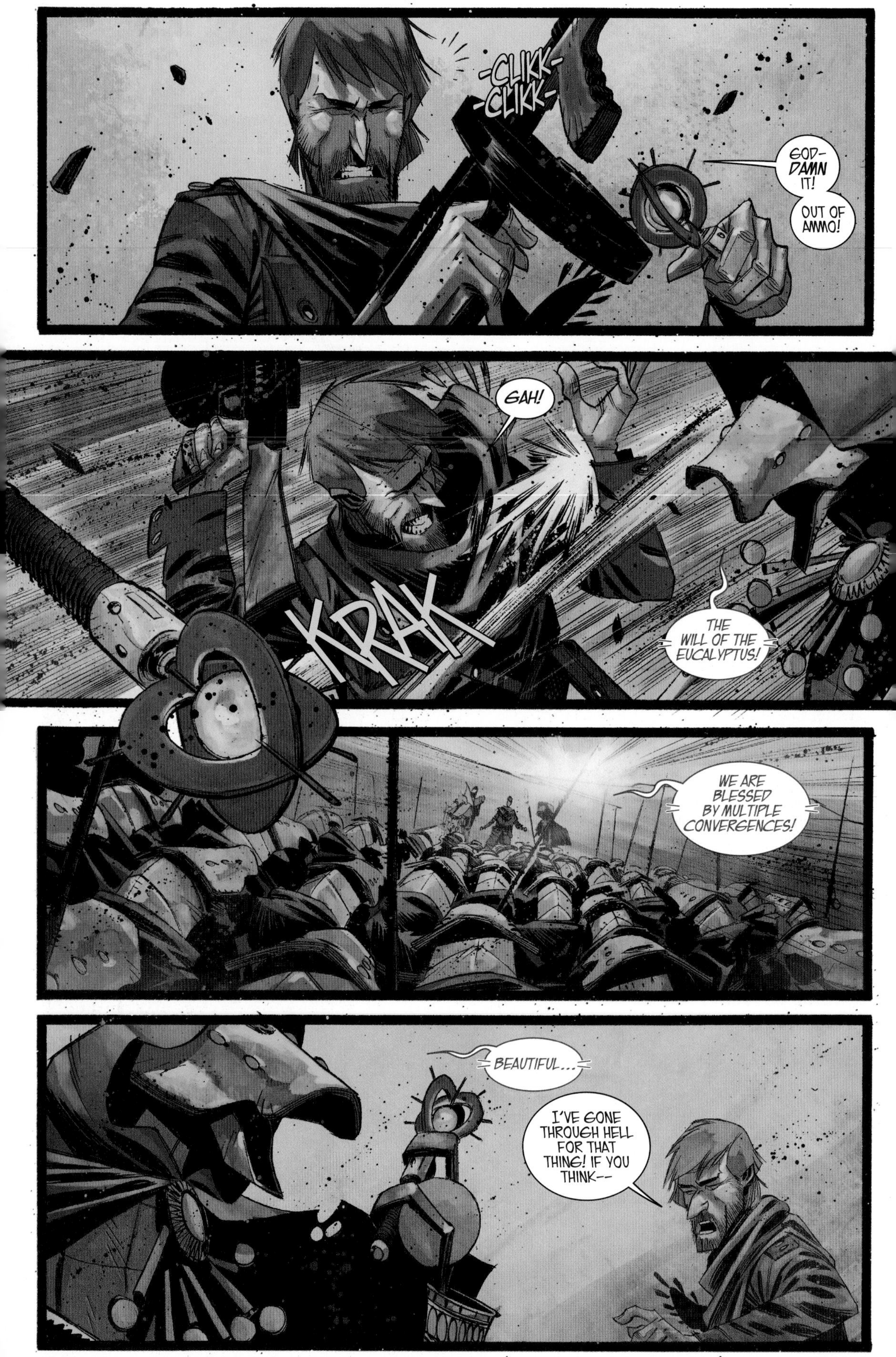
-CLIKK-
-CLIKK-
GOD-DAMN IT!
OUT OF AMMO!
GAH!
KRAK
THE WILL OF THE EUCALYPTUS!
WE ARE BLESSED BY MULTIPLE CONVERGENCES!
BEAUTIFUL...
I'VE GONE THROUGH HELL FOR THAT THING! IF YOU THINK--

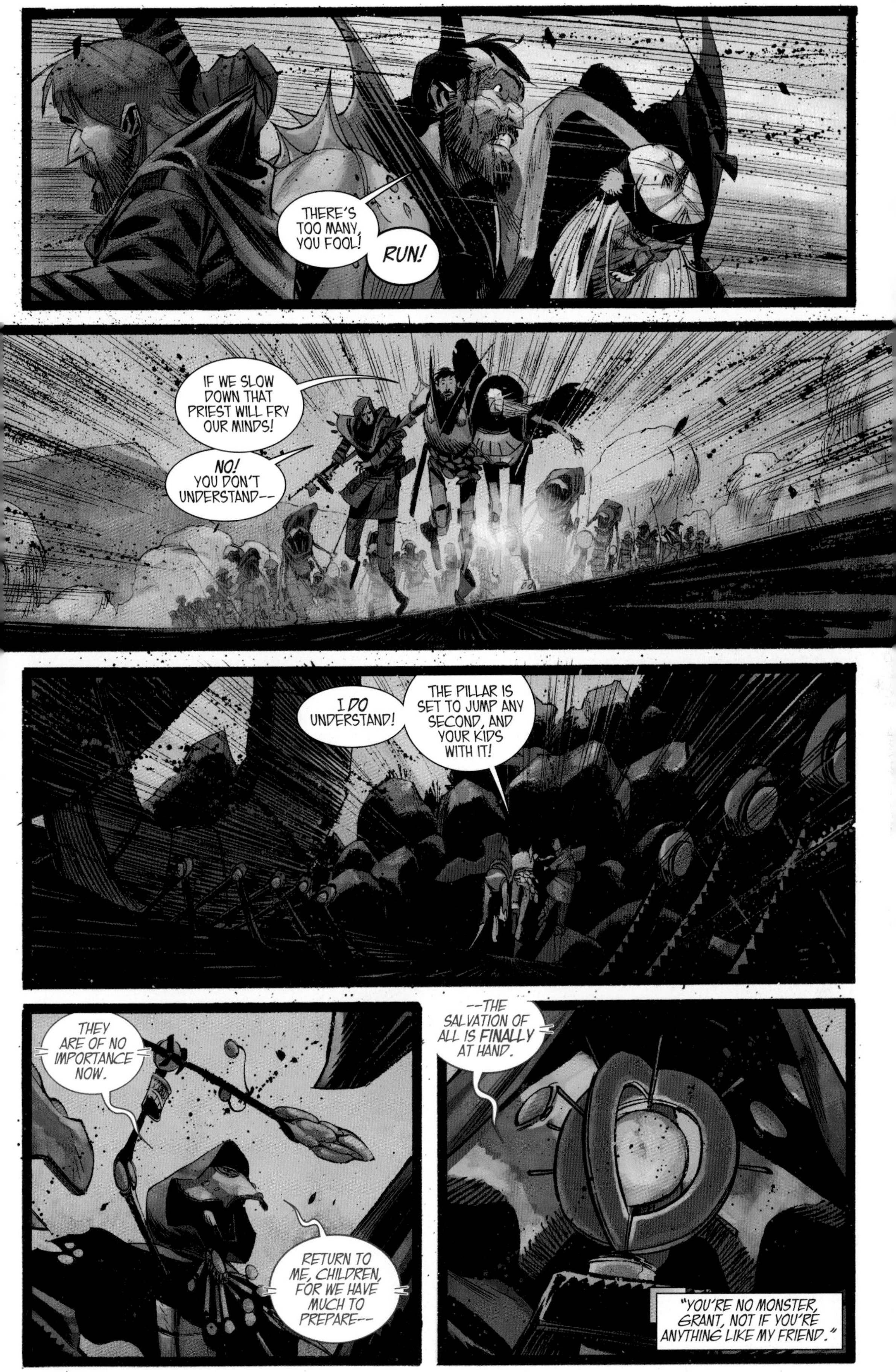
THERE'S TOO MANY, YOU FOOL!
RUN!
IF WE SLOW DOWN THAT PRIEST WILL FRY OUR MINDS!
NO! YOU DON'T UNDERSTAND--
I DO UNDERSTAND!
THE PILLAR IS SET TO JUMP ANY SECOND, AND YOUR KIDS WITH IT!
THEY ARE OF NO IMPORTANCE NOW.
RETURN TO ME, CHILDREN, FOR WE HAVE MUCH TO PREPARE--
--THE SALVATION OF ALL IS FINALLY AT HAND.
"YOU'RE NO MONSTER, GRANT, NOT IF YOU'RE ANYTHING LIKE MY FRIEND."

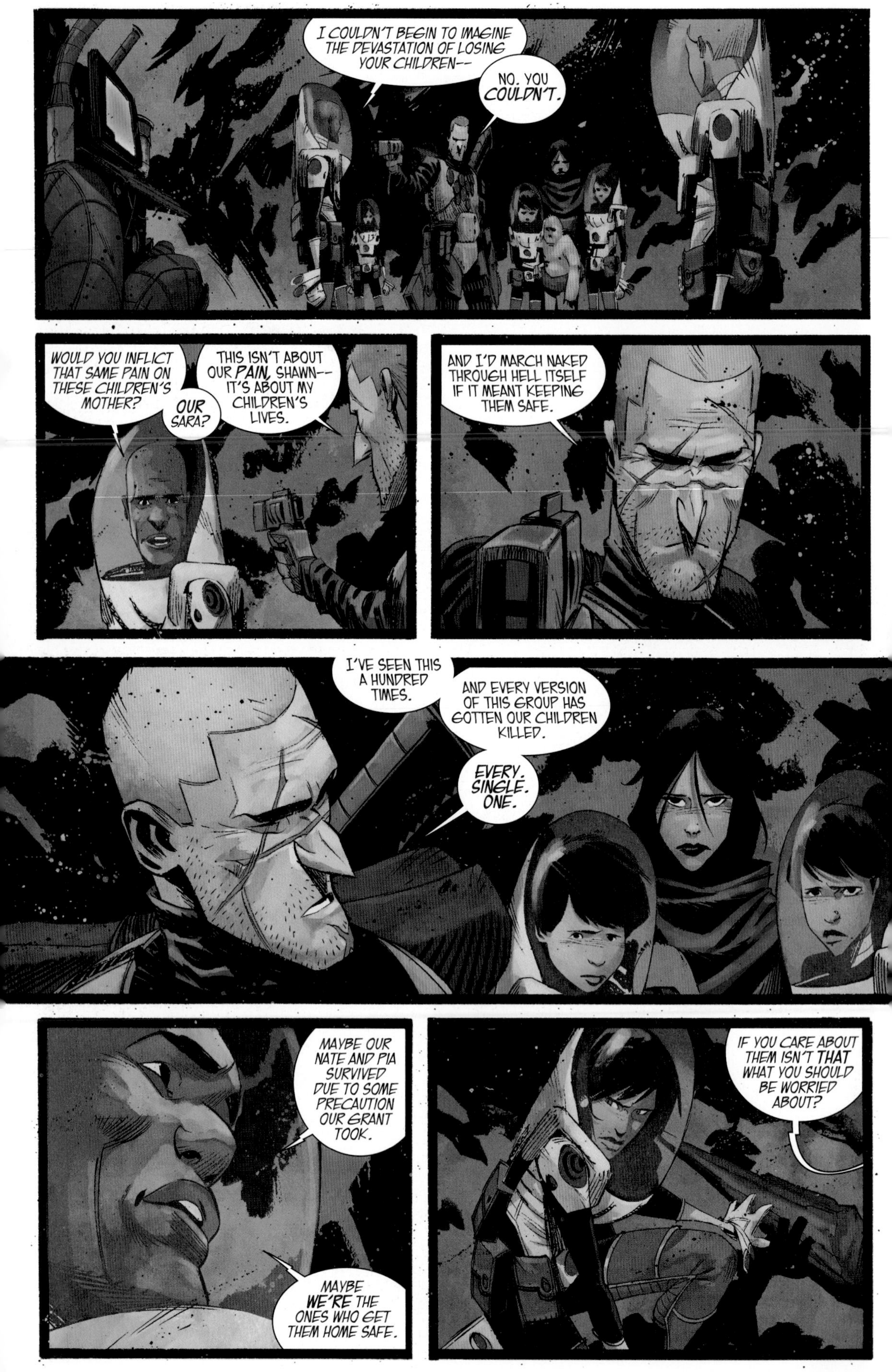
I COULDN'T BEGIN TO IMAGINE THE DEVASTATION OF LOSING YOUR CHILDREN--
NO. YOU COULDN'T.
WOULD YOU INFLICT THAT SAME PAIN ON THESE CHILDREN'S MOTHER?
OUR SARA?
THIS ISN'T ABOUT OUR PAIN, SHAWN-- IT'S ABOUT MY CHILDREN'S LIVES.
AND I'D MARCH NAKED THROUGH HELL ITSELF IF IT MEANT KEEPING THEM SAFE.
I'VE SEEN THIS A HUNDRED TIMES.
AND EVERY VERSION OF THIS GROUP HAS GOTTEN OUR CHILDREN KILLED.
EVERY. SINGLE. ONE.
MAYBE OUR NATE AND PIA SURVIVED DUE TO SOME PRECAUTION OUR GRANT TOOK.
MAYBE WE'RE THE ONES WHO GET THEM HOME SAFE.
IF YOU CARE ABOUT THEM ISN'T THAT WHAT YOU SHOULD BE WORRIED ABOUT?

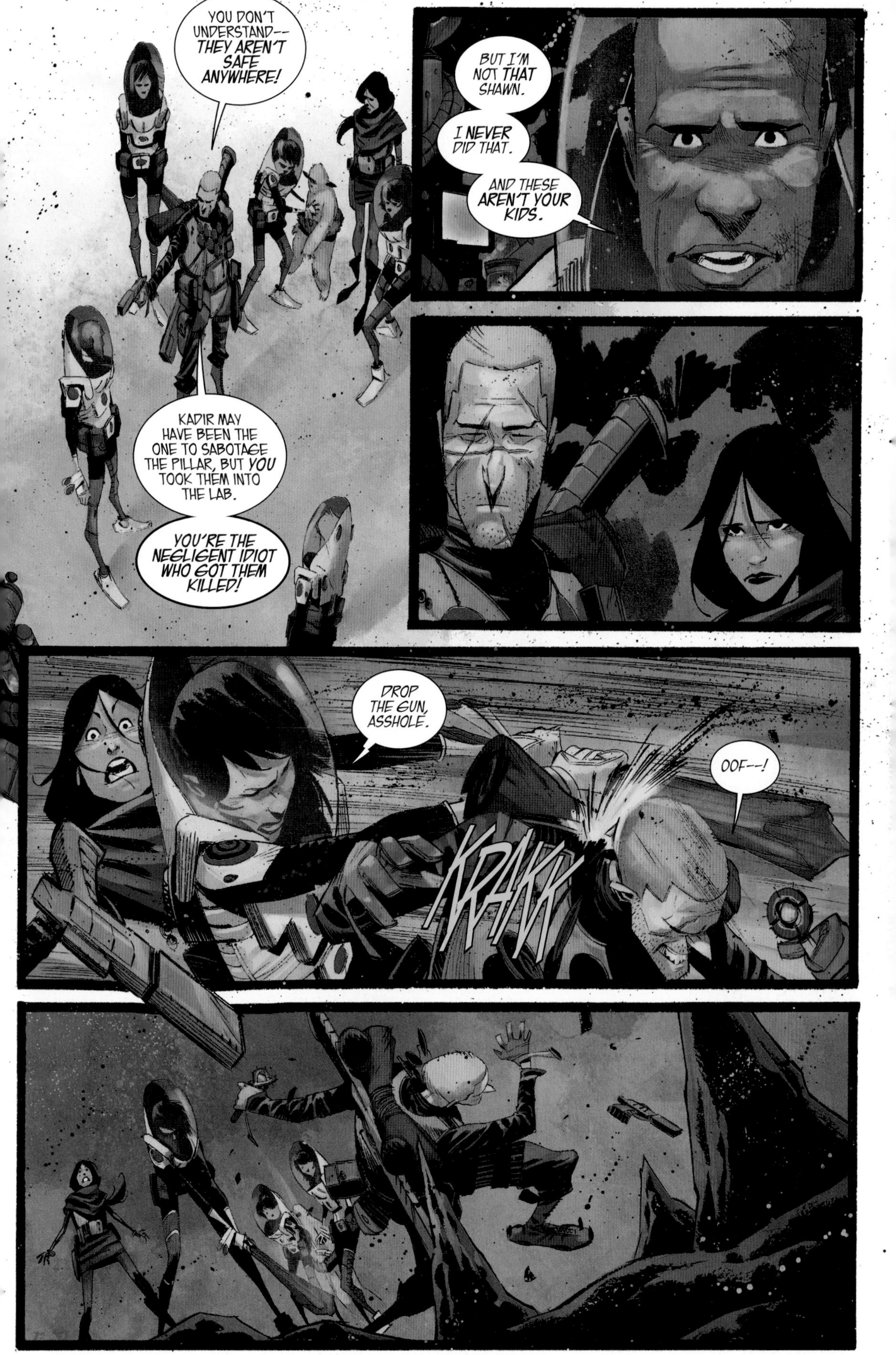
YOU DON'T UNDERSTAND-- THEY AREN'T SAFE ANYWHERE!
BUT I'M NOT THAT SHAWN.
I NEVER DID THAT.
AND THESE AREN'T YOUR KIDS.
KADIR MAY HAVE BEEN THE ONE TO SABOTAGE THE PILLAR, BUT YOU TOOK THEM INTO THE LAB.
YOU'RE THE NEGLIGENT IDIOT WHO GOT THEM KILLED!
DROP THE GUN, ASSHOLE.
OOF--!
KRAKK

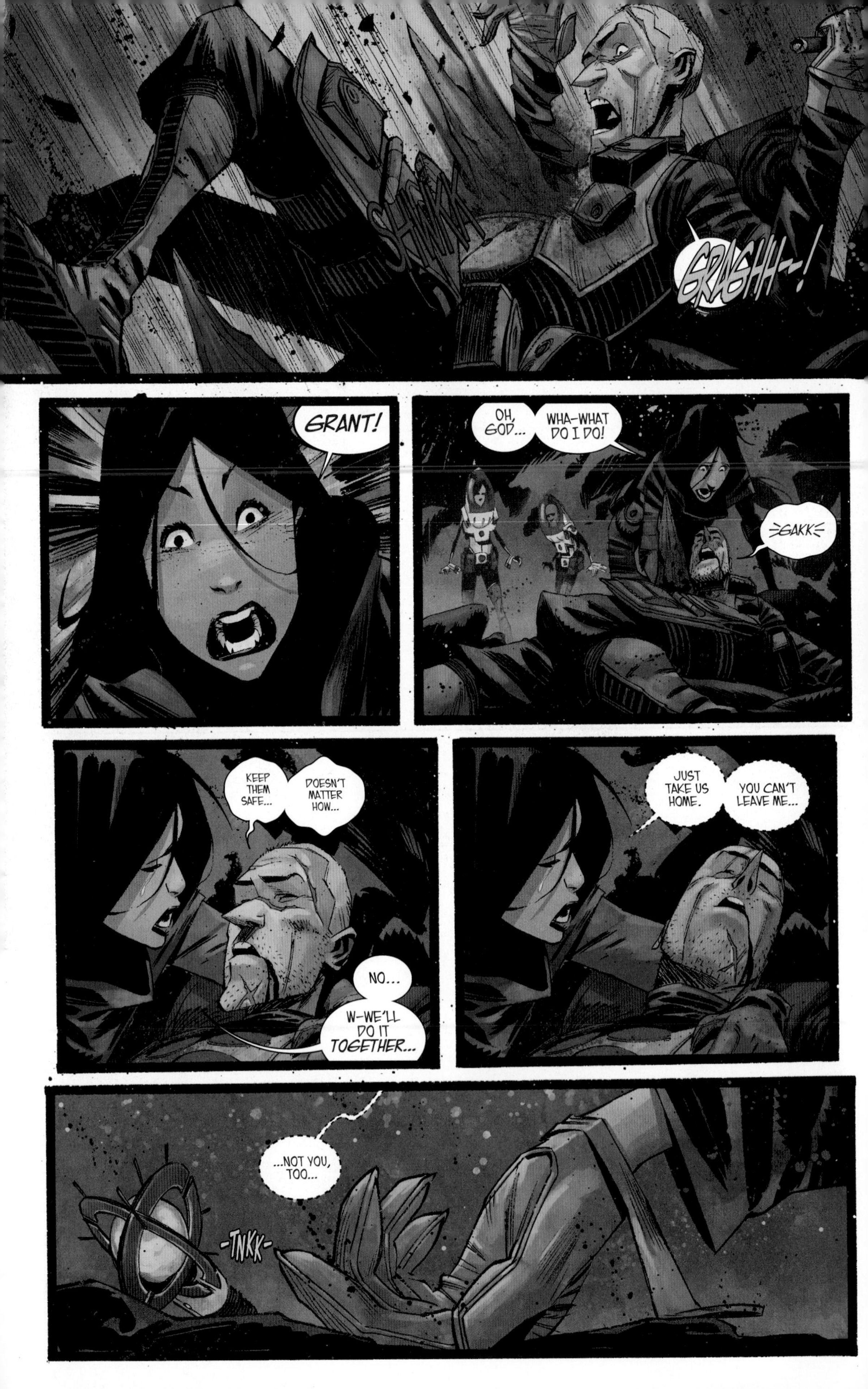
SHKK
GRAGHH--!
GRANT!
OH, GOD...
WHA-WHAT DO I DO!
GAKK
KEEP THEM SAFE...
DOESN'T MATTER HOW...
NO...
W-WE'LL DO IT TOGETHER...
JUST TAKE US HOME.
YOU CAN'T LEAVE ME...
...NOT YOU, TOO...
TNKK

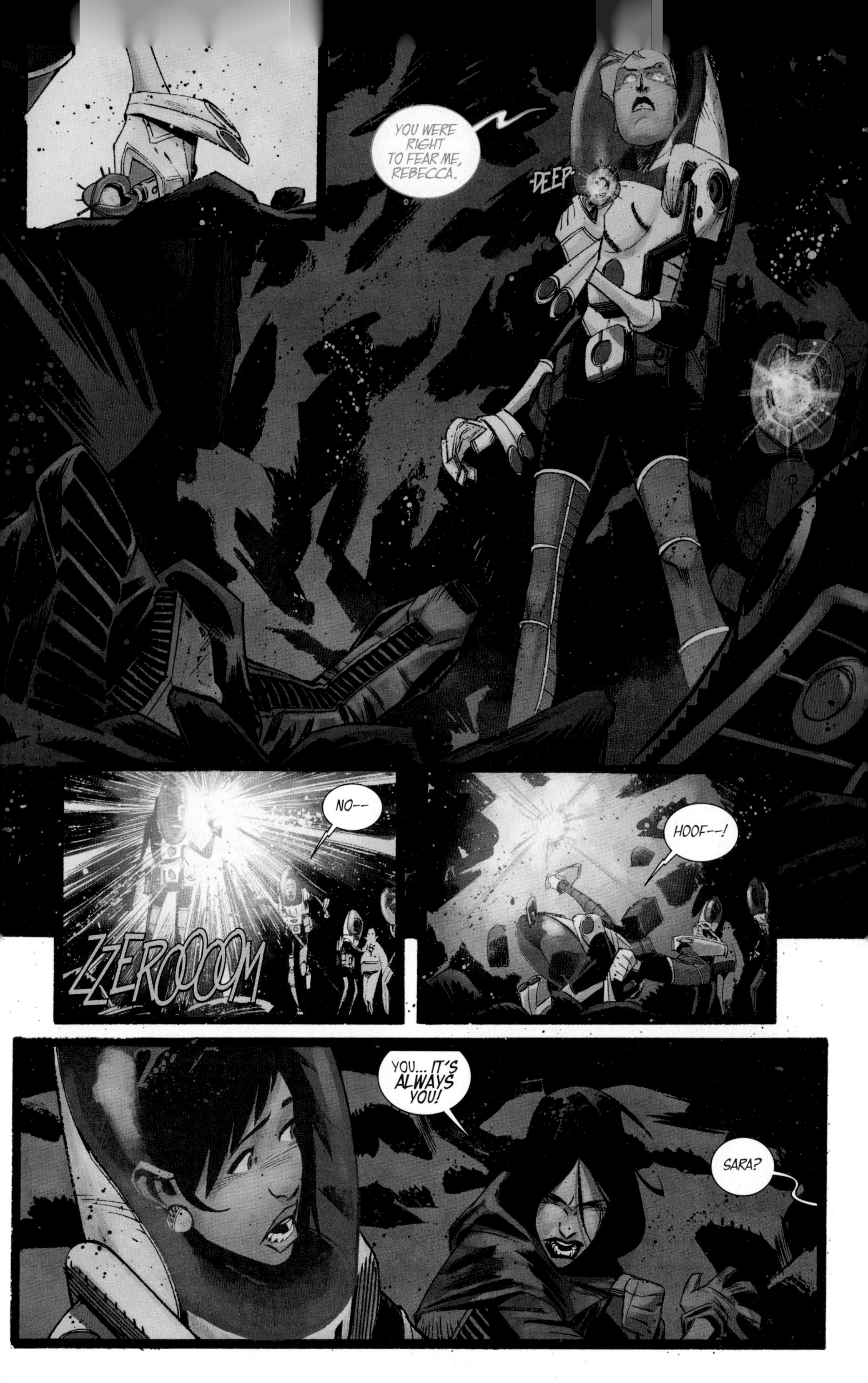
YOU WERE RIGHT TO FEAR ME, REBECCA.
DEEP
NO--
ZZEROOOOM
HOOF--!
YOU... IT'S ALWAYS YOU!
SARA?

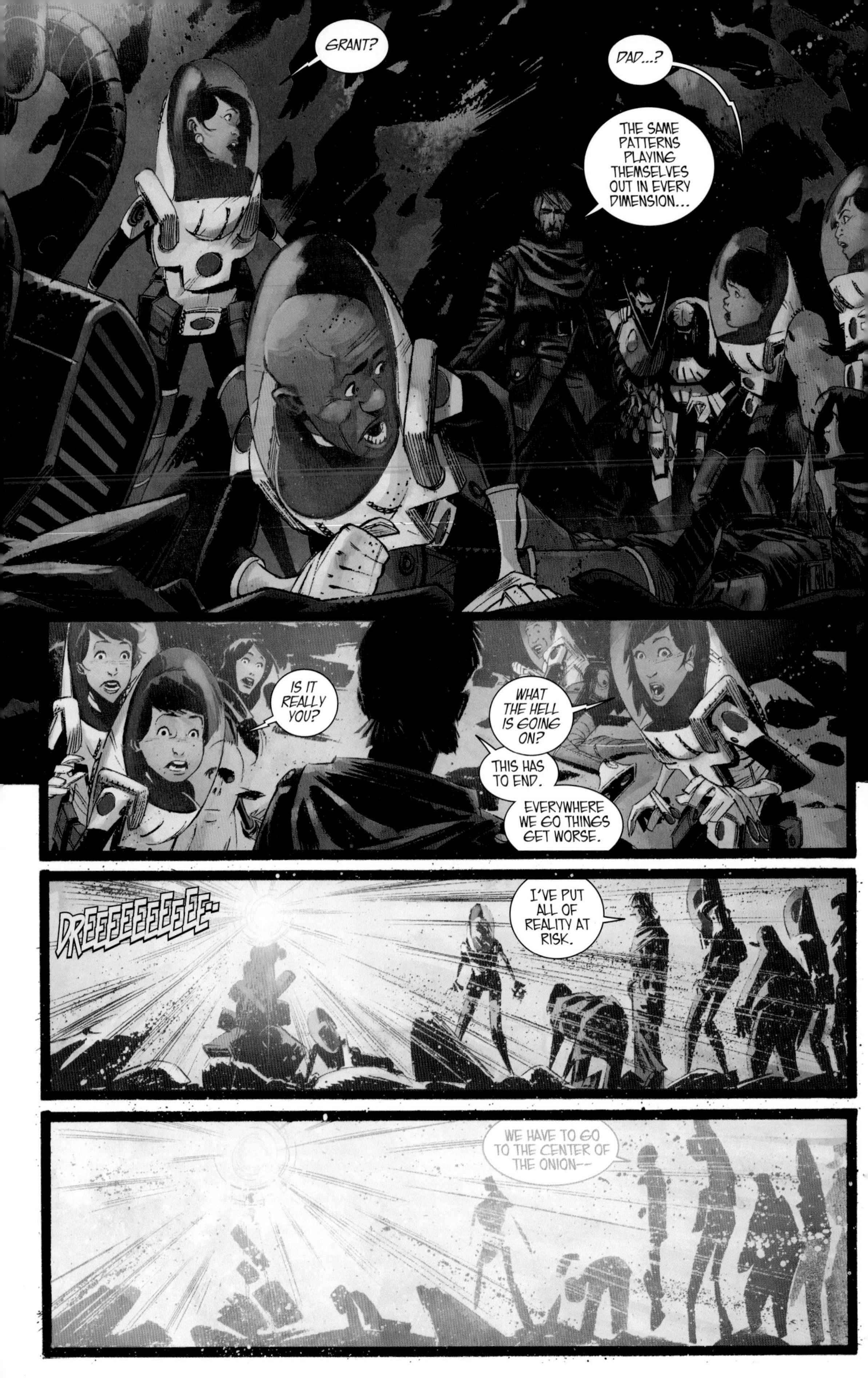
GRANT?
DAD...?
THE SAME PATTERNS PLAYING THEMSELVES OUT IN EVERY DIMENSION...
IS IT REALLY YOU?
WHAT THE HELL IS GOING ON?
THIS HAS TO END.
EVERYWHERE WE GO THINGS GET WORSE.
DREEEEEEEEEEE--
I'VE PUT ALL OF REALITY AT RISK.
WE HAVE TO GO TO THE CENTER OF THE ONION--

"--AND WE HAVE TO STOP ME."

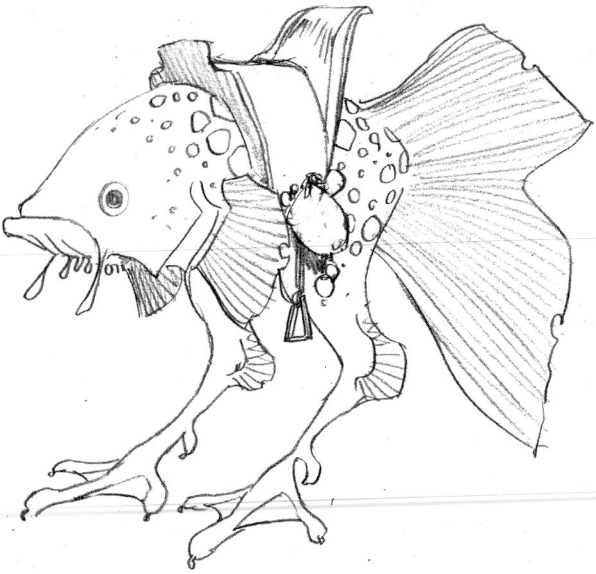

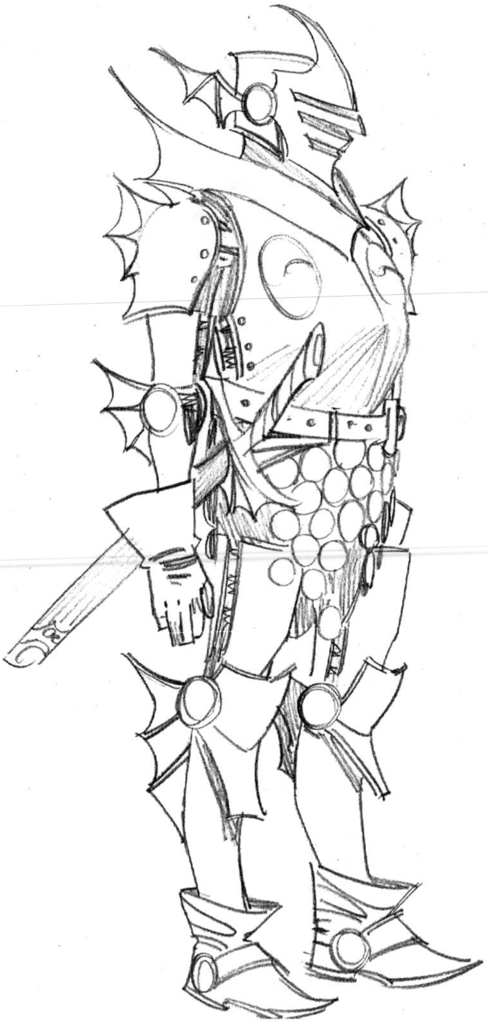

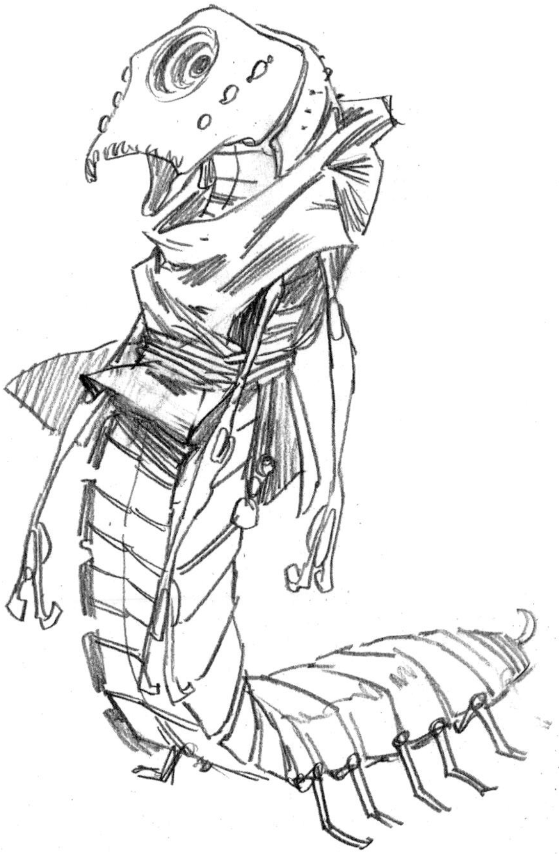

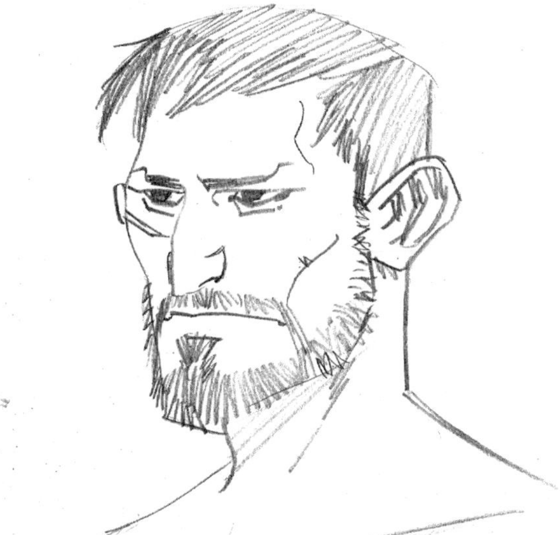

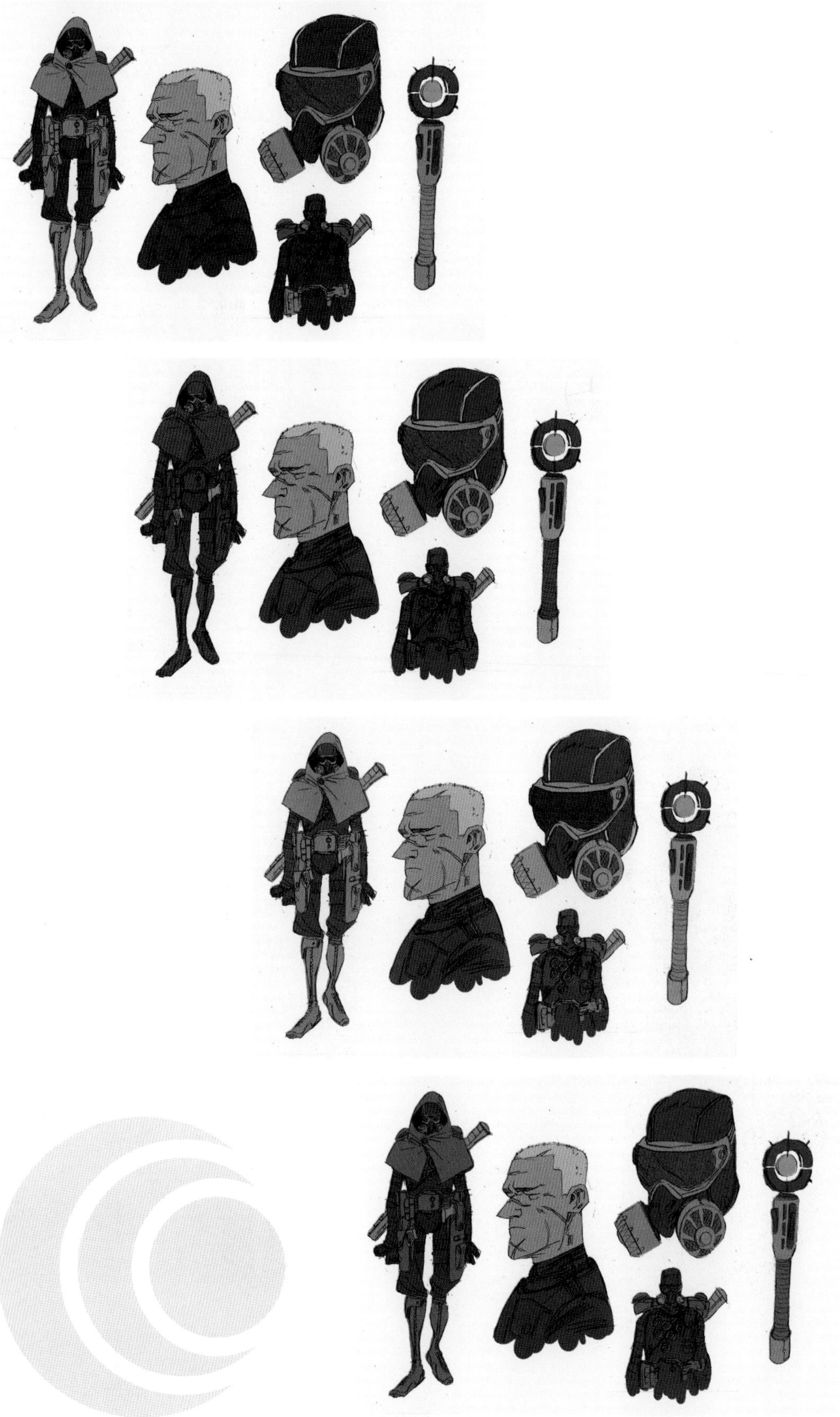

COLOR STUDIES BY DEAN WHITE

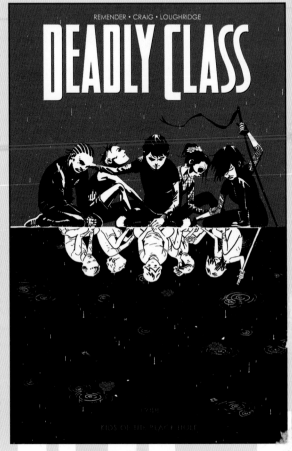